KOINONIA

From Hate, through Dialogue, to Culture in the Large Group

Sheila Thompson, Patrick de Maré, Robin Piper

Photo by Hanne Maier

KOINONIA

From Hate, through Dialogue, to Culture in the Large Group

Patrick de Maré
Robin Piper
Sheila Thompson

Routledge
Taylor & Francis Group
LONDON AND NEW YORK

First published 1991 by Karnac Books Ltd.

Published 2022 by Routledge
2 Park Square, Milton Park, Abingdon, Oxon OX14 4RN
605 Third Avenue, New York, NY 10017

Routledge is an imprint of the Taylor & Francis Group, an informa business

First issued in hardback 2019

British Library Cataloguing in Publication Data

De Maré, Patrick B.
Koinonia: from hate through dialogue to culture in the larger group.
1. Medicine. Psychoanalysis. Group therapy
I. Title
616.8917

ISBN 978-0-946439-82-9 (pbk)
ISBN 978-0-367-32528-2 (hbk)

I have been studying how I may compare
This prison where I live unto the world;
And for because the world is populous
And here is not a creature but myself,
I cannot do it; yet I'll hammer it out.
My brain I'll prove the female to my soul,
My soul the father; and these two beget
A generation of still-breeding thoughts,
And these same thoughts people this little world,
In humours like the people of this world.
For no thought is contented.

Shakespeare, *Richard the Second,* Act V, Scene 5

CONTENTS

THE AUTHORS ix

ACKNOWLEDGEMENTS xii

FOREWORD *BY PAMELA STEINER* xiii

Koinonia 1

Introduction 3

CHAPTER ONE
The story of the larger group approach 9

CHAPTER TWO
The median group 23

CHAPTER THREE
Dialogue 41

CHAPTER FOUR
Culture and Koinonia 75

CHAPTER FIVE
Object relations theory.
Systems thinking and structuralism 107

CHAPTER SIX
Ecological perspectives 165

Postscript 177

APPENDICES

Spiral course of introjected, projected, reintrojected and reprojected objects via the larger groups matrix 180

The psychoanalytic, the small-group, and the large-group settings 182

The three cultures 184

The Large Group Section brochure 187

The large group diary 189

REFERENCES AND BIBLIOGRAPHY 251

INDEX 256

THE AUTHORS

DR PATRICK DE MARÉ was born in London in 1916, of Swedish parentage. He was educated at Wellington, Cambridge, and St George's Hospital. He qualified as a doctor in 1941 and enlisted in the RAMC in 1942, when he was trained for Army psychiatry by Rickman and Bion at Northfield Hospital. He ran an Exhaustion Centre throughout the European campaign, at the end of which he returned to Northfield, where he joined Foulkes and Main in the Northfield experiment.

After the war he became a Consultant Psychotherapist at St George's Hospital; in 1952 he set up the Group Analytic Society with Foulkes, and later he participated in setting up the Institute of Group Analysis and the Group Analytic Practice. He also worked with Benaim and Lionel Kreeger at Halliwick Hospital, the short-lived therapeutic community.

In 1972 he published *Perspectives in Group Psychotherapy* (Allen & Unwin) and in 1974 Lionel Kreeger and he published *Introduction to Group Treatment in Psychiatry* (Butterworth), which was dedicated to the patients and staff at Halliwick Hospital.

In 1975 he started a large group under the auspices of the Institute of Group Analysis; in 1976 he was joined by Robin Piper. That 'large' group settled down to a steady membership of about 20 members and is currently operating as a 'median' group.

ROBIN PIPER trained as a social worker at the London School of Economics. He worked in child and adult psychiatry and later specialized in family therapy at the Marlborough Family Service.

He went on to train as a psychotherapist with the British Association of Psychotherapists and currently works full-time in private practice as a psychotherapist.

He is a member of the Institute of Family Therapy, the British Association of Psychotherapists, and the London Centre for Psychotherapy.

He is married, with two children.

For nine years he was co-conductor with Patrick de Maré of the large group at the Institute of Group Analysis.

SHEILA THOMPSON qualified as a psychiatric social worker in 1955 and subsequently worked at the Hospital for Sick Children, Great Ormond Street, at the Portman Clinic, and with Newnham Community Mental Health Service.

She has spent some years living in East Africa, where she worked with refugees, and in New York, where she pursued an interest in family therapy and in the care of patients with terminal cancer.

Her most recent post was as Principal Social Worker with St Joseph's Hospice Home Care Team. She is now a freelance teacher/writer on group work, bereavement, and terminal care.

She has been a member of the Group Analytic Society since 1970, and she is a founder member of the Large Group Section.

She is co-author with Dr J. H. Kahn of *The Group Process as a Helping Technique* (Pergamon, 1970) and *The Group Process and Family Therapy* (Pergamon, 1988), and she is a contributor to *The Evolution of Group Analysis*, edited by M. Pines (Routledge & Kegan Paul, 1983).

ACKNOWLEDGEMENTS

With gratitude to Juan and Hanne Campos, from 'Grup d'Analisi', Barcelona, for the central role they played in getting this book off the ground and for all their help and encouragement.

With acknowledgement to those who have pioneered the Median Group Section of The Group Analytic Society, in particular Heulwen Bawaroska, Raymond Blake, Tony Clayton, Eric Ferron, Sally Griffin, Teresa Howard, Hanne Maier, Don Montgomery, Josephine Lomax-Simpson, and Helen Schick.

FOREWORD

Pamela Pomerance Steiner

The past

Ten years ago I was an American living in London and working for the Green Alliance, an organization whose purpose was to stimulate discussion between Members of Parliament and proponents of the environmental paradigm. I had worked as an environmentalist for a number of years by then and had seen little of the progress desperately needed. My recent divorce had propelled me into psychotherapy. I was so impressed by the changes occurring in myself in response to the therapy that I came to believe that future progress on behalf of the environment could occur only through some new way of working for political change that reflected the kind of approach changing me. I had long been able to ask the question raised in this volume, 'why is it that intelligent people perpetuate cultures that are so self-destructive?' Now I imagined finding some sort of answer through systematic, established psychological understanding and practice. My psychiatrist pointed me in the direction of the Group Analytic Society's introductory training course in group analysis.

In October 1979 I began the Society's 40-week introductory course, consisting of an hour's lecture on one afternoon a week and the 90-minute small therapy groups conducted by the Society's training group therapists. At that time I still knew nothing about the history of group therapy, or the training for it. I took for granted what I now realize was the extraordinary opportunity for large group learning, of which Patrick de Maré was the moving force.

Furthermore, I was still so ignorant about myself and other people, and about this new world of therapy and therapists, analysis and analysts, small groups and large groups, that I enjoyed finding myself thought of as idealistic and felt it worthwhile to argue for. For instance, in the large group (about 120 that year), I talked about Darwin's discovery of a peaceable kingdom among the different species on the Galapagos Islands. The implication was that learning to talk in a large group might lead to more peaceable existence politically. This picture was immediately dismissed in the group as idealistic rubbish, except, of course, by Patrick, who kept validating the expression of difference of ideas. I recall the hush in the group when Bion died, during that year. Everyone there but I knew who he was. I don't recall whether the meaning of Bion to the large group we were then in was discussed.

I did not get to know Pat apart from the large group until early 1981, when I participated in a three-day workshop, the 'Wider Context for Groups'. A large crowd convened by Pat opened each of those four days. It evoked strong, excited, often upset feelings. For me it was the start of putting social and political perceptions into an entirely different perspective. At the end of that workshop Pat told me about the on-going weekly large group. I attended this group for eighteen months, until I moved back to the United States.

I began to apply some of this large group learning to my environmental work. One of the Green Alliance Debate series, 'Breaking the Chains of Centralisation', occurred with the approximately 60 people present, including the main speakers, prominent government people, Pat de Maré, and Eric Miller of the Tavistock Institute of Human Relations, sitting in a large, single circle. The expected frustration was certainly generated, and yet dialogue managed to occur, despite the general sense of extra difficulty.

Another occasion was the day-long conference on nuclear energy policy for Great Britain. There were the usual formal hierarchical arrangements—e.g. speakers on a rostrum, facing the audience; what was different was the mix of speakers and participants. The full spectrum, from conventional/government culture to the radical green culture on energy policy, was represented in both speaker and participant groups. All sides were given equal legitimacy by the chairman, an intelligent and subtle QC who had seen the need for a new, non-binary way of talking. Real listening resulted.

Pat and I continued to meet during the summers, discussing and arguing about aspects of the large group. Among other things, he kept urging me to start one; I kept saying I wasn't ready. My understanding and skills were not up to scratch, and I didn't feel up to what I saw as the inevitable lengthy time and frustration of attempting to get such a group off the ground. In the meantime I completed my group therapy training in Boston and was working as a clinician. I became a doctoral student at Harvard University, focussing equally on political, clinical, and developmental psychology.

In May 1987 I was to facilitate the three-hour opening session of the Fourth Biennial Conference (NOMOS IV) for Latin American bankers, businessmen, government officials, and military officers held through the Center of International Affairs at Harvard. I had told NOMOS's organizer about Pat's approach to median/large group work, in which the task was to talk to each other as well as to understand the process as it unfolds, and as a result Pat was invited to conduct a large group at this event.

> Dr de Maré acted as convener in a large group discussion involving all 65 of the NOMOS IV participants [seated in a single large circle]. The discussion, while apparently aimless, fulfilled an important purpose for the participants. It allowed people, in Dr de Maré's words, 'to express their minds in a social situation' and to explore the dynamics of a large group.
>
> Most NOMOS participants spend the majority of their time coping with immediate problems in small, hierarchical, clearly oriented groups. This discussion . . . allowed people to free-associate in an unstructured, egalitarian environment approximating the Greek ideal of *Koinonia,* fellowship. The discussion impelled participants to think in abstract terms, to listen to and talk with one another, and to get to know each other as individuals. Its goal was to transcend the limitations of everyday conversation, with all the inhibition, conformity, and repression that it involves, to go beyond a series of monologues to the establishment of a general dialogue. [Kybal, 1987, pp. 115–116]

The NOMOS reporter recalled that de Maré cited the ancient Greek practice of having up to five thousand people gathered to talk to each other in amphitheatres. She went on to describe the NOMOS conversation:

> The ensuing discussion—rambling and chaotic as it may have seemed—eventually brought about a confrontation of two opposite states of mind. A number of participants expressed frustration and dissatisfaction because the discussion lacked an apparent objective, procedure, direction, or leader. Only goal-oriented and structured discussions, they felt, could be useful, and therefore the current discussion could not be very fruitful. Other par-

ticipants believed that getting people to speak out was valuable in itself, and that no other goal than having a large group discussion was necessary. A third set of participants remained passive.

Dr de Maré ... made no attempt to resolve this clash of viewpoints. ... As the conversation spun on, and the rift between the two camps widened, Dr de Maré wondered aloud whether anyone had learned anything.

'You can't predict what happens in a larger group', responded one participant. 'It is very difficult to dominate. And that's the richness for me. The main benefit here is that you're exposed to unpredictable reactions. You may come up at the end with ideas that are unpredictable.' Another disagreed: 'I don't see it. I don't agree that we should operate in groups without a leader. A general dialogue is not useful. We're only going to get things done in small groups with specific goals and purposes.'

One participant attempted to bridge these seemingly irreconcilable views. He pointed out that it was very difficult for high-powered NOMOS decision-makers to free-associate without an apparent goal. He suggested that the discussion should be injected with a small issue—even a minor or trivial one—in order to ease people into the difficult task of confronting abstract ideas and appreciating one another's minds. Otherwise, he concluded, the discussion would appear aimless. Finally, someone suggested that the dialogue did have a definite goal—'to communicate'.

'It is aimless', said Dr de Maré, as the session drew to a close. Therein lay his message. Only in seemingly aimless discussion could a higher aim be realized: to understand large group dynamics, and to learn to communicate more freely with each other. Such understanding is crucial for decision-makers in whatever organization they work; it is the type of understanding that NOMOS participants came to Bretton Woods to acquire.

A few days later Pat de Maré was honoured at a dinner event hosted by the Northeastern Society for Group Psychotherapy and a small group therapy foundation run by Michael Lawler, a senior member of that society particularly interested in Pat's work.

The future

> Whilst psychoanalysis explores the individual, and small groups examine the family, only larger group settings can feasibly explore the social and cultural contexts in which we all reside usually as helpless onlookers. [Pat de Maré]

Pat has observed that first the legitimacy of on-going one-to-one work had to be established, then that of small group work, and now, he hypothesizes, on-going median and large group work should follow. The need for larger group work should be as evident now as it was to Freud, writing, somewhat wistfully, as I read it, in *Civilization and Its Discontents* (1930a) that, 'One day someone will venture to embark upon a pathology of cultural communities'. Pat de Maré writes:

> The culture of the group is the group equivalent of the individual mind. In so far as this culture can be inappropriate [for the culture's tasks], and even pathologically destructive, so it can be seen as the equivalent of neurotic disturbance in the individual.

If there is resistance, and there always is, some of it seems to come from our own community:

> As an example of cultural defect, it is remarkable how the areas covered by psychiatry, by psychoanalysis, by psychotherapy and group therapy all avoid a critique of the cultural contexts in which they are being practiced. Attempts to explore this context are treated as 'unrealistic'.

But practice seems to be evolving. I will mention just three different current situations in which median/large group work could be thought of as the next logical step.

First, for some years in the Boston area psychoanalysts such as John Mack and Daniel Jacobs and other clinicians have reported hearing from their individual patients about threats to global security, both environmental and nuclear. A group of women psychologists are meeting to discuss possible interpretations of patients' issues as reflections of large group dysfunctioning when faced with threats to global survival—interestingly, the patients themselves are not linking their issues to the global ones but see them rather in terms of intrapsychic and family dynamics.

These clinicians do not treat the concern about these issues solely as inappropriate avoidance of personal issues assumed to be more painful, as is often the case with traditional therapists. However, while they do believe that discussion of global threats is an issue for clinical work, they do not make the logical step Pat has taken in postulating a large group for addressing these issues.

The second situation is that in which political psychologists are working at the level of large group issues. Harvard social psychologist Herbert Kelman holds problem-solving workshops on the Israeli–Palestinian dispute, starting with the same small group therapy model of the Institute for Group Analysis. He has expanded the model to be both a small and a median group at the same time. That is, the first and second parties (the Israelis and Palestinians) number eight, while the mostly silent third party can number over twenty. Kelman has long seen the need for on-going group meetings to enable learning to be integrated more easily into work situations, but has not had the funding to accomplish this.

Psychoanalyst Vamik Volkan has been developing the idea of the need for mutual mourning between groups who have historically battered each other over decades or centuries, such as the Greek Cypriots and Turkish Cypriots and the Catholic and Protestant Irish. His idea of the need to mourn in order to heal societally inflicted wounds was also used at a conference in Jerusalem attended by children of former Nazis and Holocaust survivors. A logical step here would be on-going large group meetings in places where conflicts are still alive.

Third is the example of a staff group in a half-way house for clients discharged from the state mental hospital but not yet able to live in ordinary, uninstitutionalized outpatient settings. This group's task is to enable members to talk about their stressful work. This is its seventh year of consecutive weekly group meetings, and I have been their facilitator for the last eighteen months.

The nine members of the group discuss their relations with each other, with the directors, and with the residents, their different roles, conflicting tasks, and the strains and rewards of this demanding, underpaid, and undervalued work. They have very occasionally talked of matters outside this small world of residents and staff. On those rare occasions such talk has been about the management of all the half-way houses in the system, and the hospital of which this subsystem is a part. This discussion takes place only from the single perspective of their place in the hierarchy.

Recently the directors of another halfway house in the system decided to have staff group meetings similar to those of my group. In planning this, Michael Lawler proposed that he should himself lead a twice-monthly meeting of both staff groups together, to which both groups agreed.

However, before this agreement was reached, it was discussed at length in my staff group. The time this new large group would take, the difficulty of grasping what could be useful about it, and the emotional discomfort in dealing with new and different people in a larger setting, were prominent objections. For some it was almost impossible to imagine that the discomfort of such a group and the experience of growth might be connected, although all had experienced this connection in the small staff group. Over the weeks a willingness to try this new and difficult task emerged, provided that no time was taken away from the present group.

This is the record of one such meeting of the staff group in which the prospect of joining the larger group was still an issue.

> The group started with one member stating she'd speak first, acknowledging that she never does and wondering if the group would wonder what it meant for itself that she did. She then reiterated an announcement she had made at a team meeting the night before, about taking a five-week leave of absence to go to a country in the Far East, to which she has been dreaming of returning since her two-year Peace Corps stint there. When an offer of a four-month return visit was made to her, she discovered that her commitment to the work in the half-way house, with its opportunities for learning about herself, were important enough to her to turn down the four-month offer and to go only for the shorter period.
>
> The group then took up the issue of legitimately expanding boundaries versus having sloppy, weak boundaries (a distinction made in the group the previous week); M. felt her leave of absence meant thought-through, task-oriented expansion and that her expansion would be brought back into the house to expand residents' perspectives, too.
>
> There was agreement, and talk with another member, T., about her outside commitments, time-consuming and meaningful to her, and their relationship to this job and compatibility with it.
>
> The group then discussed differences in cultures (they used this word) and of the different ways to learn about them. They mentioned the differing cultures of different half-way houses, of countries, and the old culture of

> their house, represented by its director and two of the residents there from from its beginnings, versus the new culture that occurs each time there is new staff.
>
> They raised the question of the value of unthinkingly following established ways of doing things, and when it was and was not appropriate to question, when to create, when to make a practice their own, and what to do if conflict followed. Next they talked about what it would mean if they disagreed with another House's ways of working.—Perhaps there are clear rights and wrongs about dealing with clients.
>
> At this point I asked whether the group was anxiously anticipating facing in the median group the other group's culture, and that they might object to aspects of it. Two members want to know if I am bringing in my stuff about the large group. I ask what others think. One associates to the Cold War, and, in response, another, who has been most unenthusiastic about the median group from the beginning, says, 'Ugh'. Another (the non-white staff member) talks about differences that would arise, asking, apparently unselfconsciously, 'Are they [these issues] black and white, or not? Are there goods and bads?'
>
> Still another reports that, with help from one of the directors, he has learned of something wrong going on in another house which is being discussed at management level but not yet here in the group. His concern is his responsibility with regard to the wrong-doing of a staff person from another group.

Numerous rich themes emerged, such as the connection between the kind of giving and learning gained in working in a half-way house and Peace Corps work in the Far East; the expanded meaning of boundaries; the difficulties of discussing cultural differences; and the immediacy with which such a task brings on thoughts of the climate of the Cold War.

For me it is thoughts of the climate of hot war and a hot planet that necessitate large group work. In my experience one-to-one therapy and group therapy are undertaken originally out of a feeling of necessity; few embark on and persevere with such therapy just for the interest of it. Similarly, there is an urgent need to understand the rhythms of past and present cultures, and, in turn, their relation to the rhythms of the planet.

Department of Psychiatry
Harvard Medical School
Cambridge, Massachusetts

KOINONIA

From Hate, through Dialogue, to Culture in the Large Group

Koinonia

KOINONIA. n. Communion, fellowship, intercourse

Liddell & Scott, *Greek–English Lexicon*

By 'Greece' or 'Hellas', the classical world, is meant all lands occupied in antiquity by peoples speaking a dialect known as 'Koine'—literally, 'common'—not the classical Greek of Herodotus and Thucydides, but a sort of carthorse of a language belonging to everybody because it belonged to nobody.

Koine was spoken during the time of which Shelley wrote:

> The period which intervened between the death of Pericles (495 BC) and the death of Aristotle (322 BC) undoubtedly, whether considered in itself or with reference to the effect which it has produced upon the subsequent discoveries of civilised man, is the most memorable in the history of the world. [*On the Manners of the Ancients*]

The main structural feature of this phase in history was a novel cultural constellation, namely democracy, the temporary ascendancy of the large group and citizenship over small group oligarchy and aristocracy.

Every citizen had the right to attend the Ekklesia or Assembly, where two to three thousand at any one time would come to vote and to listen to the cleverest men in Athens.

Despite the restricted nature of citizenship (women, slaves, and foreigners being excluded), Athenian democracy has been described as 'the fullest in history', 'capable of realising energies that lifted Athens to one of the peaks in history', 'never before or since has political life, within the circle of citizenship, been so intense or so creative'. 'The city', wrote Simonides, 'is the teacher of the man' (Durrant, n.d.).

There were also vital defects, and finally the Athenian democracy had to pay dearly for them. There was the encouragement of demagogy and of rhetoric, the wasteful ostracism of able men, and the lack of organization. In the end Athens fell prey to the oligarchic dictatorships of Sparta, Macedonia, and Rome.

But before that, in this climate of democratic exchange, the word 'Koinonia' was first coined—a word later to be used in the Acts of the Apostles (2.42; 4.32–35; 5.12–16). It refers to the atmosphere of impersonal fellowship rather than personal friendship, of spiritual-cum-human participation in which people can speak, hear, see, and think freely, a form of togetherness and amity that brings a pooling of resources. To this day communion in the Greek Orthodox Church is referred to as Koinonia.

Introduction

What is this book about? Essentially it is about an operational approach to dialogue, culture, and the human mind, through the medium of a larger group context. The approach is similar in many ways to the group-analytic approach of Dr S. H. Foulkes. We have tried to link the most intimate aspect of individual beings naturally and spontaneously in the socio-cultural setting of the larger group. This endeavour seems to us to have uncovered very significant areas, since the larger group, by the very nature of its size, offers a structure or medium for linking inner world with cultural context and is able to establish a unique dimension, that of a microculture. Psychoanalysis and small groups till now have not been able to handle this aspect empirically. The larger group now shows us the other side of the coin to the inner world, namely the socio-cultural dimension in which these interpersonal relationships take place.

This has led us to explore how objects, including part objects of the mind, can be related to systems and structures in a manner that has not yet been attempted; and it brings up the vexed question of the relationship of systems to structures and of culture to social context.

We start off by tracing the development of the large group approach and by drawing up specifically large group features, and we follow this by looking at the small group-analytic principles of Foulkes in relationship to the larger structure.

It has become increasingly clear to us that the hate arising out of the frustrating situation of the larger group is distinct from libido and constitutes the basis for endopsychic energy of mind: hate also provides the incentive for dialogue and becomes transformed, through dialogue, into the impersonal fellowship of *Koinonia* (a Greek word meaning impersonal fellowship which we are applying to this stage of the large group process).

Out of dialogue emerge, first, more primitive subcultural features, and, second, the microcultural systems that are a specific feature of the larger group. These systems cannot be created in the psychoanalytic situation in which the analyst represents the assumed culture, nor in the small group where the hierarchy of family culture inevitably prevails.

This process enables us to examine both our subcultural assumptions and also the macrocultural assumptions of the society around us. The larger group microculture then constitutes a counter-culture.

We discuss various other approaches to the larger group, namely those of anthropologists, sociologists, and various socio-therapists. A distinction is made between the three systems of free association, group association, and dialogue, each with their specific cultural assumptions, and we go on to explore the relationships of various systems to each other and also the establishment of distinct cultural structures, which can be examined in relationship to each other in the light of transposition and transformation.

In chapter three we look at dialogue itself, distinguishing it from monologue, duologue, and dialectic. Dialogue is seen as affiliative, and we recall Pericles' comment that rhetoric destroys democracy, as distinct from dialogue, which promotes a Koinonic culture.

This leads on to the phenomenon of lateralization in larger groups, a horizontal quality (synchronic) as distinct from the vertical (diachronic) dimension—like the grain of wood, which cuts across the line.

We have become increasingly aware that the medium is not the message; we are in agreement with Anzias' (1967) definition of structure as the sense of the system.

We have been impressed by the philosophy of Susan Langer (1967), with her emphasis on language as essentially discursive; we are reminded of Heidegger's comment that the uniqueness of the human individual lies in his potentiality for discourse, and we are intrigued by Thienemann's book *The Interpretation of Language* (1968), which is analogous to the interpretation of dreams. We wonder when someone is going to write an interpretation of philosophy.

We realize that the exchange of words in dialogue is more central and basic than the exchange of integers in numeracy. There is far more alienation between man and man as a result of silence than there can ever be as a result of alienation from the products of labour, which is a secondary result. Secondary also is the written word, which Plato termed the language of the dead.

Ricoeur (1981) made the point that we do not think behind symbols, but symbols actually constitute our thinking. For us this occurs only in the use of symbols in dialogue since symbols are continuously changing their meaning.

Post-structuralism talks of intertextuality; in these terms, it would seem that dialogue is post post-structural.

We have examined not only the effect on structure of the size of the group, but also the crucial matter of seating arrangements: lecture-rooms and platforms, horseshoe amphitheatres with rostra, the opposition of two sides, and the very rare occurrence of single circular seating.

We suggest that the first ecology of all is socio-cultural and human. This ecology was promoted by the Greeks in their struggle for democracy; by arranging circular formations in their amphitheatres, they promoted dialogue and the evolution of the most sophisticated culture the world has ever known.

In chapter six we explore the crucial role numbers play in ecology. Alas, the world is either constrictively oligarchic or chaotically polygarchic. We need to have regard for the human scale, which cannot handle groups with a membership of more than a hundred thousand: beyond this point, global disaster lies.

In chapter five we have examined the imponderable relationship between object theory, systems thinking, and structuralism, revealed operationally in larger group settings. The splits between objects and systems that occur in the mind can become renegotiated through the medium of dialogue in the larger group—'re-membered'.

We are interested in the dialectic distinction made by Engels between horde and family: the more evolved the social organization of the horde, the looser the family ties, and vice versa. This is in contrast to Freud's socio-biological construct of the horde as the family writ large.

Dialogue goes in the opposite direction to the dream work, clarifying rather than disguising. Different structures promote different systems of thinking:

1. The primary process of the individual in the dream in psychosis or in free association occurs in monologue.
2. The binary syllogistic logic is characterized by the two-person dyad, like the digital computer, the either/or, the good or bad, the correct or false.

3. The dialectic is typified by the three-person setting.
4. The lateralized tangential, multipersonal thinking of dialogue, reminiscent of the more-or-less quality of the analog computer, characterizes the larger group. The larger the group, the more predominant this type of thinking becomes. After a certain point it results in the precipitation of microcultures involving the meaning of structure, the metastructure.

All these thoughts have led us to the conclusion that the human psyche is governed, not only by the pleasure and reality principles, but by a third principle, that of meaning, understanding, *verstehen*. It is this third principle that gives a curiously unscientific quality to our deliberations, since science itself is not concerned with totalized human meaning, but with patterns of cause and effect and with 'reality'. It was this quality that perhaps led Freud to remark in his preface to the *New Introductory Lectures* (1933a [1932]): 'It looks as though people do not expect from psychology progress in knowledge, but some other kind of satisfaction.'

The essence of the group-analytic approach to larger groups lies in the elaboration of a microcounter-cultural dimension that has been made possible by the group's increased structure. These evolving microcultures make it possible through dialogue to distance individual members from the surrounding social macroculture, and also to distance them from the group's original instinctual subcultures, e.g. from family culture and from other frames of reference and developmental stages, viz. oral, anal, genital, part objects, depressive and paranoiac positions and pre-oedipal, oedipal, and post-oedipal.

All three cultures—sub, micro, and macro—are self-regulatory feedback systems in themselves; but when they encounter each other, they constitute a structure and introduce mutually transformational features, e.g. infra- and superstructures, surface and deep.

The split cohesiveness of intrapsychic part objects can become coherent through projection into the subculture, and eventually into the microculture of the group matrix via dialogue. This constitutes both a reflection and an action, transforming the cohesive system into a coherent structure.

In the median group we consider the most significant feature to be the transformation of the chaos of mindlessness and hate in the initial rudimentary stages to the Koinonic culture of dialogue in its later, more complex phases. It is as if the space of mind is initially peopled by subhuman subcultures based on infantile developmental phases and then becomes re-peopled through dialogue by later, more appropriate, and more human communions and inner dialogue.

CHAPTER ONE

The story of the larger group approach

The introduction of large groups convened along group-analytic lines brings a new approach to our thinking about groups.

Basically, what we are doing is to apply Foulkesian group-analytic concepts to the larger situation: we are increasing the size of the group-analytic group.

The increase in size is crucial. When the group of eight becomes a group of twenty, we begin to have a different level of group activity, representing a different dimension of human experience. We have gone beyond the confines of the familio-centric group; in this larger setting the group acquires another range of meanings, and cultural context becomes the central issue.

Group analysis, building upon the foundations of psychoanalysis, made it possible to move beyond the bounds of one-to-one dyadic therapy. The large group approach, in its turn building upon the foundations of (small) group analysis, now brings the possibility of moving beyond the bounds of family- and network-centred therapy.

The particular preoccupations and methodology of psychoanalysis, and also to some extent of small group analysis, have meant that the direct consideration of cultural factors has been deferred for a long time.

In classical psychoanalysis the focus upon the individual and his personal unconscious has led to attempts to exclude the socio-cultural context as much as possible. Any introduction of cultural factors has tended to be seen as an impediment, or as resistance, hampering or deflecting the exploration of the patient's inner world. The context of reality against which the interpretation of the transference relationship takes place has to be represented by the analyst in his own person.

In small group analysis the social context is introduced, but to an extent that is determined by the size of the group. For the most part the context is taken to mean the family; problems of interpersonal networks are evoked and transferred into the group, and interpretations and understanding tend to be formulated in family terms.

Therefore, from their very nature and purpose, neither psychoanalysis nor small groups are in a position to grapple with culturally assumptive structures. In these settings, therefore, these are so assumed as to be virtually unconscious. Only in the larger group can the increase in numbers produce a definable group context in its own right, with group features in the foreground.

Thus large groups can be said to take over where small groups leave off. They provide a setting in which we can explore our social myths (the social unconscious) and where we can begin to bridge the gap between ourselves and our socio-cultural environment, which hitherto has often appeared bafflingly beyond our reach. Context now becomes central. It is a situation that has operationally speaking remained relatively unexplored until recently.

If psychoanalysis and small group therapy are primarily concerned with pre-oedipal and oedipal matters, the larger group is involved with post-oedipal considerations, and, like social psychology, it takes the group (as distinct from the individual) as its basic unit. While small groups focus upon the psychoanalytic, biological unconscious, large groups are tilted towards socio-cultural awareness.

Citizenship is only adequately observable in a larger setting, as the small group, by its very nature, displays only the most rudimentary evidence of social as opposed to family dynamics. To apply an unmodified psychoanalytic or small group model to the larger group is like trying to 'play ludo on a chessboard'. For instance, imprinting a family culture on the social context produced Freud's primal horde construct, which, as Freud himself acknowledged, is a mythical caricature.

The large group potential has always been implicit within group analysis, although it was not until the Second European Symposium of Psychotherapy in 1972 that the first large group was instigated.

Foulkes himself was well aware of this dimension when he wrote that 'group therapy is an altogether desirable contribution to people's education as responsible citizens' (1948). When he first introduced small group psychotherapy at Northfield Military Hospital in 1944, he also developed a group approach to the whole hospital in the form of a small co-ordination group. He himself acted as the link between these different groups, but there was no large inter-group meeting per se—that is, the small groups did not meet each other, and therefore it was left to Foulkes (like a Shaman) to represent the large group in his own person. He stood for the whole of the hospital, and to that extent Northfield did not directly represent itself.

After this experience, the next logical step would have been to consider setting up a larger group and applying Foulkesian small group principles to this larger situation, but this did not happen then or for some years later. During the interim, Foulkesian small group analysis continued to expand and develop.

After Northfield and demobilization, Foulkes gathered around himself people who continued to have an interest in group analysis. In 1949 he established weekly seminars in his consulting rooms; and three years later the Group Analytic Society (London) was founded to study and promote group analysis in both its clinical and its applied aspects.

The Group Analytic Society has always constituted the creative centre, the main tree trunk from which developments have branched out—in research and education, in the launching of the journal *Group Analysis,* in the application of group-analytic concepts to other disciplines, and not least in the establishment of the Institute of Group Analysis, with its general or introductory course and the qualifying course for group analysts. The Society also acted as a springboard for the development of family and marital studies, which in due course separated off to become the Institute of Family Therapy shortly after Foulkes died in 1976.

Applying Foulkesian principles to larger structures may, today, against the above historical background, appear as quite self-evident. Yet it was not until 1972, at the Second European Symposium of Psychotherapy held at the Maudsley Hospital, that the first large group, with over one hundred participants meeting in a single circle, was launched by de Maré and Lionel Kreeger. In this they were inspired by Freud's prophecy that one day someone will venture to embark upon research into the pathology of cultural communities, and by E. Neumann's (1954) comment that 'the task of evolving a collective and cultural therapy adequate to cope with the mass phenomena now devastating mankind has now become the primary issue'.

It is important to realize that a larger group technique had not until that time been seriously considered. There was little recognition that this powerful but unpredictable and chaotic structure is sensitive and potentially thoughtful and requires more structuring—more, not less.

At this time, de Maré (1972) wrote:

> What does the future hold? I think it is likely to be concerned not only with small and medium sized groups, not only with the controversy over therapeutic community and community therapy, but with much larger psychotherapeutic groups with a membership of fifty to a hundred, conducted by several co-conductors, non-directive and a-programmatic, with tiered circular seating arrangements reminiscent of the amphitheatre. In this situation group dynamics become extremely clearly defined; and atmospheres, attitudes, ideas and ideologies make themselves evident not as cloudy, idealistic non-sequiturs, but as definitive climates which can be seen as either impeding, coercing or promoting communication, and which themselves are the object of study. In these larger groups is more clearly seen the antithesis, the polarisation of conscious and unconscious.
>
> The problem for the individual is the intrusion into the individual situation of the repressed unconscious. For the large group, on the other hand, it is consciousness that is in jeopardy, both for the individual and for the group's equivalent of consciousness, namely communication and organization. The problem for the rudimentary large group is its mindlessness; not how to feel, but how to think.

The year 1975 saw the publication of a collection of papers entitled *The Large Group,* edited by Kreeger. It also saw the establishment of a regular weekly median group by de Maré. This group began with forty members, rapidly fell to thirty, and finally stabilized at twenty. It has continued ever since.

In 1984, under the auspices of the Institute of Group Analysis, de Maré started a seminar group to discuss more actively the theory and application of large groups, with a membership generally rather more sophisticated and more involved with theory than with therapy. This group formed the substratum for future developments and went on to establish, in 1987, the Large Group Section of the Group Analytic Society. Under its auspices a 'Black and White' Group was successfully established the following year. This is a group in which people of different ethnic origins meet regularly in order to learn to talk with each other and establish a dialogue through which cultural issues can be explored; it represents a specific application of large group concepts to the field of race relations.

In summary, the aims of the Large Group Section are:

to create a forum where those interested in large groups can come together;

to encourage the application of similar groups in a variety of institutional and other settings;

to provide support, information, experience, and training for potential large group convenors;

ultimately to help humanize our sociocultural context through an understanding of dialogue and culture.

In May 1985 de Maré presented the S. H. Foulkes Annual Lecture. This was, in effect, a large group experience: 350 people were seated in four concentric circles to take part in a discussion of large group issues, and a good deal of interest was stimulated.

Following this, Dr Harold Behr's editorial in the August (1985) issue of *Group Analysis* discussed the advent of the large group approach. He wrote that all group analysts have had a taste of large groups, and 'many have even conducted them; that is to say, they have sat through them as small group leaders on a course or workshop with no clear idea of how to intervene except to signal the ending of the session'. Describing de Maré as a group analyst who has done for the large group what Foulkes did for the small analytic group, he commented that the large group reflects our sociocultural environment in a way that the small group cannot possibly do, pointing out that the group is not meant to provide psychotherapy for the individual so much as to contribute towards the process of humanizing society. Large groups, ends Dr Behr, should take up the challenge and set about creating a climate in which they can form an established part of our culture.

* * *

On the basis of the experience gained over the last fifteen years, we can summarize the specific features of the large group approach as it contrasts both with psychoanalysis and with small groups.

The larger group of twenty and upwards to at least one hundred can be approached by the same principles as Foulkes used in working with small groups.

These principles consist of:

1. Face-to-face single-circle seating arrangement.
2. Regularity of attendance and meetings, usually once or twice a week.
3. Free-floating discussion. To quote Foulkes (1948) himself: 'The basic rule of group analysis is the group counterpart of free association: talk about anything which comes to your mind without selection. It works out in a different way in the group situation from the individual situation just as it works out differently in the analytic situation from the procedure of self-analysis. Free association is in no way independent of the total situation. The way it works out I have described after observing it for a number of years as free-floating discussion or conversation.'
4. The conductor does not lead, although he/she is capable of assuming leadership. He/she refrains from setting topics or goals, is non-directive, and remains relatively disengaged as to his own person.

5. There is no given task, no occupation, no programme and no goal, not even the goal of becoming a 'good' group.
6. What happens in the group is related to Foulkes' construct of the group matrix, which is characteristic of his approach. He described the matrix as 'the common shared ground which ultimately determines the meaning and significance of all events, and upon which all communications, verbal and non-verbal, exist'.

In practice, we have discovered that the figure of 18 to 20 members appears to be the appropriate size for the next stepping-stone in an approach to large groups. Groups of this size can be called median groups.

A large or median group setting needs to be handled with the care to detail already conceded in psychoanalysis and small-group-analytic psychotherapy. The large group is as complex and sensitive an apparatus, in fact probably more so since it is a learning situation as distinct from an instinctual one, and involves an emphasis on meaning as distinct from gratification or reality. As it is more frustrating and less gratifying, so it is harder to establish and maintain. The emphasis is upon the socio-cultural, not on psychotherapy.

Experience has shown the concentric circles and tiered seating originally envisaged to be contra-indicated, as face-to-face contact needs to be maintained. Conducting should be confined to one or two convenors, certainly not several: this is because the use of multiple convenors leads inevitably, by the very nature of the structure it creates, to unevenness in the flow of dialogue and to the likelihood of the formation of splinter groups within the larger whole.

In psychoanalysis text takes the form of free association; in small group analysis it takes the form of group association; in large groups it becomes dialogue. The development of dialogue is central. This dialogue can be seen as an extension and expansion of the free-flowing discussion of group association, its development promoted by the permissiveness and acceptance that Foulkes encouraged.

In psychoanalysis the intrapsychic subtext and the dyadic text occur in an unchanging standardized setting, which virtually excludes context. In the larger group this context is more broadly based against the group's own continuously emerging miniculture. Cultural issues as distinct from social play a central role. Individual symptoms become collectivized as subcultures from the subconscious, which mould the flow of dialogue. The subcultures clash with the socioculture and become transformed into growing minicultures through dialogue.

Dialogue is something that has to be learnt like a language. The avowed and only purpose of the larger group is to enable people to learn how to talk to each other, to learn a dialogue. The object is not simply talking for talk's sake, but talk as an exchange. As dialogue becomes established, it leads on to the development of an impersonal fellowship in the group, to which we have given the Greek term *Koinonia*.

Dialogue marks a different way of thinking and communication—tangential and analogic, as distinct from the binary digital logic of the one-to-one dyad. It is articulate, circular, lateralized as distinct from linear, meaningful as distinct from causal. Dialogue has an enormous thought potential: it is from dialogue that ideas spring to transform the mindlessness and massification that accompany social oppression, replacing it with higher levels of cultural sensitivity, intelligence, and humanity.

If the small group situation mainly evokes interpersonal experiences first known within the family, the large group context contains a different range of meanings for the individual. These meanings are not only intrapsychic and interpersonal but also contextual, including the impact on the individual of contextual traumas and mass impersonal forces. Individual experiences recalled in the large group include traumatic experiences of all kinds and their after-effects: from war and revolution, persecution and oppression, to job loss and redundancy, moving house and moving country, the impact of cultural change and threats to cultural identity. Topics that come up in the large group include social and macrocultural aspects that are part of the human situation—illness, death, class, race, politics, economics, philosophy, current affairs, religion, and art, the handling of universal human emotions. In the larger setting these themes can be treated in their own right as meaningful, in contrast to being trivialized as intellectual defence. Dialogue—and therefore, by the same token, psycho-sociological conceptualization—does not reflect a defensive attitude towards unconscious group processes any more than consciousness is a defence against the unconscious.

Large groups, in general, are often experienced as intimidating, inhibiting, and frustrating. Outside the more familiar small group framework, it may at first be difficult for the individual to find a voice. The central anxiety in the larger group takes the form of panic (a major issue in separation anxiety) manifested in individuals as phobia, the extreme form of mental anguish. Mass formation and packing (as in wolf pack) and the intense revenge motif of mob violence constitute the group's equivalent to counter-phobic measures.

Since the large group is by its very size frustrating, it generates hate. As long as dialogue remains rudimentary and relatively unstructured, the group continues to operate through subcultures and socio-cultural assumptions. If, on the other hand, hate can be organized through dialogue, it liberates endo-psychic energy and becomes gradually transformed into the impersonal fellowship of Koinonia. Koinonia is the opposite to panic.

Mass formation represents a flight away from the attempt to develop conscious lateralized thinking (dialogue) back into a mindless dyad of leader and led, which represents a return to a binary relationship between two parties. Splitting and the polarization of opinion into, for example, government and opposition can have the same effect.

Dialogue goes in the opposite direction to the subculture by cultivating mini-counter-cultures from whose independent standpoint it is possible to explore not only the subcultures but also the current social or macroculture of the surrounding society. It is empowered to do so by the very nature of the group's increased size.

The miniculture of the large group emerges as a result of dialogue. This emerging miniculture then provides the group with a perspective from which it is able to view socio-cultural and subcultural assumptions that are being taken for granted. The large group minicultures have the effect of expanding consciousness and so provide an ethico-cultural springboard that can distance itself from the unconscious biological and sociological cultures: these can then be demythologized. The intransigence of these cultures is only so because of their unconsciousness.

Cultural changes in the large group take the form of transformations and transpositions from previous cultural contexts, as distinct from the sublimation and transference of smaller settings. For example, the larger group is sensitive to social pressures prevalent as macrocultural assumptions of the surrounding society, whereas the smaller group, being more slanted towards the unconscious, may more readily accept therapeutic assumptions. An example could be found in the discussion of homosexuality, which until recently was treated by the surrounding macroculture as a criminal offence.

By analogy, the larger group is the opposite of the hologram. In the hologram, if the large plate is shattered, each splinter carries a complete representation of the whole. In the larger group, each member, through dialogue, projects a total transformation into the group miniculture. As an example, in India the individuals representing the British Raj were stereotyped; individually they maintained a relatively uniform structure throughout the complexity of the situation.

The larger group behaves like a tree trunk to the branches and twigs of smaller groups and individuals, both sustaining and being sustained by them.

It might be said that the larger the group to begin with, the more primitive are its responses, so that the larger group displays features similar to the unconscious of psychoanalysis. These features incude a facility for splitting, projecting, introjecting, displacing, contradicting, mythologizing, regressing, distorting; they also include being morally and ethically 'imbecile', pleasure-oriented, dependent, and timeless, with a certain mindlessness and illogicality. There is, however, one prime exception: In the large group there is the enormous opportunity for dialogue. As Freud said, there is no conversation in the unconscious. There is, therefore, this discrepancy in the large group: on the one hand it is primitive and unconscious, and on the other hand it is potentially sophisticated in that dialogue proper is able to explore and confront the unconscious subculture with characteristic precision and definition.

In the larger group, therefore, in struggling with dialogue, we are not only responding to the pressures of the reality principle and to the gratification of the pleasure principle. We are involved at the same time in establishing a third principle as we learn to understand ourselves in terms of community and not merely as organisms. The third principle is that of meaning.

It follows that dialogue proper is neither a reaction formation nor a counterphobic measure but constitutes a transformational process; it transforms mindlessness into understanding [*verstehen*] and meaning [*meinen*].

In brief, the larger group is a microculture of society, with the distinction that we can address it and be answered by it. It is the watershed between the world and the personal, individual, experiential mind. It has features of the unconscious mind, with the unique distinction of being like a dream in dialogue; it offers us the opportunity to humanize both individual and society concurrently.

CHAPTER TWO

The median group

> The chronicles of King Arthur relate how King Arthur with the help of a Cornish carpenter invented the marvel of his Court, the miraculous Round Table at which his Knights would never come to blows. Formerly, because of jealousy, skirmishes, duels and murders had set blood flowing in the most sumptuous of feasts.
>
> The carpenter says to Arthur: 'I will make thee a fine table, where sixteen hundred may sit at once, and from which none need be excluded and no knight will be able to raise combat, for there the highly placed will be on the same level as the lowly.'
>
> Marcel Mauss, 'The Gift'

The features that are specific to median and large groups can be considered under the following four headings:

1. *Structure.* This refers to the context of the larger group itself, in this instance approximately twenty members meeting weekly in a circle.
2. *Process.* This refers to the dialogue that arises as a result of the members being placed in this context.
3. *Content.* This refers to the subject matter, themes, and topics.
4. *Metastructure.* This refers to the changing cultural patterns that ensue: the dialectic between individual and group, bringing about culture—the meaning of the structure to the individual member at any one time.

(1) Structure or context

Here we have to consider the size of the group and the way in which the meetings are arranged. In the case of our median group, we have approximately twenty people meeting weekly for ninety minutes, with seating arranged in a circle.

We have seen that the significant structural feature of the larger group is its size, which brings group features into the foreground. Because of the increased size, the larger group constitutes less of an instinctual and more of a learning situation, involving matters of meaning as distinct from gratification, of head rather than of heart.

Unlike the small group, whose size is deliberately and exclusively limited to between eight and twelve members, it is conceivable that a large group can slowly expand and grow to a number that has yet to be established. Increasing the size of the group is something that we still have to learn to do, as we learn how to evolve from a familiocentric to a social culture. It could take several years to discover how to increase the size of a particular group—from twenty to, let us say, thirty members. Experience in the median group shows that there is a difficulty in developing sufficient fellowship for the group to be able to affirm positively the advent of a new member and to differentiate this arrival from the intrusion into the family of a new-born infant.

The large group can be said to go in the opposite direction to psychoanalysis: instead of excluding context in favour of relationship, context becomes paramount. We explore the conscious rather than the unconscious.

Foulkes wrote of small groups that the individual is the object of treatment, but the group is the main therapeutic agency; the group is treated for the sake of its individual members and for no other reason (Foulkes & Anthony, 1957). In the larger group this is reversed: The group becomes the object of treatment, and the individual is the treatment agent. The large group can, of course, like any other group, take on a psychotherapeutic culture, but this is looked on as accidental. As Turquet (1975) wrote in 'Threats to identity in the large group', referring to the Leicester Conferences, 'Members come for study and learning, not as patients. Any therapeutic gain is a chance though acceptable by-product.' We are concerned in large groups with humanizing the group as opposed to socializing the individual.

Following experience in larger groups, we have become interested in the way of thinking known as structuralism, involving concepts of surface and deep structure: and this not simply as a uniform system of social relationships abstracted from concrete behaviour, but as a two- and later three-level model (e.g. Levi-Strauss's 'surface socialization' as based upon a deep underlying bar on incest). This is explored in chapter four.

(2) Process

Turning to process, we see that in psychoanalysis text takes the form of free association, in group therapy group association, and in the larger group dialogue.

Since people have to learn dialogue like a language, a feature of the larger situation is its frustrating nature. The situation is all the more frustrating to begin with because the initial network of communication is so rudimentary. The hate generated by this frustration eventually becomes transformed through dialogue and constitutes the basis for mental, endopsychic, or ego (as distinct from instinctual) energy. Through dialogue this newly released energy becomes the driving force of thought.

Whilst the thinking agency in the individual is mind, the equivalent of this in the larger group is culture. Culture is the outcome of the contradiction between individual and social structure.

This contradiction has been discussed by the social theorist T. H. Marshall (1963). He has written about the double thrust in society between the politico-economic structure on the one hand and cultural status on the other. On the one hand we have the stratified monologue of hierarchy, and on the other the culture of citizenship, which involves levelling, affiliation, and free speech.

The individual therefore comes up against a structure that is, as we have seen, neither realistic nor gratifying; and from this opposition is generated the mental or ego energy (or hate) that provides the basis for thinking and dialogue. It is dialogue—'the Supreme Art', as Plato termed it—which gives rise to the impersonal fellowship of Koinonia. 'Opposition is the Friendship', as William Blake wrote in 'The Marriage of Heaven and Hell'.

In the larger situation the process of thinking has two dimensions: (1) the one-to-one vertical dimension, and (2) the lateral dimension, which takes into account the presence, the minds, and the experience of other people, and which is reminiscent of the lateral thinking described by de Bono.

In the narcissistic state the lateral dimension is undeveloped, and the one-to-one vertical dimension takes precedence. This limitation of lateral awareness can be disguised by a superficial conformity or conventionality and so go unrecognized. An example can be found in individual psychotherapy, where the therapist may be unexpectedly landed with all the power of a primary, instinctual, narcissistic attachment unmodified by the social, lateral dimension, a condition sometimes referred to as 'psychotic' or 'borderline' transference. Freud considered that people suffering from narcissistic disorders are incapable of developing relationships, and that it is this which distinguishes the psychoses from the transference neuroses. It has emerged, however, that psychotics are capable of the most passionate one-to-one relationships, but these relationships have the characteristic of being linear and of excluding lateral attachment to others—that is, they are impervious to social implications. In the larger group, relationships of this type can be very strikingly displayed—for example, when the right thing is said but at quite the wrong time.

(3) Content

Out of dialogue emerges a third dimension, neither of reality nor of pleasure but of meaning, linking personal values (in psychoanalytic terms pre-verbal, oedipal, and familiocentric levels and the specific modalities of each erotogenic zone), to their equivalent cultural consensus in the social structure.

For example, group bonding and Koinonia could be interpreted as a transformation of the frustration of sibling incest and competition. The blood relatedness of siblings is total as distinct from the partial blood relatedness of parent–child and is accordingly the more strongly frustrated by the social structure: biologically natural incest versus an artificial socio-cultural exchange. The ability to symbolize rather than reify, to transform hate and fratricide into the Koinonia of fellowship, into impersonal friendship and tenderness that is not erotic since Eros is libidinal, arises from antilibidinal social forces. If this relationship is successfully transformed, it constitutes the powerful tie binding people together in groups; if it is not successfully transformed, it can result in the psychotically cruel manifestations of unstable political situations.

The wolf-pack/scapegoat dichotomy is a simplistic reduction of the social lateral response into a one-to-one linear relationship. As Freud (1921c) put it: 'The hypnotic relation is a group formation of two' and 'Hypnosis is distinguished from a group formation by this limitation of number.' For Freud, group psychology was a mob or horde psychology.

In this connection it is interesting to recall a variation in the story of Narcissus. Pausanias, a second-century Greek scholar, reports that Narcissus, to console himself on the death of his twin sister, his exact counterpart, sat gazing into a pool to recall her features by his own, rejecting the nymph Echo and his lover, Amenias, who pined away, and provoking the vengeance of the Gods. Finally Narcissus drowned himself. Fraser, in *The Golden Bough* (1890–1915), reports the widely held superstition that it is unlucky, even fatal, to see one's own reflection. The reflection was therefore not of himself, but that of his sister. Echo calls him, but he cannot respond, since the echo is even fainter than the reflection. The tale is the most poignantly nostalgic of all the Greek myths.

Essentially the problem we pose, and for which we recommend an operational solution, is that today we suffer not from a lack of thoughtfulness generated by individual minds, but from the shattering of such intelligence and mindfulness by effete pathological cultures. Culture we regard as the equivalent of group mind: group culture is group mind.

We are troubled by the discrepancy between individual mind and culture; how effectively to hasten mutuality between them? We pose the possibility that culture can be explored more adequately in a setting that is larger than the small group. We note that Walter Schindler (1980) models his small groups on family interpretations seeking to resolve family conflicts of the past in the proxy small group of the present. He separates the family from the social dimension and suggests that the latter should be considered under a separate heading, namely that of political psychology.

We posit that the latter level, that of the political adult peer culture, cannot appropriately, technically or operationally be contained or generated in the small group setting, but demands a larger setting of more people. Our experience during ten years has confirmed this. Psychoanalysis and small group analysis manifest pre-oedipal, oedipal, and family constellations. The median group attemps to approach the post-oedipal community. Perhaps at a later date a larger group technique will be practised for more global political situations. Freud (1930a [1929]) cited one source of human suffering as the inadequacy of our methods for regulating human relationships in the family, in the community, and in the State. He considered that civilization has been built up on renunciation of instinctual gratification and that culture . . . exerts a heavy toll of aim inhibited libido in order to strengthen communities by bonds of friendship. In spite of this renunciation primary hostility of men towards one another continues to threaten society with disintegration.

The question is whether this hate is primary and instinctual or whether it is secondary. For us in the median group, instinct is a form of physical energy, whereas hate is endopsychic energy, epiphenomenal and anti-instinctual. As we see it, hate comes before guilt but after Eros. It is a form of ego energy that is neither creative nor destructive per se, not to be subdued or denied but to be affirmed, cultivated, and transformed. We make no apology for using the word 'hate'. We see it, like hunger, as a psychological absence and not as a biological presence such as aggression. What we are talking about is the anti-instinct occasioned by what Freud termed *Ananke,* a Greek word meaning external reality, necessity, or fate. Freud describes ego instinct as libidinal; but for us this is a contradiction. Guilt is a secondary consideration, which denies hate and renders it invisible, an anti-anti-instinct. Freud (1917e [1915]) wrote that 'Eros and Ananke were the parents of human culture. . . .'

The construct of a primal horde of brothers bonded by a homosexual tie could be restated as a band of brothers bound, not by a homosexual tie, but by a deeply repressed incestuous instinct transformed into hate, alias mental energy, as a result of frustration by external influences, and further transformed into the bonding of groups by the impersonal fellowship of Koinonia, which indeed has to be learned as much as does the handling of external reality. *The crucial feature then of the median group is its potential to transform the subcultural mode of the pregenital or the microculture of the oedipal familiocentric group into the framework of its social cultural equivalent, previously rendered invisible by being ignored.*

Kleinian metaphors are often apparent in large group behaviour as if the whole group culture symbolizes the world of the breast or the mother's body, into which these fantasies are projected and then transformed into cultural themes. Whilst St Paul saw the church in terms of a family group, Christ preached that such ties had to be abandoned in favour of a more universal linking.

Another Greek word that relates to *Koinonia* is *Eutropelia,* literally meaning 'good turning' or 'versatility of mind'. It refers to the ability to see things in divergent rather than convergent ways so that the familiar becomes strange and the strange familiar, tickling our sense of humour and provoking laughter.

We have found that the very size of the larger group can provide sufficient cohesiveness to act as ballast, or cement, neutralize the destructive individual attacks (often between two members), and so provide an alternative to surrendering or packing, like a pack of wolves. The larger context can present a powerful front that can absorb violation by a steady pressure of persistent negotiating. This is an example of 'ego training in action' acting as a good match, as Foulkes (Foulkes & Anthony, 1957) remarked, for the ancient superego, in the form of the group matrix, a network response. In the larger situation the network is in strikingly greater evidence. The cementing process of dialogue gives us a technique for treating the schizoid friability of groups in their early stages. The only answer to mass violence is collective dialogue.

(4) Metastructure

In an attempt to disguise their inappropriate and infantile nature, subcultures, rendered invisible both by projection and by having stemmed from an incoherent pre-verbal level into the microculture of the group as a whole, produce one of Freud's (1930a [1929]) pathological cultural communities. It is this aspect of content that we have referred to as metastructure; it corresponds to the 'superstructure' of structuralism and is essentially cultural. It concerns the varied meanings that the context of the larger group holds for the individual.

The larger group presents us with a broader span, a panorama ranging from the inner world at one end to world denizenship at the other. It thus offers us a setting in which we can study the different transformations by which cultural patterns emerge from pregenital pre-verbal subcultures and oedipal microcultures. These patterns range, as we have said, from the instinctual pre-oedipal Kleinian (oral–anal) level at one end, proceeding through the Oedipus (phallic) complex of parents and sibling, the family-centric culture, with its small group microcultural systems, to the social culture at the other end. In this process they pass through various transformations, which can be looked at in relationship to each other. Class distinction, racism, economic status, sexual deviation, professionalism, assumptions of attitudes and values in general, whether humorous, hostile, destructive, creative, promotive, or nurturing, can all be explored.

There is, for instance, the relationship between incest on the one hand and marital status on the other. There is much in marriage that is a successful transformation of incest, as it is universal, powerful, repetitive, and exclusive, and if disturbed it results in primitive, even psychotic responses. The larger group, in manoeuvring a cultural transformation from hate to friendliness, plays a major role in nurturing genital primacy. Genitality not only expresses an instinct involving a relationship, but a total social learning situation, the outcome of the latency period at puberty. Hence perhaps the reputed success of sexual dysfunction clinics. Genitality is inevitably and essentially two-faced—both erotic and social.

Whilst psychotherapy treats mind and the small groups handle the group matrix, the larger group involves the equivalent of group mind in the form of culture. The small group has to learn how to express feeling, the larger group how to express thought. Assemblages losing cultural metastructures erupt either into mob violence (hate), or fragment into chaos (panic), stultify into states of institutionalization, or demand to be anaesthetized, e.g. through drug addiction. Culture, therefore, is at the interface between individual and social context: it is the outcome of the dialectic between them, just as agriculture is the cultivation of the soil by the individual, or science, art, philosophy, and religion are the cultivation of the universe by mankind. The larger group can therefore serve as a situation for exploring and discovering its own projected sub- and microcultures—'anthropology in the making'. We do not need to go to Africa.

The median group functions as a transitional object or as a rite of passage. It presents itself as a possible technique for the treatment of the traumatic neuroses of contextual catastrophe, such as war or mob violence, which induce panic embedded in the mind like splinters of a mirror, as in the eye of the boy Kay in Hans Christian Andersen's 'The Snow Queen'. It also offers itself as a potential technique for the renegotiation of earlier contextual traumata—for instance, leaving home for boarding school, from school to university, from university to employment, from the single to the marital state, for inter-disciplinary and inter-cultural splits such as expatriation. Ronald Fairbairn (1952) has written that the core of neurosis is the panic of separation anxiety. Marie Stride wrote in *Group Analysis* (1977, 1978) that the origin of narcissism lies not so much in self-love as in the symptomatic feelings of acute dread of the outside world.

We have found that the individual threshold of panic can be raised in the course of the median group meetings, and group members can go on to make successful changes in their external lives, which had previously been thought impossible. In the split with reality of psychosis, dialogue in the larger group can establish an extremely powerful, undeniable ballast of context, forming a reality that cannot be sidestepped but which is open to negotiation. Whilst psychoanalysis faces inward reality and is intrinsic in that sense, denying context in favour of a total focus on relationship, the larger group looks out extrinsically at the surrounding culture and society. The one is biologically determined while the other is sociological and has to be learned: the former, you might say, is a system and the latter a structure. Koinonia, citizenship, impersonal fellowship, is not an instinctual by-product of sublimated Eros; on the contrary, it has to be learned as a sociogenic process of civics, and, if it is a sublimation of anything, it is a transformation of hate.

To underplay the cultural context of metastructure in any way is to overlook a crucial dimension of social reality. Unfortunately this part of our social heritage is often ignored; it comes in with the milk and therefore can be disregarded. Taken out of the cultural context and pushed into individual terms, culture often looks like insanity. Culture can, in fact, render personal insanity invisible by camouflaging it behind its own peculiarities. Negative response to a vindictive national tyrant may be interpreted and explained away, even when in social terms the tyrant remains an unadulterated monster who has failed to make a successful transformation, remaining instead a disastrous victim of his own psychotic internal objects, untransformed, uninterpreted, and regarded as an inevitable expression of social reality or of 'human nature'.

Fortunately metastructure, through dialogue, contains the seeds of its own potential restructuring. When placed with other people in the collective situation, the individual is involved in the text of the infinite surface diversification of dialogue, which is a creative process. Basic themes similar to the twelve notes of the chromatic scale can give rise to an infinitude of melodic arrangements. The frustrated biological energy flow of hatred in the collective situation is reconstituted in the form of a projection into the cultural context. It is a reflection of the inner world, providing a decipherable meaning that is also at the same time a translation. This spans the entire range, from the inner world to the total cultural context, in a gigantic transformation.

The fourth member of the tetrad then is the metastructure, or cultural context. This in turn starts off a new cycle of events, resulting in further transformations or acculturations.

* * *

Twenty members, as distinct from eight, create a more powerful, a more complex situation, which is distinguished primarily by this cultural texture, so that whilst membership of a small group may generate an infinitude of familiocentric microcultures, membership of a group of 20 may enable us to experience a wide range of social cultures literally untenable in the smaller group and primarily based on the successful negotiation of frustration and hate through dialogue and its transformations.

The world today is dominated by oligarchy; we still have to learn the praxis of assemblages, the intermediation between individual citizen and society through the tree trunk of larger groups of which oligarchies are the mere twigs.

In the small group it is the conductor who is the main receptacle for projections of parental authority figures, and the individual ego is able to become freer and stronger through identification with the rest of the group. In the larger group, however, the group itself constitutes the canvas onto which the superego is projected, and the conductor, now more appropriately known as convenor, gives support to the role of individuals at an ego level, encouraging freedom of dialogue and interpreting the nature of social and cultural pressures.

Whilst H. Ezriel (1950) maintained that the group situation was neither more nor less than a transference situation in a group setting, Foulkes (1948) was clear that there are significant non-transference aspects present in the group, notably a network of human relationships. In the larger group we see this particular aspect amplified to take on a wider range of changes with distinct qualities as microcultures: for example, there could be the family oedipal or sibling culture, a court of justice, a forum, a primal horde. It is the quality of these 'microcultures' that the convenor attempts to recognize, since they often constitute impediments to dialogue.

For us there is no instinct of destruction but an anti-libidinal hate, which becomes transformed by splitting into a superego structure and a source of neutral endopsychic energy. The external world is preserved from destruction by the hatred becoming both re-structured and re-systematized by the mind. In the larger group this split is re-negotiated by exposing the structure of the larger group to the systemic flow of dialogue.

In relation to the hate motif, it is interesting to read that Fenichel (1945) and others wrote that mental functions should be approached from the same angle as the nervous system, as manifestations of irritability. There are forces at work opposing the discharged tendency of the states of tension, of the reflex arc. The study of these inhibiting forces is the immediate subject of psychology. Without these counter forces there would be no psyche, only reflexes. This tension results in the urging quality of mental or psychic energy, constituting a dynamic force with quantitative aspects described as 'economic'. Every increase in mental tension is felt as displeasure within a structure that has been seen in terms of the tri-part ego, id, and superego.

You might say that the larger the number of people meeting in a group, the more primary is the response in the individual, so that the larger the group, the more likely it is to behave along lines that replicate the laws of the unconscious, i.e. by splitting, condensing, and displacing, by being illogical, contradictory, and symbolic. There is, however, one primary exception, as Freud (1900a) has pointed out: 'The unconscious has no conversation.'

The processes that take place in the median group can be schematized as follows:

1. *The individual member* placed in a mutually frustrating structure with others either stays and hates or panics and runs away: 'Every man for himself!' The individual, *the singleton,* is narcissistically self-centred (Turquet, 1975).

2. If he stays long enough to hate (from the point of view of the group, hate is an achievement), the individual becomes a *membership individual.* Dialogue ensues

and transforms hate into endopsychic energy, which in turn mobilizes further dialogue (FIGURE 1).

3. *The membership individual,* by a process not unlike holographic mimicry, becomes restructured, with a characteristic sense of loss identity (FIGURE 2).

The mind, to preserve reality from destruction, including the destruction of other people, defuses hate and transforms it by introjection into

(a) the impregnable superego of abandoned and lost love objects, which is a structure;

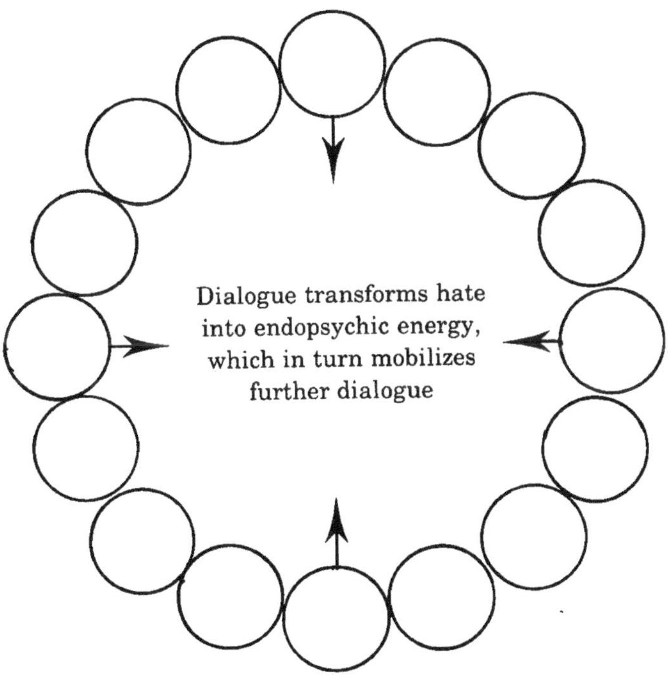

FIGURE 1

3. (b) endopsychic energy, which is a neutral system.

    In the group they meet together in negotiating dialogue.

4. In 1900 Freud wrote that there are no conversations in dreams. Dialogue, on the other hand, is quintessentially conversational. Members can choose to talk to each other, as distinct from violating each other—can choose Koinonia. So can the convenor!

The humanizing and individualizing of the social dimension run a distinctly separate course from the socializing

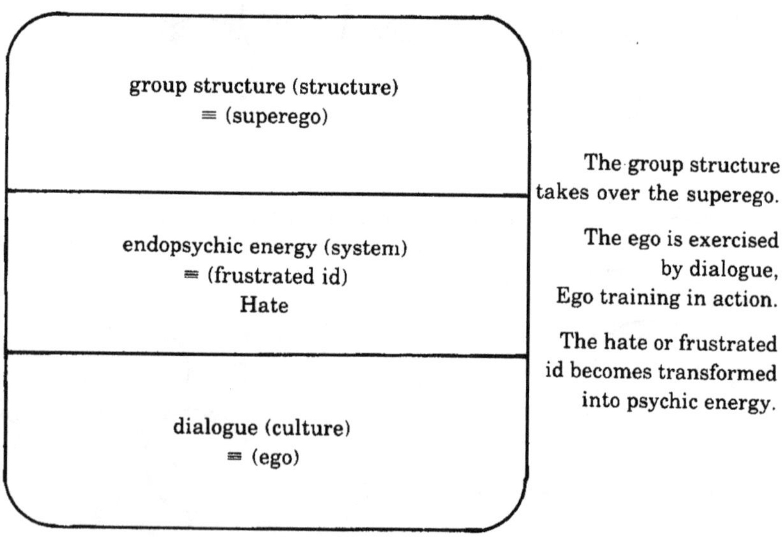

FIGURE 2

of the human individual, and are equivalent to cultivation. They are based on the learning achievement of friendship by speaking to hate with dialogue. It is the humanizing of hate that provides the drive towards social contextual structuring. (The very word 'human' relates to a term derived from cultivation: humus—the land.)

The larger group is antithetically distinct from the small group because of its involvement with Koinonia—impersonal fellowship. It is axiomatic we keep the distinction between the two courses of love and friendship completely clear; they easily become confused and there is a tendency to treat one as the other, e.g. in seeking friendship through sexuality, and in treating sexuality as friendship.

To reiterate, friendship is barred as much as sexuality and causes as much embarrassment; it is frequently misrepresented and misread as sexual. Authentic fellowship can only be successfully derived from hate by comprehensive dialogue. Friendship is often treated with suspicion since its transformation is often incomplete, psychic energy being mingled with untransformed hate. The relationship between the two needs to be disentangled if 'minding' is to occur.

The mind is capable of timelessness and spacelessness and can be experienced as threatening, but thinking is an alternative that has to be nurtured and cultivated and tasted out in dialogue. It is not simply (as Bion, 1961, would have it) a negative tolerance of frustration, but it is, rather, a viable alternative to destructiveness.

Whilst the small group is by definition oligarchic and evolves different meanings towards its small structure (e.g. family, committee, jury, cabal, enclave, which we have termed subcultural or metastructural), the larger group opens itself to the possibility of a greater range of superstructural microcultures. This is analogous to Chomsky's

(1968) rules of universal grammar in which deep structures, the infrastructures, influence the diversity of surface structures of ordinary speech, thereby transforming them. In the larger group there is the additional level of the superstructural, cultural, or group mind.

Dialogue, whether internal dialogue such as monologue or duologue between two people, or polylogue between several people, takes place under the influence of the three structures of superego, ego, and id isomorphically. A person can be as unaware of his cultural assumptions as he is of his unconscious.

We postulate that the median group enables us to view our macrocultural assumptions more effectively than other settings can do, since it is capable of evolving its own microculture from which to look at other cultural assumptions, including its own subcultures.

All neurosis (coming from the personal infrastructure in conflict with the social structure) may have superstructure or cultural ramifications that create more problems than the neurosis itself. For example, the cultural attitude towards homosexuality (still treated in many places as a criminal offence) may be as problematic as racism. It is vital that we treat the camouflaging cultural assumptions as crucial, particularly as they frequently manifest themselves in a conspiracy of silence—the 'culture of silence' (Paulo Freire, 1972).

CHAPTER THREE

Dialogue

> Some people have to say something, others have something to say.
>
> Comment made at one of the meetings

Dialectic is a term used to describe the process of reasoning by dialogue. Its beginnings are usually associated with the Socrates of the Platonic Dialogues, and with the art of debate by question and answer. The Platonic Dialogues, however, took place in symposia composed of between two and eight people and therefore are distinct from dialogue in the larger group setting.

The term 'dialectic' has taken on various meanings. Aristotle attributed it to Zeus. Plato conceived of it as the science of first principles, the ultimate clearest highest sort of knowledge, the 'Supreme Art'. Aristotle distinguished between dialectical reasoning, which proceeds 'syllogistically' from opinions generally accepted, a process of criticism wherein lies the path to the principle of all inquiries, and demonstrative reasoning, which begins with what is actually occurring (as in empirical science). Eristic reasoning was the art of specious reasoning for the purpose of victory in argument.

In modern philosophy dialectic took over from the medieval duality with the antinomies of Kant, the dualities of thesis and antithesis, of noumena, things in themselves, and phenomena, things as they appear to us in sensations and perceptions. A large part of *The Critique of Pure Reason* is occupied in showing the fallacies that arise from confusing matters that are experiential with matters that are not, such as applying space and time to 'things-in-themselves'. Dialectic is in fact a method concerned with ideas.

Hegel made the oppositional antonym dynamic by introducing the triadic movement, 'the dialectic' of all knowledge, of thesis, antithesis, and the new element, synthesis, distinguishable from the previous antonyms of Kant. The resulting spiral leads finally to the Absolute Idea, to God (and, incidentally, for Hegel, to the head of the Prussian State).

Marx, in *Das Kapital,* reversed Hegel's concept, turned it upside down, and applied it not to idealism but to materialism, in the form of dialectical materialism. Neither absolute idealism nor materialism are in themselves dialectical; both therefore reveal a basic discrepancy. However, later Lenin applied the dialectic not to a basic economism but to society, distinguishing a social infrastructure and a cultural superstructure, a process that has revealed itself clearly to us in the larger group. This dialectic has taken the form of dialogue between individuals and the socio-cultural structure, leading on to changes in culture. Social and cultural are radically polarized, a crucial distinction not previously made so explicit.

In other words, Plato's dyadic question-and-answer principle gave way to the mutually contradictory antinomies of Kant, which led Hegel onto the synthesis of a higher unified truth, the dialectical process, a continual unification of opposites in the complex relation of parts to a whole—the thesis–antithesis–synthesis of Fichte. Hegel's version gave primacy to the spirit—the world was secondary. Marx and Engels turned Hegel's approach upside down, the infrastructure became Nature, material, means of production, economism. Cultural and social matters such as class followed suit in the superstructure of society, culture, and consciousness. For this somersault Engels coined the term 'dialectical materialism'.

The big shift was brought about by Kant when he suggested that thinking, instead of evolving smoothly, takes place antinomically, in conflict and in revolution.

Aldous Huxley, in *The Importance of Language,* writes:

> To learn to use words correctly is to learn, amongst other things, the art of foregoing immediate excitement and immediate personal triumph. Much self control and great disinterestedness are needed by those who would realize the ideal of never misusing language. Moreover a man who habitually writes and speaks correctly is one who has cured himself not merely of conscious and deliberate lying, but also (and the task is much more difficult and at least as important) of unconscious mendacity.

Dialogue is affiliative (a term derived from a word meaning the abnegation of father), on the level, levelling, lateralizing, multi-personal, multipolar, and egalitarian, and therefore multidimensional. Arguments, on the other hand, binary oppositions, rhetoric, polemic performances, and duologue, the true and the false, are all basically hierarchical, or highly compartmentalized, not unlike the binary system of the digital computer.

A hierarchical hiatus between monologue and dialogue was made by Wittgenstein when he stated in *Tractatus* that what 'can be said at all can be said clearly and what we cannot talk about we must pass over in silence'. He made a split between clear speech and silence. It is the nature of this split itself that interests us, the boundary zone in which we live and indulge in small talk and dialogue. The small group also uses dialogue, but not as it is used in the larger group, not with the same complexity and intensity. It is this perhaps which is 'shown' and which 'cannot be said' in the Wittgensteinian sense: it is the nature of this unclear interface, continuously being remodelled in dialogue, which concerns us. It is the hiatus, the excluded middle within the actual boundary itself like a no-man's-land, which constitutes the territory of dialogue. It is this territory that is crucial for mental development, whether the interchange is dyadic as in logic, or triadic as in the small group dialectics, or else is the multipersonal lateralized dialogue of larger groups.

Language itself is not dialogue, since language is a structure and dialogue is a process. So when Wittgenstein says, 'language disguises thought', he confuses issues, since it is dialogue that transforms thought into language and the reverse, in a two-faced system. Wittgenstein said that all philosophy is a critique of language. We would amplify this: Dialogue is a continuous critique of language.

Whilst logical propositions cannot be confirmed by experience any more than they can be refuted by it, dialogue is one continuous process of reflected experiences. It is a commentary, a tangential analogic concourse by which 'the sap of reason quenches the fire of passion'.

Analogies that parallel the unconscious mind can be found in the larger group in its early phases. It can be compared to the cauldron of energy in a state of chaos, which preceded the gigantic monsters. It is constantly frustrated and generates a state of monstrous fury. In it there is a lack of organization, and of a collective will; contrary impulses exist side by side without cancelling each other out. There is nothing that corresponds to a sense of time. Any expansion in meaningful dialogue is as mind-blowing and as uncomfortable as consciousness itself.

Rycroft pointed out in his *Innocence of Dreams* (1979) that the unconscious has one positive attribute—that of being filled with energy. Otherwise it is entirely defined in negatives.

We see this energy as a mental or psychic energy derived from the transformation of the hate arising from frustration.

The process can be schematized as follows:

> Frustration → hate → psychic energy → dialogue → thinking → understanding → information → Koinonia or impersonal friendship.

Koinonia constitutes a holding network or group matrix and brings about the change from persecutory to friendly, thereby enabling sexuality to emerge as genitality.

The task is to establish a link, by means of the transformational process of dialogue, symbols and rituals, between hate and the opposite of hate, which is not love but the impersonal fellowship of Koinonia. This cannot be done quickly, since, although the unconscious is already present in the collective situation, it takes time to discover and establish the collective consciousness.

Earlier in the same book, Rycroft, writing of Freud's formulation of mind as a mental apparatus within which energy moves or remains static, quotes Freud as saying that we really have no idea what psychic energy is or what the concept means.

For us mental or psychic energy is transformed hate. Lacan (1977) distinguishes it as drive. Rycroft (1979) refers to Susanne Langer's (1967) suggestion that symbolization is a basic human need, not a symptom, produced by frustration. We would emphasize that it is not libido that demands symbolization, but frustrated libido or hate; and socially speaking, if we are to survive at all, this hate has to be discharged in non-instinctual forms of behaviour. All sublimations depend on symbolization and all ego development depends on the sublimation of hate, a process that is not instinctive but social and has to be learned and cultivated.

Rycroft points out that Susanne Langer, in the use of her terms 'non-discursive' and 'discursive' symbolism, makes distinctions between different types of thinking, which orthodox Freudian analysts refer to as primary and secondary processes. He quotes from Langer (1967):

> Language in a strict sense is essentially discursive; it has permanent units of meaning which are combinable into larger units; it has fixed equivalences that make definition and translation possible; its connotations are general, so that it requires non-verbal acts, like pointing, looking or emphatic voice inflection, to assign denotations to its terms. In all these salient characters it differs from wordless symbolism, which is non-discursive and untranslatable, and does not allow of definition within its own system, and cannot convey generalities. The meanings given through language are successively understood and gathered into a whole by the process called discourse; the meanings of all other symbolic elements that comprise a larger, articulate symbol are understood only through the meaning of the whole, through their relations within the total structure. Their very functioning as symbols depends on the fact that they are involved in a simultaneous integral presentation.

This whole process of discourse, of establishing the meanings of symbolic elements within a total structure, can only take place through dialogue. The mobilizing drive in this process is an irreversible fury, which is secondary to the primordial instinct of fusion or identification, and which is a state of being. Fury denotes total destruction and world extinction, equivalent to Ernest Jones' (1953) 'aphanasis', which he described as 'the fundamental face of the total and permanent extinction of the capacity including opportunity for sexual enjoyment'. It is prior to fear of death, to separation anxiety, to pain, grief, guilt, or depression. It is primal mental anguish without fantasy or meaning, a total blackness sometimes seen in dreams that can only be compared to panic. It is the cardinal obliteration of the organism, and perhaps it is this which enables the mind to conceive of zero, of nothingness, and of negative values. In its transformed state, which is its only alternative, it constitutes mental or endopsychic energy. It is hardly surprising therefore that 'we really have no idea what mental energy is'. It cannot be reversed, it can only proceed to transformation, through structuring, organizing, minding, cultivation, and it can only be defused by negotiation, dialogue, symbolization, by humanizing, or establishing meaning. Susanne Langer (1967) wrote that symbolization is a basic human need. It is an imperative.

Dialogue builds, looking to conclusions in the future: it moves in the reverse direction to propositions and arguments, which start off with conclusions.

In addition, dialogue has the following properties: It has the fullness and precision of the analog as distinct from the binary digital form; it functions without final truths; it has the continuous evolvement of a totalizing system; it is a general way of interacting; it concerns connection, relatedness, wholes, both structures and systems, and is not only dependent on the dialectic process of thesis and antithesis; it is tangential with nuances of relation and meaning, including pauses and silences; it is concerned with continuum, not simply with boundaries; it allows for different communications taking place simultaneously; it both influences and is influenced by atmosphere and cultural context; it can become open, free-floating, untamed, evocative, and provocative, empathetic and rich in ambiguities, full of non-verbal meanings, with poetry, timing, style, quality, complexity. Being multipersonal, it does not follow the course of syllogistic logic. Dialogue uses language and transforms it. Larger group dialogue can, given the opportunity, do the same to culture.

The 'word', as Anthony Wilden (1968) points out, can never become one with the subject's desire, and this may account for a generalized resistance against dialogue.

Throughout the writings of the structuralists lies a consistent baulking at the distinctions between the use of language in dialogue and language itself, so that writers like Ricoeur (1981) focus on the written texts as the basic tool of culture, i.e. for Ricoeur, 'Man is a language', 'the intertextuality of hermaneutics'.

It is not surprising that Ricoeur was forced to resign his rectorship by leftist students. He took a strong position against both conservatives and revolutionaries but failed to maintain the strength of his position, since he excluded the exercise of actual dialogue, which could have transformed the power of binary opposition into the circularization of a powerful lateralizing system. The first act of consciousness, he wrote, is meaning. For us the first act of consciousness is dialogue.

Along the same lines Lacan (1977) never distinguished between thought and language; in fact, he deplored dialogue as idealistic. He made no distinction between culture as an ongoing evolving mobile system and culture as a socially established structure. Since for us cultures can only be altered by evolving or generating other cultures, this is a crucial issue, particularly as new microcultures are generated by dialogue in larger groups. The actual praxis of language is rarely referred to by Lacan, although this is a central issue in the establishment of settings in which dialogue can be given the time, space, and opportunity to emerge. Instead, there is constant ambiguous obscure flirtation with a vast variety of ill-defined ideologies, vague macrocultures (e.g. national, American, etc.), with fragmentary allusions to other disciplines such as music, politics, poetry, psychology.

For Lacan (1977) form is everything and content very little. Despite all this, however, in company with the post-Freudians, he placed a vital emphasis on the enormous significance of cultural influences—something that the medical profession has tended to deny.

To quote Lacan from the Écrits (1977):

> The omnipresence of human discourse will perhaps one day be embraced under the open sky of an omnicommunication of its text. This is not to say that human discourse will be any more harmonious than now. But this is the field that our experience polarizes in a relation that is only apparently two-way, for any positing of its structure in merely dual terms is as inadequate to it in theory as it is ruinous for its technique.

He also wrote,

> The third paradox of the relation of language to speech is that of the subject; who loses his meaning in the objectification of discourse.

For Lacan dialogue is an 'objective' omnicommunicated text. We, on the other hand, consider that discourse is intersubjective and does not have to be related to objectification. Dialogue is not a polarized relation of dualities but an interjective multipersonal exchange, which goes beyond the psychoanalytic dyad. It is post-oedipal. Lacan writes as if dialogue had never occurred. If this were indeed the case, there would be all the more reason to decide to take it seriously, since it is capable of expressing meaning, as distinct from gratification or 'reality'.

Daniel Levinson (1978) considers that 'deep structures', rigidly codified, occur on a continuum through culturally determined configurations to a highly idiosyncratic personal structuring of experience. The range is from deep structure to idiosyncratic structure, or from biological destiny to aesthetics. We would see it, not as an idealistic, automatically progressive continuum, but as a dialectic between the highly idiosyncratic personal level and the rigid, violent codified 'deep structure' of values often culturally inappropriate, which society supports; such a dialectic can lead to more appropriate cultural configurations.

Levinson (1978) considers that there is a range from 'deep structures' to an idiosyncratic structure, from biological destiny to aesthetics, but the process and methodology through which this occurs is not clear. Dialogue is not mentioned. The individual, it seems to us, however, is already in a state of dialectical tension. This tension is between our biological structure of pre-formed, continuous and timeless instincts and each person's unique position as a single event in space.

Levinson (1978) states that whatever one thinks structure to be, whether one is interested in a man's durance or in his poetry, the *unifying* aspect of structuralism remains. 'It is clear that structure is not something out there; it is a dynamic ordering of experience. . . . "Structure" has commonly been used to describe any whole with organized interrelated parts; thus a beehive, in this sense, is clearly a structure, but not a manifestation of structuralism.' He goes on to say that the first tenet of structuralism is wholeness, seeing the world in terms of an organization. Nothing can be considered except as an entirety, no part of a system can be understood outside its context or out of its relatedness to other parts of the system. Meaning depends entirely on this unification, and we are interested in the unifying system of dialogue. This implies as strict a perspectivism for psychoanalysis as for other sciences, macroperspectively as well as microperspectively in its own time.

Levinson (1978) sees categories as unrelated in content, but reflecting the same pattern of form, as isomorphs or transformations of each other. Thus, although the content differs, form is imposed on the content by the human mind. 'Transformations are homologies or isomorphs, not analogies; analogies, one will recall, being superficial similarities of phenomena which have no real correspondence. In other words, awareness of the larger structural field in which we work is essential, for we are enmeshed in this both macrospectively and microspectively. Levi-Strauss considers that anthropology is ultimately microanthropology.' The relevance of this for the larger group method is obvious since it represents microanthropology in the making.

Much in Levinson's thinking can be related to that of Lacan. Lacan's formulations become clearer in the light of the role of hate and dialogue within the structure of the larger group. His term 'discourse' limits dialogue on the whole either to the duologue of psychoanalysis or to the monologue of the discourse of the other, or to the texts of writing and poetry and intertextuality. He focuses on the structural aspect of psychoanalysis as distinct from its dynamic systemic aspect. He regards the establishment of meaning as disastrous—in the sense that dialogue is driven by dehiscence, by lack. Once meaning is established, further dialogue is unnecessary.

For us, dialogue should be the sine qua non of linguistics, the actual praxis of language, yet people have to learn how to talk as a separate and additional process to learning a language. We have developed speech, but we cannot use it. Group dialogue appears generally to be boycotted. Dialogue—the supreme skill—is confused with dialectic, discourse, rhetoric, logos, intertextuality, intersubjectivity of logic and time, code, message, discursivity, speech, language, and linguistics, as well as with 'la parole', with reason, with trans-individual reality, with debate, argument, free association, and group association.

For us the first and deepest insight, the initial unique and major contribution that Foulkes (Foulkes & Anthony, 1957) ever made, was that of the simple but quintessential significance of free-floating group discussion. He wrote that we do not know the value of interpretation. So often interpretations seem to be an endless series of metaphors, some more apt than others. They may aid dialogue but cannot of course replace it.

Lacan (1977) gets very close to the idea of dialogue when he says that there is no word without a reply. His term 'aggressivity' is very close to our term 'hate'. He makes the masterly observation that obsessive intrasubjectivity is to be opposed by hysterical intersubjectivity, that language without 'dialect' is found in psychotic language, the language in which words are used as things not of a means of exchange.

> In madness of whatever nature, we must recognise the negative liberty of a word which has given up trying to make itself recognized, or what we call an obstacle to transference; and, on the other hand, we must recognize the singular formation of a delusion which objectifies the subject in a language with dialect.
>
> It is in the word that all the reality of its effects resides; for it is by way of this gift that all reality has come to man and it is by his continued act that he measures it.

If this is true, one is inclined to ask why this gift is not used, and not as a series of disjunctions, not dialectically, but in a continuous, multifacetted system of dialogue.

It is the Other (or the others of the larger group) who mediates between the mind and the world and establishes meaning, something essentially public. The Other, according to Lacan, is that pre-existent unconscious 'world of rules' into which we are born and for which there is no inherently private language. This results in the splitting of the inner world from the outer, the self from the I. The collective external world of the community is a world whose values and prohibitions are absolved from speech. Therefore, symbolism ranges between the more primitive and concrete on the one hand, and the more developed, discursive kind of representation on the other hand. Lacan therefore distinguishes between drive, which is mental, and instinct, which is physical and biological. Where we part company from Lacan is in considering that the mental level is frustrated instinct and therefore must be non-instinct.

Lacan is faced with the split, as it were, between the dependence of sexuality on biologism on the one hand and on symbolism on the other, and he settles for a partial dependence of sexuality on symbolism. As we see it, there are two aspects of sexuality: the one that is biological, naturally incestuous and oedipal, which does not include genital primacy, and the other that is genitality, which, in the biological situation of the family of origin, is socially prohibited. This prohibited aspect becomes transformed (socialized) at puberty, sometimes with inaugural initiation rituals, in the social setting as distinct from the family context, and is now blessed and sanctioned. Whilst the biological elements of sexuality do not have to be learned, the social and cultural manifestations of genitality do indeed have to be taught, e.g. we have sexual dysfunction clinics. Hence love and marriage, like Janus, are inherently two-faced.

Lacan (1977) calls the opening up of the gap between the mother and the infant 'dehiscence', and it is this gap that precipitates the infant into symbolism. Language, through its capacity to represent absence symbolically, offers to make good this gap. Lacan commends Kant for his use of the word *gap* and for his attempt to introduce the concept of negative quantities into philosophy.

Access to the unconscious is gained through the dialectic of analysis, which restores full speech and in that sense is a form of speech therapy. The unconscious is the discourse of 'the Other', which becomes very much amplified in 'the others' of the large group. The dialogue in the large group therefore increasingly distinguishes between the brute and the biological on the one hand and the social and cultural on the other. So Lacan distinguishes between the brute of demand and the symbolism of man's desire.

The frustration of the gap results in a process of substitution, which becomes the psychic representation of the need, something similar to Winnicott's concept of the space between mother and child where creativity is developed in play. Winnicott (1958) wrote:

> The word infant implies 'not talking' (infants) and it is not unuseful to think of infancy as the phase prior to word presentation and the use of word symbols.

The infant breaks out of the miasmic condition of need through the sumbolism of language; through which desire can be expressed and understood. But the registration of desire in language is a social phenomenon since language is social; language gives the individual recognition, affirmation, and attention through symbol acquisition. Psycho-sexuality, therefore, is something that is learned, and symbol acquisition is central to psycho-sexuality. 'Le non du père' transforms brute frustration by becoming 'le nom du père'.

Symbol formation might be related to Melanie Klein's (1948) emphasis on the moment when the infant is able to conceive of the whole person, both good and bad, rather than the part persons altogether good or altogether bad. Group dialogue is an ongoing process of expansion towards wholeness.

Richard Wollheim (1979) recalls that Freud once told Salvador Dali: 'It is not the unconscious men look out for in your paintings, it is the conscious.' This is certainly what we look for in the course of witnessing the median group's increasing capacity to move from monologue and bickering arguments to a collective, conscious, Koinonic state of dialogue. The imaginary is at one end of the continuum and symbolism is at the other. Group dialogue creates generality, shareability; it bears meaning. It moves from the brute fact of imaginary and frustration, to the language of a collective Conscious.

Lacan (1977) expresses a respect for speech when he says:

> For some years all my effort has been required in the struggle to bring to the practitioners (of psychoanalysis) the true value of this instrument, speech, to give it back its dignity so that it does not always represent for them those words, devalued in advance, that force them to fix their gaze elsewhere in order to find their guarantor. 'What happens when the subject begins to speak to the analyst?' What is it that strikes one first? Is it the sense of impediment, failure, split, in a spoken or written sentence; something stumbles!

The sense of gap, of central lack, of discontinuity, of negative quantities, of seeking as distinct from discovering and finding, are all clearly described by Lacan, but he does not appear to have our concept in which frustrated desire gives rise to hate, which then becomes the mental energy behind the drive to transform, and takes the form of symbol formation in the language of group dialogue. The actual practice of language in the process or system of dialogue in the larger group has given an added dimension to our appreciation of linguistics.

Thass Thienemann (1968) points out that when language became the substratum with which the clinician had to deal, the medical concept of 'cause' became replaced by the concept of 'meaning', 'cause' being anchored in the objective sphere whilst 'meaning' is personal, an individual variable.

Dialogue, unlike dreams, does not disguise but discloses the essentials of meaning. Thought without words does not exist; thinking is silent speaking. Logos, the word, was the beginning of all things.

Meaning cannot be cut to pieces, it cannot be measured or quantified. Sign, symbol, and meaning are co-relative concepts. What appears as sign or symbol on the objective scale is experienced in subjective reality as 'meaning'. Meaning is rooted in subjective life experience of reality.

Symbolic understanding is a distinctive attribute of man, the ability to deal in ideas in contrast to the signal behaviour of animals. Symbols are a manifestation of culture, having a historical and social context distinct from the a-historic context of physical science, which deals not with the specific socio-historical space/time of the individual but the symbolic relationship of cause and effect. Symbolism is a creative act and relates to Mythos as distinct from Logos. Talking of totems, Levi-Strauss (1968) wrote, 'natural species are chosen not because they are "good to eat" but because they are "good to think"'.

Language interposes itself between man and reality; it is the tool for thinking and is the most elaborate realization of this intermediary sphere. In dialogue tension arises between the discursive content and the non-discursive connotation of the intended meaning. It seems that symptoms relate to an unsuccessful attempt to link the non-discursive with discourse. And therapy, amongst other things, in the dialogue of the large group, arises when an articulated translation occurs between the already established structure of the group culture and the ongoing system of dialogue.

Language reveals how objects have been perceived for countless generations—e.g. 'Skol', the Scandinavian word for 'cheerio', is derived from the word *skull,* which was used as a drinking vessel by the Vikings. In other words, in understanding etymology we have at our disposal an archaeology that pre-dates historical archaeology and is as royal a road to the unconscious as dream interpretation: not surprisingly, it has met with as much resistance. In this context it is interesting to note that 'semen' and 'word', sowing and speaking, have a common derivation, so that sexual potency is related to the capacity for thinking and often meets with a similar envy. Thass Thienemann (1968) also points out that the words *brother* and *sister* (in English) had no common name until recently, no doubt being too disparate to be allowed to be grouped together; similarly, the words 'generate' and 'know' and 'knee'. The word 'intelligo' properly means 'to pick up and collect', in the same manner that the Gestalt psychologist singles out the figure from the ground as the basic operation for the perception of meaning.

The prime quality of language is that it is 'trans-individual' (similar to Durkheim's [1972] 'collective consciousness'); it is handed down culturally so that the culture is the primary carrier of this cumulative memory. Language is therefore the most immediate record of unconscious fantasies of pre-consciousness and of collective motives. Everyday mythology is encased in language that is essentially vulgar and profane and has a greater continuity with prehistoric ages than does myth. It has been suggested by Freud that not only dispositions but 'mental contents' can be inherited; they could alternatively be transmitted culturally. Little surprise, therefore, that the psychoanalytic technique carried with it a new moral philosophy, which does a great deal more than treat symptoms. A whole cultural movement is involved.

It has rightly been said that man cannot perceive things in themselves, but only their 'meaning'. So that whilst expression is a primary function of the body, communication is a primary function of the mind. Prof. Ernest Hutten (1981) has written: 'Meaning rules human action, whereas cause determines physical processes. The rules of meaning rather than the laws of nature explain human behaviour.'

In brief, language and dialogue, our archaic heritage, are spoken through the individual. As a collective unconscious structure, etymology offers us a supreme method for exploring personal unconscious fantasies in relation to the culture of the whole community. Little surprise, therefore, that descriptive linguistics is not interested in etymology any more than behaviourism is concerned with dreams; they are both structural approaches per se, which leave out the dynamic systems approach existing in the situation as a whole. For the behaviourists, transliteration does not exist. Thass Thienemann (1968) writes: 'Language was primarily figurative, symbolic, descriptive and concrete, like picture writing.' Only later did it develop into conceptual communication through a vast process or system of transformation.

The basic duality described by Hegel, the polarity of the subject and object, constitutes the basic structure of consciousness. This brings about an experience of 'incompleteness', the 'I' and the world being categorically distinct yet inseparable, as the inside and the outside are inseparable and relate through language. Anxiety, anguish, and birth are also words that are closely associated. The word separation is derived from *separare,* to engender one's self.

Symbolism is the characteristically human element in cognition. It constitutes the great departure from animal mentality and is the prime feature of dialogue and of the socio-linguistic structure of man's environment.

In comparing psychic and physical energy, it is clear that physical energy is spatio-temporal and that psychic energy is qualitatively distinct, if not positively antinomic. Matter and motion, space and time, are physically and universally inseparable as space–time and can only be made distinguishable by the mind. The mind, in other words, offers a conceptual frame; the question then arises as to the structure of mind itself with its mobile system but no mass, in space and time.

What we are suggesting is that the body and mind problem only exists in the 'mind' and is of linguistic—i.e. symbolic—origin. It is only when we provide the cultural structure of a large group, engaged in dialogue, that we can safely say 'we now have a medium in which the mind can be observed in operation in actual practice'. We see it as offering us a structure like a discipline that enables us to examine the mind functioning as a system. It is on this account that we have found observing the large group situation to be extremely revealing, in the way that any scientific task becomes immensely informative if it can be examined functioning in its appropriate frame of reference. Our observations, in other words, are rooted in the actual field of ongoing problems and take in mind as a highly mobile phenomenon, elusive as to defy simple definition. For us culture is more like the medium that bacteriologists use for the purpose of isolating and examining organisms. But we feel that this mode, this larger group model, has not been sufficiently explored in any comprehensive yet spontaneous sense. Psychotherapists and group therapists, as distinct from behaviourists, deem 'mind' to be their subject matter, but, alas, so often they work in isolation without the medium of a culture.

The larger group offers a way of approaching culture with some semblance of scientific criteria; it provides a medium that is 'isolated', controllable, repeatable, offering facilities for research and qualifications rather than quantifications, uncovering the sources of old obfuscations by showing up subtle fallacies. Going down to biological sources may very well reveal feelings, but this is in no way the same as totalization in which the subjectivity of the mind is revealed, culturally, through dialogue. Speech is a two-way mirror, and to quote Langer (1967): 'Symbols, concepts, fantasy, religion, speculation, selfhood and morality present the most exciting and important topics of the science of mind.' But speech, as a two-way mirror, puts symptoms in terms of symbols not signs; it is open to negotiation, sharing, and exchanging in a manner that is a network, as distinct from the linear system of S.R. theory.

Lacan (1977) makes no distinction between the discourse of two individuals and the discourse of dialogue between several people. Nor does he distinguish between language as a structure and language as a system exercised in speech as dialogue.

We have discovered that the larger group deals in a currency that is less inward-looking, therefore less involved in the free association of individual minds, and is in fact less free; dialogue is therefore primarily outward-looking towards others, is dependent on culture, and can result in a sense of constricted oppression which itself has to be tested and contested. However, Lacan must be referring to dialogue when he states that we must recognize 'the singular formation of a delusion which objectifies the subject in language without dialect'. He also writes: 'It is in the word that all the reality of its effects resides; for it is by way of this gift that all reality has come to man and it is by his continued act that he maintains it.' Again one is inclined to ask why we do not use it more.

This seems to be the nearest Lacan gets to recommending dialogue—dialect becoming dialogue and providing the ultimate theory of the proper function of aggressivity in human ontology. For example Lacan (1977) writes:

> In itself dialogue seems to involve a renunciation of aggressivity; from Socrates onwards, philosophy has always placed its hope in the triumph of reason. And yet ever since Thrasymachus made his stormy exit in the beginning of the 'Republic', verbal dialect has all too often proved a failure.

In contrast, we consider that dialogue must continue as long as it fails to handle hate. When it succeeds, no further dialogue should surely be necessary. According to Lacan (1977), 'The notion of aggressivity is a correlative tension of the narcissistic structure in the coming into being of the subject!' In other words, the generating of hate is ceaseless, and, by the same token, dialogue never ends. Over ten years of meetings we have never found the larger group to be lost for words.

'Civilisation and Its Discontents' in German is *Das Unbehagen in der Kultur*. 'Civilization' is derived from the verb 'to civilize', from 'civic' or 'civil', and means qualities of politeness and amiability on the part of superiors to inferiors in contrast to barbarism and feudalism. Modern civilization usually means contemporary urban and industrialized society. There is a relationship between civilization and high culture, but as often as not they are contrasted, since culture is a far more complex social phenomenon, a technique of techniques, of values, ideas, and beliefs. The German word for 'civilization' is *Zivilisation*. We suggest that civilization causes frustration and *Unbehagen,* i.e. unease and anxiety, which constitute the endopsychic energy that can create culture. Civilization is now generally used to describe an achieved state or structure of organized social life, whilst culture is a mobile growing system or dynamic process.

The relationship between hate, dialogue, and culture is crucial. These are processing systems, and we cannot allow ourselves to remain passive and helpless towards them, even though language and civilization are structures that give the appearance of being immutable. At a conference of ecologists (The Fourth World Assembly, 1981), Ivan Illich raised the question of what might be done in order to improve our current situation, and it was pointed out that we might start there and then by altering the established lecture structure of a rostrum facing rows of chairs. This met with no response, as such structures are so generally accepted as to be taken for granted.

The contrast between passive renounced instinctual gratification, on which civilization is built, and the active frustration of hate to which the evolution of culture owes its origins is a theme that runs right through *Civilization and Its Discontents* (Freud, 1930a [1929]). It ends with the pessimistic conclusion that individuals become neurotic under the pressure of civilizing trends, and that any attempt to apply psychoanalysis to civilized society is 'doomed to fruitlessness'. In any case, 'what would be the use of the most acute analysis of social neuroses since no one possessed power to compel the community to adopt the therapy'. However, 'in spite of all these difficulties we may expect that one day someone will venture upon this research into the pathology of civilized communities'.

Freud (1930a [1929]) wrote: 'In the neurosis of an individual we can use as a starting point the contrast presented to us between the patient and his environment which we assume to be "normal".' For us it is clear that this 'normal' refers to a vast panorama of differing cultures, most of which have yet to be cultivated; and which also need to be differentiated from the family culture and the cultural superego. Freud poses for us the question that we are trying to answer in the technique of the larger group—'The fateful question of the human species seems to me to be whether and to what extent the cultural process developed in it will succeed in mastering the derangements of communal life.' Perhaps he should have left it at that, but he goes on to add, 'caused by the human instinct of aggression and self-destruction'. For us this is not an instinct but an anti-instinct, which constitutes the essential basis for endopsychic energy and which does not demand that the forces of nature should be subdued, but, rather, that they should be transformed totally.

Hate, then, is not the adversary of Eros but the inevitable irreversible outcome of the frustration of Eros: if there is any adversary to Eros, it lies in this frustration and in the reality of *ananke,* of external necessity. We have to cope with ananke and thereby we evolve dialogue, mind, and culture. With hate we handle the situation of the lack characteristic of the 'real' of Lacan. Lacan's 'real' is that which always 'returns to the same place, refractory, resistant, impassable, approached but never grasped, the umbilical cord of the symbolic, the ineliminable residue of all articulation, the domain outside symbolisation'.

People often ask how it is that members never stop talking, that dialogue, like breathing, never ceases; perhaps the answer is that hate occasioned by lack never ceases either.

Linguists have described discourse as a stretch of language, larger than the sentence, which takes into account sentence sequences as well as sentence structure. Dialogue is much more than discourse. It is not disputation or argument, but Plato's 'supreme art'. Dialogue goes beyond the notion of contradiction in the course of discussion; beyond logical metaphysics, since it is a creative practice; beyond Hegel's higher and unified truth, since it is not a unification but a process beyond a primacy of either spirit or matter.

The particular way in which dialogue develops in larger groups deserves to be distinguished by a new term, such as 'polylogue', but so far we have not been successful in finding one. We are reminded of Leibniz's comment: 'People (monads, souls) are like mirrors placed in a circle around a market place; each presents a different picture than each of the others do, but these cannot contradict each other as they reflect one and the same object.'

The opposite of polylogue, you might say, is alienation and isolation and estrangement, 'the estrangement of man from man'.

In *Alienated Labour,* written in 1844, Karl Marx wrote that the reason the labourer has become alienated from the products of his labour is that labourers have become alienated from each other. Deliberate dialogue amongst the workers hardly exists; there is even less dialogue than amongst the middle classes. Thus the workers are divorced not only from capital but also from the responsibilities of dialogue. Marx wrote: 'As a result therefore, man (the worker) only feels himself freely active in his animal functions, eating, drinking, procreating; in these human functions he no longer feels himself to be anything but an animal self estranged both from nature and from himself.' 'He mortifies his body and ruins his mind.' Marx hoped that universal human emancipation would ensue once private ownership of production (nowadays this has become mainly financial ownership) had become democratized. He entirely misses out the interim stage, in which people learn to talk to each other responsibly. Integers, e.g. money and words, do not by themselves take responsibility, nor does the economism of the materialistic infrastructure.

Marx wrote:

> An immediate consequence of the fact that man is estranged from the product of his labour, from his life activity, from his species being, is the estrangement of man from man. What applies to a man's relation to his work, to the product of his labour and to himself, also holds of a man's relation to the other man and to the other man's labour and object of labour.

It is true that this may be an immediate consequence, but it is certainly not a final and inevitable one. People are not ensconced in a capitalist society, but in their own frozen cultural structures, whether 'bourgeois' or 'working-class', whether slave, citizen, or world denizen: change lies not only in the exchange of integers and words but in the actual praxis of dialogue. Words as a medium of exchange, in the form of dialogue as distinct from monologue, speech, and rhetoric, existed long before the institution of money. Dialogue is the hallmark of the human species and is an a priori form of currency; it is a skill that has to be learnt and used if humans are to survive the onslaughts of human mismanagement, let alone Nature.

People speak to each other in a creative, emerging manner. Mind does not emerge automatically: it is an outcome of a dynamic tension continuously in dialogue, a continuous miracle of psycho-genesis; it is a miraculous process, miracle being a word derived from a subjective experience of wonder, of astonishment, of curiosity, of surprise, joyful, delighting, concerning anything that is creative or new. For us society, culture, and mind are not 'natural'; they are as artificial as cultured pearls. Mind is essentially like language, a large group phenomenon.

Natural language is distinct from formal—i.e. scientific and mathematical—language. The formal abstract symbolic character of pure mathematics (symbolic logic) is the most successful method for handling natural science and avoids the pitfalls and imprecisions of natural language. Nevertheless it was from natural language that formal or artificial language emerged. Whichever way you look at it, dialogue is not only the supreme art, it is the first act of science (or should we say the second, since the first act is for people to meet).

Einstein describes science as an attempt to make the chaotic university of our sense impressions correspond to a logically uniform system of thought. This could be applied to dialogue as a system in which people meet in the first place in discourse to sort out the diversity of our minds. Russell's theory of logical types (in *Principles of Reconstruction* appears to break down, for here the class (the group), and the members (the individuals), appear to lose their distinction 'transpersonally' in dialogue. The very essence of dialogue is contentious and paradoxical, neither true nor false. The medium of exchange does not consist in an academic exchange of signs but a richer, far more complex interchange of symbols.

Following upon structuralism, a movement known as 'post-structural' has emerged. Whilst structuralism is involved with describing the transformation of various structures as distinct from the actual content or meaning of those structures, the post-structuralists are exploring intertextuality. That is, they are concerned with examining the texts of different disciplines, comparing, linking, and contrasting texts in philosophy, literature, anthropology, linguistics, and concerned with subtext, text, and context: they are therefore primarily concerned with meaning.

Socrates described writing as the language of the dead. Or as an orphan! He also considered dialogue to have been neglected. Along similar lines, Foulkes (1948) encouraged spontaneous free-floating discussion to its full extent. Any failure in this he regarded as defensive. Group association is a living, highly intimate process and like dialogue meets with all the resistances characteristic of free association. By the same token it is rarely practised, being too frustrating, even though it establishes the foundations for language and for mind. Noam Chomsky (1968) wrote: 'Language both mirrors human mental process and shapes the flow and character of thought.' He asks how an essentially closed body of technique such as linguistics 'could be applied to some new domain, say to analysis of connected discourse to other cultural phenomena beyond language'. Language is determinate, whilst indeterminacy is the principal feature of intelligence and of free-floating dialogue.

An effect of existentialism has been to establish the authority of the individual system in the context of the structure of surface events. On the other hand, one effect of structuralism has been to establish the authenticity of the influence of shared factors outside the control of the individual. Therefore, post-structuralism is an attempt at a dialectic between the existential and structural approaches, but it is still not dialogue. It is curious to read how close certain structuralists have come to expressing such a possibility. Chomsky (1968) describes how de Saussure went beyond the tradition of linguistics proper in stating that sentence formation is not strictly a matter of 'langue' but is rather assigned to what he called 'parole', outside the scope of lingistic proper and a process of free creation unconstrained by linguistic rules.

Chomsky (1968), quoting from the sixteenth-century Spanish physician Juan Huarte, noted the generative ability that is revealed in the normal human use of language as a free instrument of thought. Wit, *ingenio,* understanding, is a generative power; intelligence has the same Latin root as 'engender' or 'generate'. Huarte, according to Chomsky, suggested that intelligence has three levels: (1) a passive perceptual level, which is restricted to that level alone and on its own is a disability resembling that of eunuchs incapable of generating; (2) a cognitive system to do with rearranging; and (3) true creativity. Chomsky considered that we live in an age of behavioural science, not of a science of mind; the creative aspects of language use have not been regarded as within the legitimate province of linguistics, and he made a plea that the study of language should occupy a central place in general psychology.

'The classical questions of language and mind receive not final solution or even a hint of a final solution from the work that is being actively pursued today' (Chomsky, 1957). This was written in 1957; in 1968 he was still writing: 'Linguistic knowledge of course extends beyond the levels of the sentence. We know how to construct and understand discourses of various sorts and there are no doubt principles governing discourse structure.'

The impenetrable problem of a scientific method in relationship to the study of mind remains; a tree of knowledge, yes! but not a tree of life. Chomsky suggests that a kind of synthesis of philosophical grammar and structural linguistics is needed. The mind is usually regarded in binary terms paralleled by the mechanics of phonetics, 'phonemes'; for example, the sound 'ma' is the opposition of closed and open lips; the basic sounds of words are in binary opposition. In society we find the same opposition of nature and culture, of *parole* and *langue,* of such concepts as diachronic and synchronic, paradigmatic and syntagmatic, metaphors and metonyms, contiguity and similarity. The mind splits, opposes, mediates, and resolves by use of a binary structural logic. However, dialogue refutes this binary structure in its very nature as a system of tangential analogues. Myths, for instance, exist on a higher level of organization than sounds and words. Levi-Strauss (1968) wrote: 'Myths get through in man unbeknownst to him.' Whole phrases and sentences create 'mythemes' (e.g. the phrase 'once upon a time'), and these are a way of structuring and ordering concepts and reality in a manner that is anecdotal and not limited to specific words. Dialogue is the ultimate system in free-wheeling, breaking away from binary logic, from dialectics and 'triangulation'. Like the group matrix, it simultaneously and spontaneously both releases and holds together. Yet it is not irrational, since it has its own laws and its own capacity to bind the rational and the irrational. It has been said that myths express man's intellectual nature whilst kinship orders his sexual nature. Myths enable us to conceptualize and to relate to our social structure. Dialogue transcends the physiological constraint of words: it conveys ideas and enables exchange to take place; it relates the external world of nature and society to the inner world of mind.

Our prime consideration to the larger groups goes beyond the study of language itself to the emergence of dialogue. Dialogue both differentiates and unites, filling in the split between structure and system. Most environmental approaches explore the material environment and overlook the foundation of cultivation, namely, the generative substructure of the mind itself. Usually the responsibility for this is attributed to economic 'forces'; but these are in fact secondary manifestations since the instigation of logic, mathematics, and money was initially introduced by dialogue. Our interest is not in a material ecology but in a psycho-socio-cultural ecology. We would wish to cultivate culture.

There is therefore in dialogue a dynamic balance between logical and expressive signs, between fact and fiction, maintained through tension by the symbolization of dialogue swinging between concretization on the one hand and relatedness on the other; in the larger group this process can go to the extreme extension not of the binary opposition but of multiple appositions, of lateralization, circulation, and ventilation, if so allowed. Unfortunately this is very rarely the case.

Dialogue links up the diachronic, which refers to the historical change of language, with the synchronic, which refers to the state of that language at a given point in time.

A typical effect of structural *un*dialogue is seen in our Parliamentary seating arrangements. In Parliament, people talk in order to dispute and to debate, to oppose and orate; they do not talk to inform. The seating arrangement in the House of Commons is the rectangle characteristic of the two-party system, leading inevitably to the perpetration of a logical binary oppositional type of thinking, rivalrous and competitive, involving change of power rather than exchange of information. The usual committee structure also consists of two long lines, with a chairman at the head of the table through whom all comments are made.

The Institute of Psychoanalysis in London meets in a hall in which there is a rostrum, faced by rows of chairs. When the Institute of Group Analysis meets in the same hall, the seating is arranged in a circle. Naturally the communication in the former is stilted and inhibited, in the nature of monologue, whereas in the latter it is a lively, spontaneous polylogue. A lecture from a platform, addressed to rows of auditors below, automatically creates a 'dependent basic assumption culture', which virtually rules out dialogue; in this setting any member of the audience who wishes to make a comment has to clamber up onto the stage and speak down a (probably faulty) microphone.

War is a typical example of relationships reduced to a binary system, a duel, a duet; when the lateralization of relationships is no longer possible, relations are 'broken off'. The problem is to relate system and structure, the one biological and libidinal and the other social, cultural, and only to be implemented by multipersonal lateralization.

The seating arrangement of, let us say, ten rows of twenty chairs facing a panel of eight, is a structure that cannot possibly do justice to the system of energy it contains. The effect therefore is to constrain dialogue to such an extent that by the end of the meeting the people have reached the borderline psychotic levels of frustration and anxiety. It was Pericles who considered that rhetoric and rostra ruined the great Greek endeavour to establish democracy.

We as human species are hurtling towards disaster, not because any one single individual wishes it, but because we have delegated community responsibility to mathematical and technological 'logic'; integers have replaced dialogue as currency.

Dialogue cannot proceed either through syllogistic or through dialectic logic, and any attempt to punctuate the process or bring it to an end fails. This open-endedness of dialogue, without cease and without restriction, is mind-blowing; its side-effects could be both therapeutic and consciousness raising. It is certainly disconcerting. Perhaps dialogue is the most extensive form of thesis possible, and in producing antithetical opposition in the form of either splits or oppression and microcultural effects, it synthesizes reflection with action—and establishes both unconscious and conscious structures such as 'social reality', which, in turn, comes under scrutiny.

Dialogue acts like interpretation in the opposite direction to dream-work, which distorts. As Foulkes and Anthony (1957) pointed out, group associations are interpretations, and we have found that they proceed and extend a great deal further in large group dialogue. Freud wrote in *The Interpretation of Dreams* (1900a), in 'The psychology of dream processes': 'The fulfilment of these wishes would no longer generate an affect of pleasure but of unpleasure; *and it is precisely this transformation of affects which constitutes the essence of what we term "repression"*' (Freud's italics).

In dialogue, again, the reverse occurs, but if the transformation is successful (the transformation of hate), it takes the form not of repression but of liberated endopsychic energy and meaning.

In the *New Introductory Lectures* (1933a) Freud wrote: 'Dream-work translates the abstract thoughts into visual images.' Dialogue does the opposite; it translates visual images into words. 'Again, the dream-work cannot create conversation in dreams.'

Whilst dream-work is intent on preventing us from waking up, dialogue promotes consciousness.

Again in *The Interpretation of Dreams* (1900a) Freud wrote: 'The waking and sleeping states are alien to each other.' For us dialogue is alien to dreaming. 'While the sleeper is isolated there is an alteration in the distribution of his psychic energy.' This for us is equivalent to the vertical axis, and in dialogue the opposite obtains—namely, a redistribution of psychic energy in sharing and lateralization.

In conversation dialogue goes beyond words and sentences, beyond statements and syllogistic logic: it produces meaning. Dialogue constitutes an ongoing process in both liberating and constraining the mind. It articulates and formulates kosmos out of chaos. It introduces dimensions outside linguistics proper, involving tensions, timing, constraints, pauses, gestures, interceptions, cross currents, general themes, tangential analogies, contrasts, narrative, poetry, and drama, withholding, avoidance by inferential silences and boycotting, unravelling energy (decibels) from information flow, introducing spontaneity and unexpected novelty, myths, rituals, metaphors and antonyms, ideologies, historicity.

Dialogue offers a link between the subjective individual consciousness such as is explored in phenomenology, and the socially institutionalized structure: it is out of this exchange that microcultures evolve.

Despite these implications, the actual study of dialogue itself is sparse. Its praxis, you might say, has been totally overlooked. Perhaps this is due to a fear of chaos and panic, the ultimate in mental anguish, separation anxiety, and isolation. Levi-Strauss (1968), whose ultimate concern is with the human mind, drew attention to the way in which women have been circulated between families like words and money. 'Marriage is the archetype of exchange.' He depicts a constant stable pattern of rules and structures recurring in different myths, underlying the widely different surface manifestations. The net result seems to have been an extreme cautionary monitoring of dialogue. Yet no body of knowledge, no structure, political, social, scientific, or cultural, is secure unless it is interwoven in a system of dialogue.

Levi-Strauss (1968) suggested that thought processes, including perceptual experience, display a binary organization. We would suggest this binary outlook is moulded by one-to-one relationships in vertical reductionism, as distinct from the multipersonal lateralization of horizontal totalizations such as we see in dialogue. His opposition to phenomenology is based on a crude naturalism; the mind is seen as a thing amongst things. Like Freud, he refuses to be involved with consciousness which is something to be left to the political thinkers, to the moralists and to the philosophers.

Paul Ricoeur, in *Hermeneutics and the Human Sciences* (1981), approaches the centrality of dialogue in referring to spoken discourse that is contextually bound to a particular time and place. He distinguishes spoken discourse from textual discourse, available to an unrestricted audience across time and place, the primary domain of hermeneutics, and to be studied in the manner in which human action is explored in sociology. Textual discourse is a unitary given form to be distanced, studied, and objectified, whereas spoken discourse is a series of meanings reached by way of unstable syntheses and detours of understanding and interpretation that make us what we are as human beings. Thoughts can perhaps be said to be distanciated distillations of spoken discourse: dialogue is an ongoing conflict of interpretations, involved in the production of meaning, unrestricted to the narrow range of logic and linguistic problems, semantic rather than semiotic narrative.

Hermeneutics is the route to philosophical reflection where the symbol gives rise to thought. Ricoeur (1981) believes that we think 'not behind symbols but starting from symbols' and that hermeneutics is the interpretative bridge of meaning between representative symbols and primordial instincts, a de-mystification of meaning, separating ordinary language from the quasi-language of the unconscious. Meaning has two aspects: an objective aspect (what the sentence means) and a subjective aspect (what the speaker means). He considers that speaking and writing are alternative and equally legitimate modes of discourse. In speaking, there is a specific audience taking part in a dialogical relationship of shared reality, in contrast to the de-contextualized, unknown audience of written discourse, or sense versus reference. Reflection cannot speak from nowhere, but is always emerging from a specific traditional, cultural background. Consciousness is a difficult task, which explains why inertia plays such an important role; we are lazy rather than frightened.

Ricoeur attempted to go beyond sterile antinomies, beyond juxtaposition of conflicting views, towards a constructive 'discourse'. By symbol, Ricoeur understood all expression of double meaning, in which a primary meaning refers beyond itself to a second hidden meaning, never given directly. Discourse is much more complex and cannot be reduced to a simple binary double; it expands to a tangential, analogic, complex flux of the contextual matrix, involving understanding rather than explanation, and the vast imaginary panorama of culture. His interest lay in writing and intertextuality as distinct from speech.

For Aristotle logic, which in *Metaphysics* he termed Prior Analytics, was not so much logic as the dialectic of popular reasoning, not a substantive science but 'part of a general culture which everybody should undergo before studying any science'. 'Three', he commented 'transcends the simple opposition of two'.

The marketplace was the first university for dialectic and the development of concepts of ultimate cosmic issues. Like psychiatry, this caused ridicule, but Socrates appropriately answered that it was human wisdom that primarily interested him. The socratic method developed dialectically in the sense of process. Ideas born in man represent the difference between brute and man, a cultivation like a midwife's function, giving birth to ideas in arduous educational processes, 'Wherein the free soul is to be coaxed and nurtured by dint of deliberation into the kind of freedom that previously was only potential' (Plato, *The Republic*).

Plato held up, as it were, a speculum to see its glint in all directions and in different lights. The single formula of dialogue represented endlessly varied approaches to the three ultimate problems of the nature of the good, the beautiful, and the true. Parmenides said that there is an art that is called by the vulgar idle talking, which is often imagined to be useless 'but in which you must train and exercise yourself while you are young or truth will evade your grasp' (quoted in Bertrand Russell, *History of Western Philosophy*).

CHAPTER FOUR

Culture and Koinonia

> Men fear thought as they fear nothing on earth.
>
> Bertrand Russell, *Principles of Reconstruction*, 1916

> The nearer in blood, the nearer bloody.
>
> Shakespeare, *Macbeth*

> In our village, only the village idiot speaks his mind.
>
> Irish priest, 1980

> We live in a world of technical brilliance and cultural barbarity.
>
> E. de Maré, 1983

The four quotations at the heading of this chapter do not refer to thought itself, but to the nature of the surrounding cultural context. In each instance it is the context that evokes fear. If, on the contrary, the context is affirmative, we can evolve a culture which the

Greeks, felicitous in words appropriate to all occasions, termed *Koinonia,* or fellowship.

Durkheim saw human association as a creative process, not simply as an aggregation; he emphasized that the psychological potential of human society is dependent upon dialogue. Most societies at some time or other have declared free speech illegal. The boy who steals an apple is not frightened of apples, any more than Adam feared the tree of knowledge.

In the one-to-one relationship of traditional psychoanalysis, context is deliberately excluded (by standardization) in order to explore the relationship of transference.

In groups, context is judiciously reintroduced, and in large groups context becomes paramount and can take on microcultural features.

Freud formulated two fundamental drives: Eros and Thanatos; he saw the problem as one of providing facilities in which the two could be developed in a common context (Freud, 1920g):

> The aim of the first of these basic instincts is to establish ever greater unities and to preserve them—in short, to bind together; the aim of the second, on the contrary, is to undo connections and so destroy things. We may suppose that the final aim of the destructive instinct is to reduce things to an inorganic state. For this reason we also called it the 'death instinct'.

For us the larger group perspective throws new light on the death instinct. This 'parliament of instincts' by its very nature frustrates Eros, which therefore becomes transformed into hate, taking on a destructive form and giving the appearance of a primary drive. It is the context that causes this, producing an anti-drive, you might say, which is by no means primary: rather, it is a non-instinct, a sentiment, as William McDougall (1920) suggested, involving a cultural attitude.

The idea of anti-libido is no more fanciful than is the postulation of anti-matter in modern physics. But whatever it is, whether it is directed against the self (the death instinct) or against others (the death wish), it appears as the psychological sentiment of hate arising as a response to the frustration that comes from without. It demands an act of discrimination from within and therefore gives rise, not to biological energy, but to the psychic energy that constitutes the very essence of thought, mind, and culture. It is the nature of these microcultural manifestations that we have set out to explore.

So we have come to regard Thanatos as the outcome of the frustration of the primary instinct of Eros, and therefore a result of anti-instinct or hate that constitutes psychic energy as distinct from physical (solar) energy. Psychic energy is essentially neutral and under the right circumstances can become constructive. Winnicott's (1958) 'facilitating environment' or Foulkes's (Foulkes & Anthony, 1957) suggestion of 'allowing aggressive energies to be set free in order to serve constructive ends' begs the question. Hate is already facilitated, already set free; in fact it has been positively created by the context and the outcome of frustration. 'Setting it free' is itself only the first step of many in the discovery of its alternative uses. It is the outlet, not the energy, that is in question. Rycroft (1979) says: 'It is not the thought that is unconscious, it is a person who is unconscious of the thought.' We extend this in suggesting that it is not the individual who is unconscious but the culture that does not allow the thought to be voiced.

In wider settings the distinction between people and their environment can be repeatedly seen in the anomaly of the brutal cultures created by kindly people (e.g. Portugal, Chile, Cambodia, Rhodesia). People who are personally good, kind, and warm live in, and presumably help to create, the most violent cultural contexts. Perhaps this accounts for the universal tendency to avoid issues of context by personalization, infantilization, and familiarization. How then do we move from personalization to ideation, how do we lose the fear of thinking?

We found, in the median group, that certain members were treating the group culture exactly as if they were in the culture of their families of origin. One member could not speak in the group any more than he could speak in his family; another could only wheedle, a third could only disclaim and protest, whilst a fourth indulged in violent wrangling. This we called *transposition* as distinct from transference; and we came to regard transposition as a core concept, the touchstone in median group therapy.

Discussing the nature of small groups, Malcolm Pines (1982) writes: 'In this setting personal redefinitions can take place.' In the larger group the reverse can also occur—namely, a bid to humanize the setting. It is the wider parameters of cultural context that are being explored and which undergo redefinition; the problem is not to find what is culturally unshareable but to discover which cultures treat which matters as unsuitable for sharing. You might say that in the median group we are deliberately trying to create a state of anomie (defined by Durkheim, 1972, as 'a state of society in which normative standards of conduct and belief are weak or lacking) in order to explore and broaden the facilities for shareability. Whilst most groups are concerned about what to do together, our concern is how to think together.

The word 'climate' is derived from a Greek word meaning 'inclination'. We can become the stultified victims of climates when the culture is implicit, unconscious, and unshared, as distinct from being explicit and ventilated by dialogue. The practical question we have to solve is when, where, and by whom can such dialogue be arranged?

An example of the distinction between relatedness and context is found in the predicament of a married couple living alternately in two different countries, England and Norway, she being English and he Norwegian. In England he became dependent on her, something that she enjoyed since she liked feeling needed; in Norway, conversely, she became dependent on him, and he resented this.

Group therapists often allude to the dimension of culture, viz. Foulkes's matrix, Ezriel's common group tension, Bion's basic assumption cultures and (in larger groups), the protomental level, Dorothy Stock Whitaker's 'recurring themes under expanding cultural contexts', Forizs' 'loop theory', and de Maré's first concept of 'metastructure' (since revised). By all these writers, culture is ascribed a secondary position; whereas in the larger group it confronts us as a primary issue.

Culture is the outcome of a dialectical conflict between the individual system and environmental 'reality'. In relationship to nature, it takes the form of cultivation, e.g. agriculture, tool making, and science. In relation to society it takes the form of different sorts of *Kultur*. In relationship to the universe it takes the form of religion, philosophy, ideology, and art. In all three of these situations—nature, society, and the universe—the common denominator is the presence of the individual mind. Societies, civilizations, religions, philosophies, ideologies, art forms, methods of production come and go, but the individual with his mind (*mynde,* the old Norse equivalent to the word meaning 'vote'), goes on forever. One individual—e.g. Socrates, Shakespeare, Mahomet, Buddha, Christ—can influence the culture of the entire world.

Those who have worked in large institutions may have been struck from time to time by the sudden onset of unaccountable but ostensibly shared cultural attitudes: at these times decisions take on a life of their own, unpredictably and inexplicably, as if people have become spellbound by 'events', and views held privately are not voiced openly. In the changing microcultures in the median group, however, it has become abundantly clear that given the time and space in which to learn to talk to each other, people's cultural assumptions are in no way allowed to remain unaccountable. On the contrary, they are constantly being questioned, and through the process of dialogue new micro-cultures come to be established. This process we have called 'transformation'.

The spur, the mental energy underpinning the creative responses (to nature, to each other and to the universe), can be made more understandable in terms of Levi-Strauss's (1968) formulation that the first dialectic of all is the imposition of the barrier to the individual's biological 'natural' incestuous nature by society, something essential to the very core of society's continued existence. Human sexuality is both naturally incestuous and socially prohibited, and from this dialectic the first major transformation, that of culture, occurs. A similar dialectic occurs between the prohibition against 'own kill' in hunter bands and 'natural' male dominance, which established the culture of womanhood, perhaps the first primary cultural phenomenon. This is also related to the revolutionary transformation from nomadic to the agricultural way of life, the first signs of settling and of citizenship.

Genitality therefore is essentially two-faced. It is intrinsically biological and extrinsically social. We are exploring the dialectical process between the naturally 'incestuous individual' and the prohibitions imposed by society. From this dialectic culture is created. As already suggested, structure, process, and content create 'meta-structure', and meta-structure is culture when the structure takes on new meanings—sometimes through a revolution brought about by a sudden jolt, sometimes through a transposition when a new structure altogether (e.g. a larger structure) has to be adopted.

'Cultural' and 'social' are therefore by no means synonymous terms; derivatively, *socios* originally meant 'associate, ally, companion united to others, mutual intercourse', whilst 'to culture' meant to till, to break up the soil, to let in the air. The relationship between them is a dialectical one—'social reality', broadly speaking, representing the interests of society and 'culture' the interests of the individual, the areas between being the area of negotiation, of discrimination.

People are constantly involved in a clash between culture and society; they live in an arena of duality between social and cultural, the old order and the new. If they move too far into the socially institutionalized setting, they become strangled, frustrated, and depressed; on the other hand, when they move towards the idiosyncratic pole, they become isolated: Idealization versus persecution!

Culture is the 'group mind', meaning a grouping of minds. In much of the writings of sociology and anthropology confusion exists between social and cultural; the two terms are often used synonymously. In effect they are polar opposites in a state of dialectical tension. It is this tension (hate) that activates dialogue. Levi-Strauss (1968) talked of a 'classic antithesis between nature and culture'. For us, on the other hand, the primary antithesis is not between nature and culture; it lies in the encounter between mental processes and society of which culture is the outcome, a multipolar network as distinct from the triadic dialectic.

The issue centres round the nature of the currency of exchange. For Levi-Strauss (1968), marriage is the archetype of exchange. 'Marriage is thus a dramatic encounter between nature and culture, between alliance and kinship.' 'Alliance with another family ensures the dominance of the social over the biological and of the cultural over the natural.' Wives are the currency of exchange.

As an example of cultural defect, it is remarkable how the areas covered by psychiatry, by psychoanalysis, by psychotherapy and group therapy all avoid a critique of the cultural contexts in which they are being practised. Attempts to explore this context are treated as 'unrealistic'. Milieu therapy, for instance, takes the form of socialization as distinct from humanization and refrains from scrutinizing our social assumptions. It avoids looking at the community (therapeutic community) in favour of treatment by the community (community therapy). Attempts to approach the social context itself, phenomenologically, are rare. Whilst psychoanalysis explores the individual and small groups examine the family, only larger group settings can feasibly explore the social and cultural contexts in which we all reside, usually as helpless onlookers. How can we study what is meant by the words 'social' and 'antisocial'? What is meant by the word 'cultural'?

The next essential and self-evident step is to adopt the group-analytic principles that Foulkes and Anthony (1957) evolved while studying small group analytic psychotherapy and to explore this uncharted territory of the larger group itself. Referring to this matter, Peter Worsley, in *Marx and Marxism* (1982), writes: 'Small group sociologies for all the light they have thrown on the internal dynamics of the milieux in which we spend most of our working life, are usually devoid of any model of societies as wholes.' The structure of society is taken as 'given' and somehow assumed to be known—or, alternatively, to be irrelevant As C. Wright Mills (Gerth & Mills, 1946) put it, these are people who fail to place small groups within a theory of society at national and supranational levels.

To understand more of the situation, we have studied ideas suggested by the ancient Greeks, and also by certain of the structuralists namely Marx, Durkheim, Freud, de Saussure, Levi-Strauss, Chomsky, Roland Barthes, Foucault, and Lacan. These ideas particularly concern surface events of structures in relationship to deep structures via transformational rules. For example, there are the social super-structure and the material economic infrastructure in Marxism; or Durkheim's social consciousness determining individual consciousness; or the primary and secondary processes of Freud; or, in linguistics, the distinction between *la parole,* speech, discourse, and dialogue on the one hand, and language itself (*la langue*) on the other (de Saussure, 1970).

For the structuralists surface events are to be explained by, or determined by, structures of which individuals are not aware. For us, on the other hand, following the example of Foulkes, the approach is less deterministic but more purely dialectical, less hierarchical and more reciprocal and affiliative ('abnegation of father').

It has been our experience that panic occasioned by public speaking, and also the traumatic neuroses, can appropriately be treated in the larger group. The same can be said of the problems of expatriation, of social persecution, of the survival syndrome. The function of the larger group method is an attempt to transform hate into dialogue and eventually to arrive at a culture of fellowship and Koinonia. The areas between people within the larger group have an 'isomorphic' equivalence within the individual mind, for instance between the 'structures' of ego, id, and superego.

We have found that the multi-personal exchange of the larger group profoundly affects the type of thinking, highlighting the distinction between classical or traditional logic and the dialectic or polylectic or dialogue between several people.

The term 'logic' was unknown to Aristotle. 'Dialectic' was the term originally used, and it referred to the process of laying bare the structure, the syllogism. Aristotle regarded this a part of all reasoning, exhibiting its formal varieties irrespective of the nature of the subject-matter. It demanded self-consistency, which was called 'prior analysis'; 'analytics' meant that it had to be scientific as well as self-consistent. In *Topics* Aristotle described dialectic as self-consistent common sense, but a common sense that fails to satisfy all the conditions of scientific thought. He taught that the matter and the form of physical things are elements distinguishable by thought but inseparable in reality. He also wrote that a thing comes into being from its privation, a concept similar again to the ideas of lack, absence, void, need, or hiatus of Lacan and Bion, which for us takes the active form of hate.

Theoretical science was divided into metaphysics, theology, physics, and mathematics; of these metaphysics alone was a substance free of any connection with matter, the chief of these pure substances being God. Dialectic was a pre-theoretical science—not a substantive science, but a part of general culture which everyone should undergo before studying any science. Traditional logic, as a result of the excluded middle, *Tertium non-datum,* ignored the essence of the laws of contradiction themselves. Aristotle's *Topics* dealt with dialectic, which he described as the commonplace of argument seeking a method that would enable us to argue about any proposed problem from the probable premises while under examination ourselves. The dialectic syllogism is not scientific since its premises are not true but merely probable.

Aristotle drew up a list of thirteen fallacies that deceive not only others but also the speakers themselves. He divided these fallacies into two groups, namely six depending on the actual words themselves—e.g. ambiguity, incorrect emphasis—and seven that are non-verbal—e.g. not realizing properly what is being said, asking too many questions, and inconsequentiality. One gains the impression that he was referring almost entirely to duologue. The dualistic law of contradiction concludes that a thing is either correct or incorrect, false or true, and there is a definite exclusion of the relationship of the excluded middle. He wrote, 'there is no third man', thereby excluding group psychology, since the smallest group is a group of three; and also excluding systems-thinking and the network approach as distinct from the linear binary one-to-one structure of classical logic.

B. F. Skinner, in his book *The Design of a Culture Beyond Freedom and Dignity* (1971) displays the usual behavioural disrespect for the human species and democracy. Ethical control, he writes, may survive in small groups, but the control of the population as a whole must be arrogated to specialists—to police, priests, teachers, therapists, and so on, with their specialized reinforcement and their codified contingencies. For us these are already in conflict with each other and will almost certainly be in conflict with any new set of contingencies. Clearly Skinner sees responsibility as an individualized matter, depending on a scientist controller, and his word 'Utopian' presupposes a lack of personal responsibility. The simple procedure of people talking to each other in dialogue is not remotely considered, with the result that the word 'Utopian', originally a neologism of Sir Thomas More's meaning 'no place', has come in Skinner's writing to mean 'slavish work'. Skinner implies that the only hope of culture lies in the hands of the isolated individual, such as the planner or the scientist, persons defending themselves against predators, or persons who are engaged in the design and redesign of cultural practices. Who is to control? he asks, and adds that cultural evolution was made possible by biological evolution, denying still further the responsibility that is entailed in participating in the simple procedure of people talking to each other. Utopia then becomes a term dismissive of humanity's responsibility, a responsibility that can occur only in cultures that promote dialogue.

An interesting example of an unchanging structure in relationship to the constantly changing surface is provided by Chinese writing. Any Chinese man or woman today is in a position to recognize much of the ancient Chinese script, which is in fact pre-hieroglyphic and pre-cuneiform, dating from 5000 B.C. The pictographs, which amount to about 6,000, are identifiable with characters appearing in the daily newspapers of China today. There is a direct continuity going right back to the Shang dynasty, equivalent to present day English-speaking people experiencing a continuity with the early Egyptians, Mesopotamians, Greeks, and Romans.

Cultures are transformed through dialogue. This transformation may be, and perhaps necessarily is, incomplete, thereby creating a discrepancy between relatedness and context, which remain at loggerheads with each other. As an example, sexual intercourse between blood-related kin within the family is forbidden by society—a prohibition that becomes part of the family culture and may continue in the offspring once they have moved out. It can then be extended to social relationships generally, so that kindness (a word derived from kinship) and tenderness may impose a continued 'purity' in socio-sexual relationships—in marriage, for instance. A marital relationship may be 'good' but sexually inhibited. A change can only be effected by transforming the oedipal familiocentric culture into a social culture. A cause of the neurotic state can be the incomplete transformation between these two cultures falling between two stools, family and social, the social culture having to be learned, as distinct from the biological culture, which is instinctual. In family therapy the therapist acts as a referee from the 'outer space' of society.

In applying the median group method we begin to understand how inappropriate microcultural patterns can change through a process of extended dialogue. We have also learned a great deal about citizenship and Koinonia.

As an example of cultural transformation, let us consider the story of Rayalaseema, a region in India with a population of about a million people, dotted with small villages of up to a thousand inhabitants. In 1972 Vincent Ferrer, a defrocked Spanish Jesuit, settled in one of these villages and was confronted by the following situation. The entire population was illiterate, nobody had a radio so no outside news got through, and the whole region, for generations, had lived in gross poverty. In thirteen of the last twenty years rainfall had been inadequate and five famines had been recorded, despite the fact that there was plenty of water a hundred feet down. Quite apart from lack of funds, there were many cultural difficulties that obstructed any social change: for instance, there were fifteen castes, between whom it was impossible to marry, and with whom it was impossible to eat (and presumably drink from the same well) or to pray. All marriages were arranged. Virtually the only people it was possible to get to know were the untouchables and the gypsies, who were largely ignored as far as cultural developments were concerned; and so it was on these groups that Father Vincent concentrated his efforts. In spite of the difficulties, within seven years he was able, by dint of sinking wells, to change Rayalaseema from one of the poorest regions in India into a showplace. (Reported by Mervyn Jones in the *Observer Colour Supplement,* 6 May 1979.)

The question remains: why is it that intelligent people perpetuate cultures that are so self-destructive? We do not have to turn to other cultures for anthropological study, we have only to step outside our own front door.

Throughout the ten-year meetings of the median group, the problematic relationship between entangled strands of hate, friendship, lust, and love, have constantly arisen as recurring themes. It has become evident that friendship and love are two entirely distinct phenomena. Because of frustration at the genital level, a person grows up in an atmosphere of love in relationship to the parent of the opposite gender and of hate in relation to the parent of the same gender. If this hate is not transformed into friendship, then genitality becomes inhibited since it is generated in a hostile context; and following this only impotence, or pre-genital manifestations—e.g. sado-masochism, homosexuality, drug addiction—are possible. It is interesting that the word 'gender' is derived from a word similar to 'engender' or 'generate'.

Marriage has many features in common with incest and represents a successful transformation of incest from the familiocentric microculture to the social culture. For instance, marriage is exclusive, repetitious, powerful, universal, unique, often appears to be completely irreplaceable, and, if disturbed by unfaithfulness, sometimes even of a most minor nature, can precipitate feelings of psychotic intensity that are persecutory and irreversible, e.g. morbid jealousy. If the transformation is incomplete, it can result in love without passion, or frigidity, occurring from the moment of the wedding ceremony. The relationship can be idealized, sentimentalized, or, alternatively, can turn into the opposite, with constant feelings of persecution.

Koinonia is a cultural and impersonal manifestation of fellowship, which nurtures genitality. It is not itself in any way erotic, springing as it does from a basically blocked eroticism converted into hate. It cultivates a cultural context in which genitality can grow, can be learned, can be engendered.

It is nature versus culture, to quote Levi-Strauss (1968), who considered that 'the former is licentious to the point of corruption, the latter pure to the point of sterility'.

We would suggest that the larger group method begins at the biological level of self-absorbed narcissistic materialism (mater). However, it is then faced with the imperative demand of the social dimension, and from this confrontation the dialectic starts, bringing with it a new beginning.

The negotiation of the split between lust and love, between the existential and the structural, between the Dionysian and the Apollonian, takes place through the intermediation of dialogue. When negotiations break down, there is either fragmentation (panic) or else there is reaction formation (counter phobic), unification by mass-, pack-, or mob-formation and scapegoating. This is liable to happen at any time, and it is this that makes larger groups frightening when information flow (dialogue) gives way to the energy flow of violence.

The majority of people who have attended a large group would agree that it has a remarkable impact, which is quite characteristic. For better or for worse, it is extraordinarily exhausting and gives the impression that in the course of it you either grow up or grow old. There is no way of feeling indifferent. Members have often suffered a sleepless night following the large group meeting.

Large groups provoke phobic responses, and since panic is indigenous to crowd situations, it is not surprising to discover that people sometimes take the opportunity to talk their way through panic. To do this raises the threshold of panic, enabling members to undertake major changes in their external lives. Fears of phobic intensity, hostility, alliances, and friendships develop suddenly with extreme intensity. The nature of the culture at any particular juncture is a central issue; for instance, the predominant culture may be one of bickering and blocking, cliché-ridden with destructive comments, and this may have to be pointed out. The question is how to foster a culture that enables and promotes thoughtfulness and creativity and helps to transform hate into a more negotiable currency.

A minority of people insist they find the situation entirely meaningless. This can often be seen to be a counter-phobic reaction resulting from traumatic experiences in previous larger group situations, e.g. expatriation.

Fellowship marks a transitional state between kinship and lawship. For instance, there are the blood pacts of brotherhood, alliances somewhere between family on one hand and an alien society on the other—neither incestuous nor social but cultural; there are also situations in which an entire group can act as a transitional object, for example the caste system in its battle against anomie. A dyadic relationship in the large group at the familiocentric cultural stage of development may be interpreted as a persecuting primal scene, or as a combined parental figure. Creative thinking generated by fantasies of procreating (e.g. 'pairing') may be seen as threatening, excluding the freshness of freely associated spontaneous thought; then a 'double bind' may arise, the group splitting into factions of idealized clichéd sentimentality—'caring', 'gut reaction', 'in touch with feeling', 'warm', 'real' on the one hand, 'indifference' and 'cold intellectuality' on the other.

The fear of ostracism and of exile can precipitate panic, but it may take the alternative form of respectable depression, kindness being preferable to victimization. Psychic or cultural death is distinct from physical death; indeed phobic personalities sometimes choose the latter as a way out, the final evasion.

In this context it is interesting to note that Max Weber initially investigated bureaucratic oligarchy in the setting of a mental hospital where he was a patient. Oligarchy is the key question in modern sociology and political science since it is mistakenly regarded as a central factor in the survival of large organizations. (Our experiences have radically refuted such contentions.)

For us it has been essential to make the distinction between, on the one hand, social oranizations dependent on small group 'bureaux', and, on the other, the wider structure essential to culture, with its more fluid quality, indigenous to larger groups. Whilst bureaucratic organization was considered by Weber to be the embodiment of rationality, intrinsically superior to all other possible structures in channelling and allocating power, small bureaucratic offices cannot, by the very nature of their small structure, view themselves extrinsically and culturally in relation to the whole. The machinery of bureaucracy, if left to itself, emerges in a mindless manner, and oligarchy cuts through the larger cultural structures like a knife through butter. The world today is dominated by oligarchy, whether of small bureaucratic offices or terrorist gangs. For us charisma is creative art related to culture, which has to confront dialectically domination by hardened lasting social institutions—including familiocentric 'cultures', i.e. system versus structure.

In dialogue we discuss the cultural dimension of citizenship which presents denizen views (analogic, tangential and lateralized) at levels not available in either psychoanalysis or small groups. Unfortunately, neither the time nor space accorded to either of these disciplines is given to larger groups, that is, to 'phenomenological' large groups 'without prejudice' and 'bracketed off' from the world. Larger groups unhampered by external ties simply do not happen, and, therefore, the opportunity to explore culture as pure culture does not happen either.

De Saussure (1970), in talking of dialogue, makes a clear distinction between words as symbols and words as signs. Dialogue can take place with words as symbols but not with words as signs. 'Signs are fixed, and not free with respect to the linguistic community who use them.' Symbols involve the interaction between private and public meanings as in dialectics, and the outcome of this is cultural. Symbols, play, rituals, metaphors, and myths are all cultural manifestations, as indeed are all transitional objects. Text itself is a transitional process whether it be free association, group association, or dialogue. It is derived from a word meaning 'to weave'.

The mind can only tolerate symbols, e.g. words and music, as distinct from emotion itself, which can only be tolerated in a transformed state. Panic (the ultimate in mental pain) and hate (the ultimate in mental energy) have to be contained in some form of symbolic currency so that they can be transformed and structured out of their biological subsystem and become functional for intellectual purposes (e.g. a poem can provoke tears).

Given time and space, the larger group, free of anxiety from pressures, can provide a locus for dialogue and can to some extent make amends for the mindless neglect the infant so often suffers during the formative years. No child fulfils his or her mental potential; the constant cry is not for love but for attention. Thoughtfulness is a slow process; it is citizenship in the making!

In his book *The Ritual Process*, Victor Turner (1969) throws light on the liminal area between structure and anti-structure, bonding and separation, between antecedent or subsequent social states and statuses of the individual. But it is clear that these distinctions could be extended to antecedent and subsequent cultural shapes in society itself. His term 'communitas' refers to an egalitarian relationship in people stripped of status and property, a concept related to Koinonia and affiliation, 'on the level'. Neither Turner nor Levi-Strauss, nor other anthropologists, with the exception of Marshall Sahlins, appear to have made a clear distinction between social and cultural in the dialectical sense that we have employed here. Ten years after pointing out that there was a distinction between cultural and social, Levi-Strauss was still using the terms interchangeably.

To illustrate the distinction, we could look at a Norwegian village seen as a paradigm of social functioning, but culturally moribund; and then at an artist like Vincent van Gogh, who was a genius culturally speaking but appears to have been treated as a social moron. The individual contains both social and cultural potentials, which constitute an ever-present dilemma, and this dilemma can never be resolved since the one is institutional and the other is existentially unique.

Social structure moulds, canalizes, exerts pressure, and structures mental energy; culture as a manifestation of group mind converts this matter–energy into information. The major conceptual shift from matter–energy to information flow, previously confused, marks a breakthrough in the history of science: a parallel shift must also take place in psycho-social thinking where the biological, the psychological, the social, and the politico-economic must be handled operationally in a unified cultural field. But until we achieve a deeper understanding of the phenomena occurring in large groups per se, as self-regulating systems, all politico-economic systems, however theoretically sound, must flounder through want of a more sophisticated large group experience.

Micro-cultures play a vital rôle in promoting or impeding relevant ideas. In the large group it is consciousness that is in jeopardy. As we have said, the problem for the large group is its mindlessness.

The larger group, then, has two very powerful features. The first feature is the way in which it generates hate out of frustration, hate that can prove quite ungovernable and can take the form of panic or violence. The second is the way in which, given the time and place to evolve a structural matrix, it can become a highly sensitive and informed thinking apparatus. Structures of redundant hierarchy can then give way to systems of affiliative self-regulation, using in addition to language such non-verbal strategies as silence, boycott, ridicule, laughter, inspiration, timing, and ambiences of all sorts to achieve it. Above all, the large group is the situation of choice for handling the panic of phobic states and psychotic (e.g. persecutory) anxiety, as panic is an indigenous feature of large group phenomena.

The hallmark of psychotic anxiety lies in its break with reality. The larger group, in creating a powerful cultural context, establishes an undeniable group mind related to reality that cannot be sidestepped yet is open to negotiation through dialogue. A group can be seen as developing spirally from structure to process and content, and these mutually influence each other so that the meaning of a structure can take on different cultures as the group continues to meet in time and place.

This leads one to infer that the culture or, as it has been termed, the 'meta-structure' constantly changes the nature of the meaning of that structure for its participants and is a crucial feature of group development. For instance, therapeutic atmosphere is a cultural concept. As social structure and personality mutually influence each other, group therapy can be viewed primarily as entailing a process in which the cultures of the group (social) structure are constantly changing. The question is, how is this arranged? And how is this implemented? In the larger group this process takes place through dialogue and becomes increasingly explicit. Once it has reached a conscious level for the members of the group, a cultural change may be adopted. The culture of the group is no longer an atmosphere that is being acted out. The members of the group can deliberately decide to discard it or alter it, or on the other hand simply allow it to sink into the background in favour of a newly developing culture, constituting, as it were, the values or the sanctions of the group.

The larger group, if it does not split up into smaller groups, is in an advantageous position to scrutinize the microcultural parameters that keep emerging. This is done, as we have said, through the activity of dialogue or discourse, and we have found that it can take more than ten years to create a culture in which people can begin to talk to each other without violation. This may be aided by the developing capacity of the larger group to condition people to contain panic, thereby successfully transforming and completing a transposition from a previous traumatic social situation. As a cultural organization, encouraged along group-analytic lines to discuss affiliatively, 'on the level', the larger group constantly remoulds 'social assumptions' in the creative moment and is therefore concerned with the meaning it has for the individual participants. Whilst social is dialectically speaking anti-nature, the microculture is anti-social in its ability to distance itself from social assumptions.

Cultural variation involving matters of race, class, religion, philosophy, ideological attitudes, values, emotional climate are manifest in a state of constant flux in the larger group setting, with clarity and vividness, not as second-order realities or defence mechanisms, but as primary considerations. We would suggest that the larger group provides a method of crossing this minefield.

For instance, the understanding of friendship in a group at a pre-genital sado-masochistic phase of subcultural development may be interpreted as weakness, and intelligence and gentleness construed as feebleness, as intellectualization, or as 'homosexual'.

It is unfortunate that the median group remains a largely unexplored territory since it has an advantage over other large organizations, which are fragmented by oligarchy. Cultures can best be created and explored in the nascent state of the microculture, the creative moment tilted towards the future. It can provide the key meanings that societies have for the individual, the individual mind being alive and human and society being mechanical. The median group in being bracketed off is culturally mobile and concerned with the politics of politics, the culture of cultures normally relegated to unconsciousness.

Psychoanalysis and the philosophy of phenomenology emerged at the turn of the century to free us from the cultural constraints of organic psychiatry. Later, in the 1930s, interest was extended beyond the relationships of psychodynamics to the context within which these relationships occurred. The expatriated Freudians, for instance, emigrating to the United States, displayed a lively interest in the political climate. Fromm was a Marxist; Adler, Erickson, and Horney were concerned with cultural factors; and Foulkes in this country was developing concepts concerned with socialization, communication, specific group features, and the group matrix. Moreno in the United States introduced socio- and psycho-drama, while in Britain Bierer, Maxwell Jones, David Clark, and others developed the concept of the therapeutic community and other forms of milieu therapy such as social clubs, activity groups, ward meetings, and administrative therapy. All this occurred during the 1930s, 1940s, 1950s, and 1960s; it was not until the early 1970s that interest was evinced in the larger group per se.

Political issues such as the mass ideologies of the 1930s, the Second World War of the 1940s, the cultural revolution in China, the student movements of the 1950s and 1960s in the West, had influenced all psychodynamic approaches, but this effect was peripheral and there has on the whole been a lack of sophistication and of personal political involvement; political developments therefore emerge in an arbitrary and mindless manner. However, during the 1970s there was a growing realization that the genetic psychoanalytic approach, the small group and family approach and the therapeutic community, are not able to cover man as a cultural being, operationally speaking in the sense of teaching social realization, citizenship, and Koinonia. The small group, by the very nature of its size, can only too easily be tilted towards psychoanalytic and family and biological constructs; by the same token it is only in the setting of the larger group, of twenty or more people, that factors specific to the situation can become open to direct observation. People cannot learn about these matters, as it were, on their own, in isolation. Cultural changes are brought about by the hard work of dialogue between each individual in the group, responsible not only to themselves but to the larger situation.

Therefore, with the best will in the world, the most free and liberated one-to-one relationship, teased out with the help of psychoanalysis and/or group therapy, and manifesting a high level of psychological maturity, may yet founder through having to survive in a context and environment that is antipathetic to cultural sophistication.

In an address to the second European Symposium in 1972, Lionel Kreeger (1975) dwelt on the topic of intimacy in large groups. He quoted from Foulkes's first book, *An Introduction to Group Psychotherapy* (1948): 'For the purpose of such highly intimate work as group analysis, numbers cannot be large.' He also quotes from *Therapeutic Group Analysis* (Foulkes, 1964). Writing about the value of a ward meeting in sensing the overall atmosphere, Foulkes stated 'more is needed however. The patient needs insight into his own conditions and life, insight into his present feelings, behaviour and reactions. Therein lie the limitations of a large meeting (thirty to eighty). For this a more intimate setting is essential, i.e. the small psychotherapeutic group'.

Kreeger quotes various writers concerning the larger group, none of whom seriously maintains that the larger group itself as an evolving structure is capable of creative discovery and cultural change. Rather it is regarded in an undynamic way as a form of social control and confrontation of deviant behaviour. Kreeger also quotes T. Wilmer's point that large groups create the need for small cohesive subgroups. Andrew Curry, in his paper 'A critique and appraisal of selective literature on large therapeutic groups' (1967), considers that conformity in the large group is a means of influencing or neutralizing group pressure, and concludes 'whatever goes on in large groups is not psychotherapy'. Edelson (1970), on the other hand, has a more dynamic approach to the large group potential in stating that socio-therapy consists specifically of dealing with intra-group and inter-group tension, as distinct from psychotherapy, which deals with intra-personal tensions. He views community meetings as task-orientated, designed to examine and resolve conflicts that inhibit organizational effectiveness; his approach is therefore diametrically distinct from the approach we are recommending, i.e. the application of Foulkes's group-analytic principles to a larger group, which is not task-orientated. Edelson reaches the surprising conclusion that intra-personal elements, if produced and examined, are task-inhibiting.

Kreeger (1975) goes on to say that Rafael Springmann, in his paper 'The large group' (1970), is one of the few who acknowledge that psychotherapy can occur in a large group situation, and that this large and mixed forum could be utilized for approaching personal dynamics. Springmann also suggests that large groups cannot take the place of regular therapeutic groups through lack of continuity and intimacy; that a large part of the group remains silent and anonymous (we on the contrary have certainly never found this to occur for any great length of time), and that 'the group leader may be left exhausted, comparable with an hour of personal psychotherapy with a psychotic, through the constant effort of harnessing this vast power to constructive therapeutic ends, of creating harmony in a potentially chaotic atmosphere'. We would like to point out that we do not see ourselves as harnessing any vast power, or of remoulding in order to create harmony. As we see it, Springman's conclusions are not surprising since he appears to see the conductor as having to do all the work. Foulkes, on the contrary, as we understand it, applied the principle of swinging from leadership by the 'leader' to leadership of the whole group in his construct of the evolving group matrix. The groups are 'leaderless' and without a specific task, and the whole work of the group is to create a culture in which the group takes over the responsibility of conducting its own affairs. What is not sufficiently appreciated is the length of time such a procedure takes and the amount of preparation that has to be done by *all* its members.

Lionel Kreeger retains a more open mind. He considers that the place of the larger groups in clinical work has still to be defined. He states: 'I think that it is true that groups are essential to the working of a therapeutic community, but that a therapeutic community setting is not essential to the running of groups.' We have noted that small groups in antipathetic settings take on the ambience of a secretive, persecuted cabal. Large group organizations, Kreeger concludes, constitute the only possible way of dealing adequately with the psychotherapeutic needs of the hospital population.

It is not sufficiently realized that in group therapy generally an essential and unique dimension has been introduced which, although it in no way supercedes individual psychotherapy, provides new parameters for treating aspects of neurosis that heretofore have been unapproachable: out of this grew Foulkes's construct of 'location', in which the ramifications and impact of a neurotic conflict on its social environment can be mapped out, and which gives an entirely new and cultural meaning to the significance of neurosis.

In the larger group method this is carried a stage further, and the process of mapping out itself is examined. We can not only look at the effect of the neurosis on the environment, but also at the influence of the culture created by the larger group in promoting neurosis as distinct from nurturing the creative cultural potentials of the individual minds involved. In other words, the only truly effective way of coping with redundant institutionalization, redundant hierarchy, redundant bureaucracy, and the problems that arise from traumatic social crises lies in pitting large group against large group, pitting microculture against established macroculture. In the larger groups we can examine the medium of one culture against another and discover, sometimes perhaps dispel, those cultures that stem from inappropriate assumptions.

In parentheses one might add that in psychoanalysis the specific modalities of each erotogenic zone carry a subcultural equivalent and therefore contribute towards the shaping of our macrocultures and microcultures—that is, the infrastructure influences and transforms the social structure culturally. By the same token the reverse is also the case: the current culture shapes the handling of sphincters—'sphincter morality!'

Duverger (1972) makes a very important distinction between mass group structures and cadres, which are groups appealing to small, but influential social categories. The importance of this rests in the fact that larger groups, whatever the latent opinions or culture may be, only too easily become victims to small power cadres, through violence, coercion, or fear; for example, we have the terrorist gangs, which will be a recurring phenomenon unless citizenship is regarded in an active and dynamic operational way. We see this problem also in bureaucratization, where the larger system is controlled by small offices and committees who never directly meet each other in a larger setting and therefore cannot establish an overall policy that is coherent and appropriate. The system therefore takes on a mindless motion of its own, creating a machinery that is often callous and subhuman—the 'Deus ex machina'. For this phenomenon we have adopted the term 'packing' (wolf pack) leading to a 'follow my leader' subculture. The culture of the group is the group equivalent of the individual mind. In so far as this culture can be inappropriate, and even pathologically destructive, so it can be seen as the equivalent of neurotic disturbance in the individual. No group exists without culture, but most societies have inappropriate 'cultures' that are always out of date.

The small group, being closer to the conflicting influences of family life, with its hierarchical barriers to communication, does not have the cultural and emotional impact that is generated through collision of ideas in larger groups. In the median group, one function of its members, including the convener, is to uncover the assumed ongoing subculture. For example, the topic of gender cannot be so easily reduced to intellectual terms and evaded in the larger group as in the small, since it is a major cultural issue. We regard the phenomenon of morphogenesis as being particularly characteristic of larger group structures, where highly adaptive, elaborate and evolving organizations can emerge in relationship to a wide variety of implicit subcultures.

The larger group treated along Foulkesian lines differs substantially from such groups as those conducted at the Leicester conferences, which meet for a fortnight. In these groups several members of staff preside, and the seating arrangements are relatively haphazard, in concentric circles or spirals. For us the larger group requires as much time as smaller groups or as psychoanalysis—perhaps more—and the seating must be a single circle. The larger group is a far more complex situation than either psychoanalysis or group analysis and demands as close a scrutiny.

A. K. Rice (1965) suggested there were three main situations to be considered: that of the individual, that of the small group face-to-face setting, and that of the large group in which face-to-face relationships, he wrote, are no longer possible.

We would suggest the larger group be provided with sufficient time and adequate seating arrangements to make primary face-to-face contact possible. We do not know the optimal size of larger groups, but it is clear to us that face-to-face contact is still possible within the group that he sees as too large, i.e. forty to seventy people.

Themes emerge in constantly changing atmospheres. As we have said, attitudes make themselves evident, not as cloudy idealistic non-sequiturs, but as microcultures—that is, as clearly defined climates that either impede or promote communication and information flow.

Rice at the Leicester conferences saw the large group in leader-centred terms, leadership being required to control the internal and confused striving of its members and to relate them to the external environment. To underline this he recommended daily lectures designed to give intellectual content to the learning taking place in the other events of the conference: these lectures were intended to provide a framework for the articulation of the experience of the conference; intellect was regarded as the prerogative of the lecturers since the large group was only capable of experience. This, we feel, is questionable since what is urgently needed is large group thinking per se, something equivalent to good-citizenship.

It is essential we differentiate large groups from the loosely structured organizations with which we are already familiar, such as therapeutic communities. The group-analytic approach to the large group demands a comprehensive exploration of large face-to-face primary groups per se, a meeting of the members regularly over a considerable time, not a sudden marathon. These meetings should be as rigorous and extensive as any psychoanalytic or group-analytic procedure, freed of current community ties and of redundant hierarchical structures. Such a setting could provide a melting pot, an opening to otherwise impervious and closed individual mental structures. What is needed is a deeper understanding of the phenomena of the large group structure itself in relation to its evolving system leading to an expansion of consciousness since consciousness itself is by derivation a process of 'knowing with others'. Within this situation one might gain experience of those ephemeral and to a great extent ignored contextual features that we call cultural, to do with climate, ambience, atmosphere, ethos, values—the attitudes and ideologies that are so characteristic of the micropolitics of all large groups and that play an enormous role in matters of morale, communication, and information flow. Activating mind through emerging cultures that are created by individual minds in dialogue is the core feature of the larger group; the larger group that starts as a mindless pack—characterized by 'votelessness', equivalent to mindlessness, with a rudimentary system of communication, with a group mind at risk of being reified and personalized in the single isolated mind of the leader as distinct from leading ideas.

The structure of a group influences the flow of thinking—e.g., the setting of lecture-rostrum or pulpit creates monologue and dependency in the audience, and axiomatic thinking. The one-to-one setting, on the other hand, makes for syllogistic logic and the mutually contradictory antinomies of the dialectic of Kant. In *The Critique of Pure Reason* Kant wrote: 'We must be able for instance, to know, according to a rule what in every possible case is right or wrong, because this touches our obligation and we cannot have any obligation to that which we cannot know.' 'We call dialectic in general a logic of illusion.'

Kant considered the outer world produces only the matter of experience, and our own mental apparatus orders this matter in space and time and causality and supplies the concepts by means of which we understand experience. Things in themselves, the causes of our experiences, are unknowable; they are not in space and time, they are not substances, nor are they 'categories'. The purely intellectual use of reason, of Logos, leads to fallacies; its only right use is directed to moral ends—leading to the 'categorical imperative', a completely isolated metaphysic of morals, unrelated to any end, neither to theology, nor ethics, nor physics, wholly a priori in Reason (*Metaphysics of Morals*). The 'categorical imperative' is equivalent to the superego that becomes humanized in dialogue.

The group of three has an equivalence to the triadic dialectic of Hegel, thesis, antithesis, and the outcome, synthesis, which in its turn becomes the next thesis. A group of three concentric circles leads to hierarchy—usually with the more active élitist inner circle prevailing.

The single circle of a larger group is structurally conducive to affiliative, on-the-level, analog thinking, tangential, multi-faceted, and 'lateral', with chains of thinking constituting themes that are neither correct nor incorrect but 'phenomenological' as distinct from logical.

We have coined the term 'transposition' for the introduction of matters from previous contexts into the group, similar but distinct from the manifestations of transferred relationships in psychoanalysis (i.e. transference). Transposition is an extension of Foulkes's constructs of group matrix and location, itself an extension of Gestalt thinking of foreground figures against the background of the total communicational network as a slowly evolving specifically group phenomenon; it consists of the pattern of an individual neurotic response mapped out against its social context. In transposition it is this background that is brought into the forefront in much the same way that one might examine the backcloth of a stage setting, constituting the Gestalt-type reversal of location that characterizes the group dynamic approach. Whilst in psychoanalysis it is the transference that constitutes the cornerstone of therapy, in group analysis it is transposition.

In exploring the large group we have taken the further step of linking it up with the structuralist construct of transformation to refer to the situation when it is not a position that is being transposed but a whole culture that is being transformed. Whilst transference explores the linear causal relatedness of the one-to-one situation, and transposition explores the multi-personal network of the small group matrix, transformation juxtaposes and transforms one subculture, microculture or social culture into another, linking up systems thinking with the broader perspective of structuralism.

Our task as citizens is not only to adjust to society but to enable society to adjust to us. Unless we look at our cultural context, we are groping around in a vacuum.

Transposition also occurs when people in groups create subcultural climates consisting of unconscious rejected fantasies and frustrated parts of themselves and produce atmospheres that are neither 'realistic nor gratifying'. These are explored from the stance of a wide range of evolving microcultures. Paranoia in the individual has to create a persecutory climate before the delusion can be dispelled. In non-therapeutic situations it does not usually reach this stage, and the experience is constantly repeated in other settings. In the group a delusory subculture may be transposed into an actual persecutory microculture and then worked through in dialogue.

For example, a group member was able to talk freely to everyone individually but was unable to talk to all when they were all together in a group. It became clear that a parallel situation had existed in relation to this woman's family, parents and siblings, in the past. She concluded that the larger group was a more effective setting for the resolution of her problem than the one-to-one or small group situation. The Oedipus conflict is of course a group conflict. Atmospheres can hang like a pall over a group, transposed as a group ethos even though transferred from separate individuals. The process of cultural transformations are much more obvious in the larger setting, where a familiocentric subculture stands out, becoming increasingly discrepant with the strong sociocentric microculture which opposes the tendency to trivialize and infantilize the context.

The traumatic neuroses that Freud noted, and which could not be explained in terms of the infantile neuroses, can and do occur at any time in life, producing symptoms that are indistinguishable from those of transference or familiocentric neuroses. The therapist may produce improvements in relationships, but in a subculture that remains a-social and familiocentric; treatment may be prolonged almost indefinitely till broken by some sudden change in microcultural circumstances, e.g. hospitalization.

Psychoanalysis focuses on the dyadic relationship in the shape of the transference; the small group introduces the familio-concentric context in the form of transpositioning; the larger group transforms one culture to another. As Foulkes and Anthony (1957) said, the neurotic person is both more isolated from society and more fixated to a group (family) than the normal. In this context we are reminded of Freud's comments in *Totem and Taboo* (1912–13):

> This difference in the treatment of the two subjects [totem and taboo] is due to the fact that taboo still exists in our midst . . . and is still nothing else than Kant's 'Categorical Imperative' which tends to act compulsively and rejects all conscious motivation. On the other hand totemism is a religio-social institution which is alien to our present feelings; it has long been abandoned and

> replaced by new forms. . . . The social and material progress of the history of mankind could obviously change taboo much less than totemism.
>
> Taboo is a command of conscience the violation of which causes a terrible sense of guilt which is as self-evident as its origin is unknown.

The vital issue for us is that taboo manifests itself as a cultural phenomenon.

CHAPTER FIVE

Object relations theory. Systems thinking and structuralism

A system is a set of units with relationship among them.

Ludvig Von Bertalanffy, *General Systems Theory*, 1968

Time is the particular instant at which a structure exists—the measurable period over which a structure endures.

James G. Miller, *Living Systems*, 1965

The mind is peopled by part objects and by images and subcultures of the past, and it is only by introducing the microcultural dimension that structural transformations can take place between systems and cohesion become coherence. Under the reciprocal influence of evolving microcultures, dialogue can become humanized by real here-and-now people and their dialogue. The subhuman subculture of the past, and the indifferent macroculture of the social environment, can be viewed against the creative microculture of the present median group, so that instead of identifying with the subcultures and social macroculture, we are now able to scrutinize them from the distance of this new perspective. Microcounter-culture is the specific metastructural dimension of the larger group, bringing about transformations in the part objects of individual subcultures and in the attitudes to the surrounding macrostructures of the social environment—e.g. the family subculture gives way to the social macroculture of a horde mentality, of a family writ large, as Freud would have it.

Structures are formed by boundaries between systems. Once a transformation from one system to another takes place, an irreversible structural change is established, e.g. insight and outsight emerge.

The structuring of hate through dialogue constitutes transformation, as distinct from Bion's passive toleration of frustration. System, being self-regulating, becomes structural once it is involved in regulation from another system, and the transformation of one system in relation to another. This process, as we see it, is 'structuralism'.

Subcultures can be said to be based on shared individual infantile and developmental stages and 'frames of reference', e.g. 'part objects', 'paranoid' and 'depressive' positions, 'oral', 'anal', 'genital' and family constellations. These stages and frames of reference first become established as subcultures directly influencing the social macroculture and can be scrutinized from the viewpoint of median group microcultural developments occurring through dialogue. As already instanced, the family subculture can become the horde macroculture.

The work of Wittgenstein and Hegel is relevant to the concept of dialogue. Whilst Wittgenstein seems to have excluded dialogue within the framework of binary logic in which things are either clear or unmentionable, Hegel saw history not as a hotch-potch of blind forces, chance and permutations, but as a purposeful consciousness of freedom. 'Man is destined to be free' through a new development in logic, namely that of the dialectic method of logic. For us dialogue is a multifaceted extension of the triadic dialectic, analogic as distinct from the binary digital dyad.

The inherent relatedness in the constructs of objects, systems, and structures becomes strikingly self-evident in larger group settings; indeed, it could be surmised that these constructs have been derived unknowingly from larger group influences. For instance, it could be said that individuals are like objects who resolve their splits by relating to each other through dialogue, thus creating systems. These systems in turn establish codes or microcultures, which impose frames or metastructures on the original structure. The change or transformation of one such subculture to the new microculture constitutes a process elsewhere known as structuralism.

J. P. Roberts, in his article, 'Foulkes' concept of the Matrix' (1982) wrote: 'Matter and mind are the explicit order of an implicit order projected onto the matrix.' He suggests that, in submerging personal consciousness in a group, the struggle to emerge again in a transcended and re-defined form can be therapeutic. This process stands out even more clearly in the larger group when it is dialogue that struggles to emerge. He wrote that object relations theory can offer a better starting point, 'since the matrix melts like a snowflake when put under the microscope'. It is important to be aware, however, that there is no object relations theory 'as such' but a large number of related but disarticulated and even idiosyncratic personal viewpoints. In a similar direction Colin James (1982) relates the group matrix to Winnicott's transitional object, which, in the space between mother and child, mediates between fantasy and reality.

Freud first referred to object relationships in *Mourning and Melancholia* (1917e [1915]):

> First there existed an object choice, the libido had attached itself to a certain person; then owing to a real injury or disappointment concerned with the loved per-

> son, this object relationship was undermined. The result was not the normal one of withdrawal of the libido from this object and transference of it to a new one, . . . the free libido was withdrawn into the ego and not directed to another object . . . but served simply to establish an identification of the ego with the abandoned object. Thus the shadow of the object fell upon the ego, so that the latter could henceforth be criticized by a special mental faculty like an object, like the foresaken object. In this way the loss of the object became transformed into a loss in the ego, and the conflict between ego and the loved person transformed in a cleavage in the ego between the criticizing faculty of the ego and the ego as altered by the identification.

The ego can only

> treat itself as an object, when it is able to launch against itself the animosity relating to an object—that primordial reaction on the part of the ego to all objects in the outer world.
>
> The relation of hate to objects is older than that of love.

In *Civilization and Its Discontents* (1930a [1929]), Freud wrote:

> Love opposes the interests of culture. . . . The rift between them seems inevitable. . . . It expresses itself first in a conflict between the family and the larger community. . . . We have seen already that one of culture's principal endeavours is to cement men and women together in larger units. But the family will not give up the individual . . . that form of life which is phylogenetically older and is in childhood its only form, resists being displaced by that type that becomes acquired later with culture. . . . [Culture] exacts a heavy toll of aim inhibited libido in order to strengthen communities by bonds of friendship between the members.

> The tendency of culture to set restrictions upon sexual life is no less evident than *its other aim of widening its sphere of operations*. Even the earliest phase of it, the totemic, brought in its train the prohibition against incestuous object-choice, perhaps the most maiming wound ever inflicted throughout the ages on the erotic life of man. [our italics]

It is the complex paradox of the subject treating itself as the object that first gave rise to the seeds of object relations theory. This led in due course, to such constructs as Fairbairn's (1952) construct of the Central Ego treating parts of the self, subject, or mind, as 'objects', described as rejecting, exciting, libidinal, or sabotaging Egos. In 'Endopsychic structure considered in terms of object-relationships' (1952), Fairbairn wrote: 'Obviously the dynamic of rejection cannot be libido. So there is no alternative but to regard it as aggression. Aggression must accordingly be regarded as the characteristic determinant of the attitude of the central Ego towards the subsidiary egos.'

The conclusion is that in the group matrix, subject and object are simultaneously aspects of the same transitional dialogue—so that the old conflict between ego instincts and objects instincts is no longer polarized but appears in multifaceted analogs.

Freud (1917 [1915]) abandoned the distinction between these *two sets of instincts* by postulating the concept of narcissism in which libido cathects the ego itself. For us this cathexis takes the form of a transmutation into the anticathexis of hate, which becomes transformed into endopsychic energy, but this transformation only takes place as a result of the work done through dialogue that is both an inner reflection and an outer world action. In melancholia 'the existence of the lost object is continued in the mind'; in the group the lost object is replaced by the transitional object of dialogue.

> The narcissistic identification with the object then becomes a substitute for the erotic cathexis, the result of which is that in spite of the conflict with the loved person the love-relation need not be given up. This kind of substitution of identification for object love is an important mechanism in the narcissistic affections. . . . The ego wishes to incorporate this object into itself, and the method by which it would do so in this oral or cannibalistic stage is by devouring it. Abraham is undoubtedly right in using this to explain the refusal of nourishment in severe forms of melancholia. [Freud, 1917 (1915)]

For us dialogue replaces this oral addiction and transforms 'the hate expended upon this new substitute object' (self-torment, unworthiness) into the very endopsychic energy that mobilizes dialogue. The withdrawal of object cathexis characteristic of melancholia and the 'anti-cathexis' of the transference-neuroses is projected into the transitional half-way house of dialogue; here it meets with the same resistance accorded to free association generally in psychoanalysis: depression oppresses the expression of creative thinking.

The transitional space of dialogue is neither subjective nor objective, governed neither by the pleasure nor by the reality principle. On the contrary, it leads to the establishment of a third principle, namely that of meaning.

Paulo Freire, an educationalist from the Third world, in *Pedagogy of the Oppressed* (1972), attacks the culture of silence: 'Within the word we find two dimensions, reflection and action—the praxis of thinking.' Dialogue is an existential necessity, essentially human, with the word (as distinct from number) as the essence of dialogue. Human existence cannot be silent, yet we must avoid the vacuity of verbalism and the blindness of activism. He suggested that we create dialogue by work and praxis and described verbalism as a sacrifice of action and activism a sacrifice of reflection. Dialogue is the mediating encounter between men through which those who have been denied their primordial right to speak their word must first reclaim this right and prevent the continuation of this dehumanizing aggression. Dialogue transforms and humanizes the world; it cannot be reduced to the act of one person depositing ideas into another. 'It is', Freire says, 'an act of creation; it must not serve as a crafty instrument for the domination of one man by another. The domination implicit in dialogue is that of the world by those who enter into dialogue, it is the conquest of the world for the liberation of men.' Naming the world should not be a matter of possessing it privately. He talks of the 'dialogical man' and of dialogue as being 'a horizontal relationship of which mutual trust between the participants is the logical consequence', and of the anti-dialogics of the academic banking method of education. 'To glorify democracy and to silence people is a farce. . . . Only dialogue which requires critical thinking, is capable of generating critical thinking.'

In the 'objective reality' of traditional logic, matter-energy, like structure-system, universally occur together. Aristotle wrote that it is only in the mind that matter and form are distinguishable; in nature they are inseparable. Morowritz, in *Energy Flow in Biology* (1968) wrote that 'the flow of energy through a system acts to organize that system', structures it like a river structures its bank. Structure-system of groups has replaced form and content of mind. When the separation becomes a 'split', then objects become split in the mind and society becomes split from culture in the group. Synchronic space-based structures become separated from time-based diachronic systems.

It is only as a result of dialogue in the group that the human mind can relate structure and system appropriately; structure contains while system moves, its motion experienced as emotion.—'The cistern contains: the fountain overflows' (Blake, 'The marriage of heaven and hell').

In small groups it is simple to apply systems thinking on its own since the small group like the family is a universal biological phenomenon, and structure as such is not necessarily scrutinized at all. The larger group, stark and monolithic, confronts us breathing subcultural fumes of fused split objects in the form of cultural assumptions; but now these objects are no longer assumed, no longer regarded as epiphenomenal; they have become central issues involving transformations within evolving microcultures.

The primary problem of large groups centres around primal hate. Can hate be transformed into endopsychic energy, and can endopsychic structures appropriate to such mental energy be constructed? In discussing large groups Freud (1921c) pointed out that the failure of the large group lay in an inability to procure for itself precisely those features that were characteristic of the individual and that are extinguished by him by the formation of the group. For us group thinking is transformationally distinct from individual thinking, and there is no question of there being precise equivalents; for example, language and culture are products of group thinking, not of individual creation. As Marx emphasized in *Das Kapital*: 'History is made by individuals but not singly.' Consciousness is culturally determined and can be 'false' to the best interests of society as a whole.

Marx and Engels saw sociology as economically determined, 'economism', constituting the infrastructure to the cultural superstructure. Marxist sociology must therefore by the same token be a biased dialectic, based on a materialism in which thought, consciousness, and culture are ultimately determined without our awareness by economic forces. Our ideologies are therefore seen as manifestations of false consciousness, cultural legacies from the past. The individual per se therefore remains an unknown quantity. Consciousness is knowledge of economics: integers, not words constitute the medium for exchange, and therefore there can be neither dialectic nor dialogue but only a one-way determinism by matter and money which become confused with each other. This is in sharp contradistinction to the ancient Greek way of looking on people who were only concerned with their private affairs as 'idiots'.

The one-way determinism by economism is equivalent to the upside-down of Hegel's massified mind and seems to have led to a mindless, dehumanized, bureaucratic materialism. Both Hegel and Marx seem to be biased in a highly undialectical manner, unless we regard them as being in a dialectical relationship with each other, an antithesis between matter and mind. These antinomies could only be resolved through dialogue; and dialogue is impossible if free speech is forbidden. Peter Worsley wrote in *Marx and Marxism* (1982): 'Economism is more decisive than anything else.' It is certainly more decisive than dialogue. But dialogue, if it is not to lose impetus, must become decisive and can do so through cultivation by a vigorous counter microculture. In capitalism dialogue is allowed but not practised, whilst in a dictatorship by the proletariat it is forbidden, by the oligarchy of a small élitist hegemony. Potentially, large group dialogue is a methodology, essentially human and democratic; it is the sine qua non of any happy human enterprise, restoring the democracy that economism has compromised.

In the mind, structure can be separated from system, society from culture, form from substance, and individual from group. In Russell's logical types, the member of a class is distinguishable from the class itself. Relations and structures are separated from each other in mathematics, space from time, and in linguistics the synchronic is separated from the diachronic. For us, looking at the larger group, the structure stands out firmly as an antinomy in relationship to the system of dialogue.

Whilst structural anthropologists and linguists have borrowed from psychoanalytic sources, Jacques Lacan (1977) has returned the compliment in structuring psychoanalysis in relation to language. As an example, he suggested that when a child internalizes the name of father (i.e. the social symbol), he also internalizes the father's hostility to his sexual desire for mother—'Le *non* du père' becomes 'Le *nom* du père'—the child transposes the brute 'non' to 'nom'. A process of socialization through language takes place, which renders the oedipal collision negotiable.

The essential distinction between structuralism and systems thinking is that structure is space-orientated, whilst systems are time-based; structures are created when one system becomes related to another.

Whilst the physical reality of objects cannot be split in external actuality into structure and system, or into space and time, the mind is able to envisage such distinctions and does so constantly. Through memory and imagination the mind experiences immobile past structures, images of objects and thoughts, and also present mobile systems and processes of emotion. An example of this is the endopsychic construct of the superego, made up of abandoned loved objects on the one hand and of the mobile system of internal object relations on the other. Another example is the distinction between the original Freudian biological basis for psychology and his later formulations of psychic structures, e.g. ego instincts.

Repression occurs when memories are cordoned off by boundaries that are so impervious as to render them timelessly immobilized, existing only as unconscious structures, influencing larger groups subculturally.

By instituting mobile systems of communication in free association, group association, and dialogue, the time element is introduced again and old ossified spatial structures are linked up with the time-based present. Structure and system can then become more appropriately conjoined. Memory links space and time, which fantasy formulation had separated. It is the mind that can separate structure from system; and it is only in the mind, whether individual or group, that these phenomena can take place. We can happily imagine a sphynx though no sphynx has ever objectively existed. When an object becomes a subject, through introjection, changes take place in the introject which are governed by the phenomenological laws of the mind. What interests us is the question of how introjects are handled.

In the interest of the preservation of the object, the mind has constructed a manner of dealing with hate by splitting it into structure and system, separating structure from flow. Indeed, the mind only negotiates in terms of speculation, for no object has ever entered the mind except as a foreign body.

In computer language, systems analysis is the first stage in describing any large tasks to a computer, the other stages being programming and coding, which are structural.

In *The Use and Abuse of Biology* (1959), Marshall Sahlins makes the salient observation that 'Biology, whilst it is an absolutely necessary condition for culture, is equally and absolutely insufficient. There is no necessary relation between the cultural character of a given act, institution or belief, and the motivations people may have for participating in it.' He sees socio-biology as an increasing reciprocal interchange between social Darwinism and natural capitalism, closely paralleled by the functionalism of Malinowski, who tried to account for cultural phenomena by the biological needs they satisfy. Sahlins describes socio-biology as 'a gigantic extension of the physiological processes of digestion', 'one-to-one parallel between the character of human biological propensities and the properties of human social systems'. In socio-biology human aggressiveness is taken as a universal instinctual taste for violence, warfare for territoriality, and social ranking. Sahlins questions the whole construct of sociobiology. Instead of a rupture between human dispositions and social forms, culture is regarded as an inevitable manifestation of human nature rather than what it so clearly is, the transformation of hate. Individuals become enemies accidentally—no longer citizens but soldiers. Therefore, like ourselves, Sahlins sees a radical discontinuity, a dysfunction between culture and nature, rather than a reduction of superstructural facts to infrastructural determinants as in a vulgar Marxism. He shares our view that a great deal that passes today for the biological basis of human nature is, in fact, a failure in cultural mediation within the intellectual void left by anthropology.

Whilst physics explores causality and biology is concerned with instinctual gratification, culture and mind are concerned with meaning. Human action is ruled by meaning (Hutten, 1981). Mind, in dealing with frustrating objects, and in order to preserve them, splits hate into two less noxious institutions, namely, structure and system.

The two directions in psychoanalytic thinking, structural (topographical) ego psychology and object relations theory, can be linked to the interplay between structuralism and systems thinking.

Emile Durkheim was one of the earlier 'Structuralists'. He set out to relate the social structure to individual human consciousness, to create an intersystemic structure with a superstructure of variation and detail relating to an underlying infrastructure of more general rules. He attempted to resolve this problem by his construct of the group mind—the point of reference for all human knowledge—impersonal, non-subjective, and superior to the individual mind and acting as a directive force to the individual agents who comprise society. Whilst Freud saw 'the unconscious mind' as fulfilling this function, Durkheim went in the opposite direction, maintaining that it was the group conscience, 'l'ésprit collectif', that was basic. Marx, on the other hand, had already suggested that the basis was material reality, 'economism'. However, Marx introduced a dynamic revolutionary approach in the dialectic, as distinct from Durkheim's positivism, which was of a static nature, and against which Durkheim appears conservative. Nevertheless they had many things in common: they both created structures, and they both saw a split between individual and society. This is shown by Marx in his construct of alienation, and by Durkheim in his theory of 'anomie', referring for instance to 'acute economic anomie', and 'chronic anomie'.

The term 'internal object' lends itself to ambiguity since the derivation of the word 'object' is from the mediaeval latin *objectum,* a thing that is thrown at the mind. Once it enters the mind, it can no longer be an object. It might clarify matters if we were to adopt the term 'introject' consistently. The introject differs from the object in that its structure can be mentally split from its system, its structural form from its substance, systems being the psychic equivalent of substance. By the same token, objects and introjects are constituted by different forms of energy, i.e. solar or physical energy and psychic or mental energy.

Projects, on the other hand, differ from both objects and introject in being externalized introjects, either split or not, as the case may be.

Since the split between structure and system does not occur in objects, it can only be seen externally when split projects are exteriorized onto the group situation itself—that is, onto a grouping of minds which is extrinsically objective but composed of intrinsic subjects. In the group the subject–object binary duality, with its linear thinking, takes on the added dimension of systemic or network-lateralization of the subject, tangential and analogic as distinct from digital. Whilst digital binary computers are universal, we know almost nothing of analog computers.

The splitting between structure and system is amplified in the large group situation. The group acts like a sounding-board that throws the split project into relief. Systems are mobile, self-regulating, intrinsic sources of biological and psychic energy. Structures are intersystemic and are not therefore self-regulating but regulate each other. Whilst systems theorists study open system survival through exchange with environmental matter-energy, structuralists explore the areas of information and meaning between systems, not simply with 'environment'.

Fairbairn (1952), who was one of the first object relations theorists, maintained that the pristine ego is concerned with the handling of bad objects. 'Repression is directed primarily against bad objects', and 'memory represents a record of relationship with the bad object'. We would like to extend this concept by adding that the ultimate repository of the hated introject is the containing endopsychic structure of the superego.

Fairbairn asks whether the libido is pleasure-seeking or object-seeking. We suggest that seeking only occurs as a result of frustration, and so cannot be libidinal. Gratification is libidinal, frustration is anti-libidinal. Hate provides the psychic energy for the mental process of seeking objects, a matrix or context in which gratification can be structured and supported, not itself gratifying but relevant, and meaningful, like a nest in relation to eggs. Mentation is only necessary when frustration occurs, and therefore mind owes its being to hate, transformed into the psychic energy that mobilizes thinking processes and in so doing lays down mental structures.

The 'bad' object, being both structural and systemic, is hated as a result of frustration, but is rendered harmless by introjection. It is split on the one hand into a structure that is impregnable, the endopsychic structure of the superego, the memory bank, the mausoleum of abandoned and therefore hated objects, and on the other hand into a system of neutralized endopsychic energy. In the larger group situation both structure and system become projected into the social project of the group structure provided that the group is itself sufficiently structured and that the systemic flow of psychic energy is able to become exteriorized, symbolized, and restructured in the form of group dialogue.

To give an example, a member rejoined the group after having left it a year previously. In his mind the group had remained as he remembered it at his last meeting, like a lifeless ruin, a structural introject. On his return he was surprised to find that the group was not only structurally different, in that one member had left, a new member had arrived, and another member had become pregnant, but the whole system was qualitatively different as well. In his further participation he was able to project the ruin onto the group as a whole in its revised structural form and to join a system of fresh dialogue; the memory of the ruin then receded. This, however, was only possible because the new structure was sufficiently secure for his ruin to become re-peopled by the new subjects.

The splitting of the introject between structure and system is a result of repression and is manifested as a project in the group, as oppression or even depression: it can then be expressed in the system of dialogue as an experience of energized liberation so that the group, instead of being depleting and exhausting, becomes energizing. However, when these systemic psychic energies remain uncontained, the project is free-floating and takes an infantile form, with fantasies that on occasion appear psychotic; and then the cultural group, though liberating, may be totally inappropriate.

Another rather more complicated example is that of a group member who had been brought up in London and therefore had English as his spoken language, but who nevertheless found that he was thinking in his mother tongue, and his mother's only tongue, which was German. As he could not speak German fluently, he discovered, as a result of participation in a group, that neither could he think fluently. It was as if he had been brain-washed and could only think in broken German. In other words, mentation continued to occur in the fixated structures of his mother tongue, which had been split off from the ongoing system of English dialogue. It was only when the structure of the group proved sufficiently secure and reliable for him to project the fixated structure into the structure of the group and utilize the psychic energy as dialogue within the system of that group that he began thinking in fluent English. This was accompanied by a clinical improvement, and his contributions, instead of being heavy and boring, became colourful and lively. Eventually he discovered that when he spoke to his mother in German, even though he was less fluent, she became less tyrannical and more amicable and affable.

To simplify matters, it might be helpful to consider objects in terms of external actual objects and internal introjects, which finally in dialogue become the new topic or 'project' (the revised object). In network or matrix terms this involves relatively static constructs on the one hand, and the systems of energy contained within them on the other. In dialogue the projects relate to each other tangentially and analogically, as distinct from binarily. The structure of an object is in a state of dialectical tension with its system. In the mind repression separates introjects into structure and system: the structures, like empty ruins, stand as frozen memories, whilst the energy flow of system is free-floating in a no-man's-land and either trying to get back to the original introject, or, alternatively, seeking a new project, however inappropriate. In psychotherapy a spiral takes place between object and introject and project, through free association, group association, and dialogue.

The superego, being a deposit left by lost, therefore frustrating, object choices, is a repository not of guilt, but of hated objects. These objects are preserved instead of being destroyed, and the superego is a memory reservoir or mausoleum of immobilized, static, preserved structures without mobile system. It is hate that splits structure from system. As Fairbairn saw it, aggression is secondary to libido, disallowing the death instinct. Thereafter, as the superego is a structure without system, it is an anti-system, an agent by its very nature for the instigation of repression of system, which can be projected as a project but only into a structure of the group. The dissociated free-floating system of neutralized endo-psychic energies provides the energy that activates dialogue within the projected structure, the structures being either the analyst or the small group or the larger group.

In the case of the larger group the dimension of culture arises as the group mind. The structure (the group) develops a metastructure or microculture of group mind, meaning or pattern, as distinct from meaninglessness or chaos, so that now clarification of these projects occurs in the form of the microculture of that group. This explains why newly constructed groups can display unbelievably sadistic 'Kleinian' manifestations of infantile pre-genital impulses and fantasies, from a projected subcultural structure of the primitive or early superego, which subculture is, to quote Fairbairn 'determined by the externalization or projection of an internal object'.

Whilst the internal object relations are the major organizers of the mind, the endopsychic structure of the superego constitutes an immobilized network or matrix already laid down which is projected into the mobile matrix of the group. The Foulksian group matrix, so central to his ideas, can become restructured in the process of group association (or of dialogue in the case of the larger group) that follows upon processes of destructuring and deculturation. Dialogue is the ultimate in free speech, and the group, as Foulkes remarked, is a good match for the ancient superego: this is even more evident in the larger group where we find the confrontation of culture by a micro–counter-culture.

To suggest, as Klein had done, that hate cannot be educated, is inconsistent, since hate forms the very essence and drive of education ('to lead a way'): direct interpretation is in any case educative, but education with a sledgehammer. The split between paranoia and idealization can be resolved by the transformation of hate into the drive that mobilizes dialogue. To us, the interesting aspect of the larger group is not its social features, but its cultural features. Culture is to social as mind is to matter.

Working on the basis that hate is the energy and the result of frustrated instinct, we have arrived at the conclusion that the larger group constitutes a structure large enough to contain and transform hate for cultural purposes via the system of dialogue. Such a structure is not evident either in psychoanalysis or in small group situations.

Therefore the two directions, in psychoanalysis, of ego psychology and object relations theory (as described by Otto Kernberg in *Internal World and External Reality* [1980]) relate to the interplay that we see in the large group between structure and system. For us the problem is the establishment of boundaries, discovering how to totalize, how to cope with 'pregenital aggression' (system), and how to establish 'a strong ego core' (structure). These are the features that are more or less assumed in the typical instance of normal or neurotic people but are apparently relatively absent in borderline and psychotic personalities. However, in the conflicts that constantly arise in the larger group, we see again and again dialogic attempts to negotiate splits.

If we read large group for superego, we find ourselves handling an operational approach, equivalent to 'ego syntonicity'. How does reality testing proceed? Kernberg calls it ego functioning, but this is putting the cart before the horse. The suggestion that differentiation between self and object representations is a structural precondition also begs the question. In the large group we are continuously working to clarify these differences. They are by no means given or assumed but are constantly being discovered in the creative process of dialogue. Truth is not given—it can only be arrived at.

The energy of the superego is said to be derived from the Id, but we emphasize again that this energy is not direct and biological, but is the frustrated energy of hate, which can become transformed into mental energy. So therefore we have the schema of (1) *instinct,* up against (2) *frustration,* leading to (3) *anti-instinct* of (4) *hate,* which is transformed into *mental or endo-psychic energy* leading to (5) *psychic energy,* leading through (6) *dialogue* eventually to a *microculture of Koinonia.*

This has led us to realize that the fundamental distinction between the issues of structuralism and systems thinking has not been sufficiently clarified. In the same way radical distinctions exist between love and hate, between social and cultural, between events and context, between binary and analog, between duologuic dialectic and dialogue. These issues could not possibly become so apparent in any situation other than that of the larger group, and, as we have also said, neither could the distinctions between structural ego psychology and systemic object relations theory. The large group structure constitutes a real blockbuster to the endopsychic structure of the archaic superego.

The structuralist movement in France reached its zenith in the 1960s and marked the fact that philosophy could look not only to the subject as ground for validation, as had phenomenology and existentialism.

Levi-Strauss, J. Lacan, M. Foucault, and others showed that the Freudian psyche could not be assimilated as a unitary founding subject. The ego had been all too readily identified 'as the true centre of the psyche, as a kind of knowing responsible subject'.

It is the purpose of our book to suggest a technique for exploring the rift between culture and subject. Subject is a word that is curiously ambiguous, i.e. it is used to denote both the experiencer (the subject), and the subject (or topic) being explored: we suggest that this ambiguity arises as a result of regarding subject as individual and of neglecting subject as cultural being, e.g. 'subjects of a nation'.

The structuring of hate in the large group perspective is central, and the idea of the toleration of frustration, as suggested by Bion (1961), evades the issue and begs the question, since frustration is the origin of psychic energy. It is not toleration that is required, but transformation. System has to be structured, otherwise there is lack of meaning and chaos. In psychotherapy we are creating structures that can contain system adequately. The system must be architectured in such a manner as to accommodate the hate. If the structure is inadequate it becomes constricting. Restructuring occurs as a result of creating extrinsic structures sufficently secure and firm to take up from the point where an inadequate internal frozen structure previously failed, and to allow once again a flow of energies to take place.

The 'no breast' and the recognition that the bad thing is a product of mind again begs the question, unless the word 'recognition' is interpreted to mean 're-structuring'. Hate is primarily energy, which requires not tolerance but full affirmation, demanding delicate canalization and transformation in order to become mobilized systemically and avoid either the waste of explosion or the stagnation of ossified institutionalization. It is here that the concept of structure as distinct from system takes on a crucial significance.

There are no concrete objects as such in the mind. Instead there are frozen states that need to be thawed out in order to become mobilized. This is only possible if appropriate structures are available, and if the 'frozen states' are offered the opportunity of becoming once again subjects under the sovereignty of a reliable structure. There are no internal objects, merely structural reflections of the ruins of extrinsic structures that have failed to live up to the system.

The concept of the group matrix is crucial and central to all Foulkes's thinking. By the same token there are no evacuated beta elements (Bion, 1961) in which physical and psychic are indistinguishable. According to Bion, the good object turns the 'no breast' into a breast and therefore transforms the 'beta elements' into 'alpha elements', which have psychic meaning: this is negotiated by an external object, not by toleration or insight but by the experience of contextual structural alternatives, which in themselves are neither frustrating nor psychic, but real. There are no internal objects, but deserted structures, which, in psycho- or group therapy become re-peopled, re-cultivated, re-ventilated by alternative extrinsic structures enlivened by their own intrinsic systems. A well-balanced mother is not a matter of choice for infant or psychotherapist. Alternative structures, on the other hand, are. Thoughts, concepts, dreams, alpha and beta elements are not objects to be dealt with, but structures in various phases of processual or systemic development. Foulkes, in his *Introduction to Group Analytic Psychotherapy* (1948), described neurotic fixations as melting in the higher temperature of the transference.

The concretization of immobile 'internal objects' is as psychotic as the 'beta elements' they portray. It is only when they become stultified that they become so rigidly reified, demanding a re-reflection in a deliberately contrived therapeutic extrinsic structure sufficiently secure to activate systemic mobilization, to become an extrinsic apparatus capable and available for thinking, 'Koinonic'. Perhaps this is what Lacan (1977) means when he says that the unconscious is structured like a language—i.e. the system of the unconscious mind has to be structured before it can consciously exist in reality.

Matter–energy can be looked at in the primary terms of structure and flow producing systems of power in states of delayed frustration. The 'esprit' of Levi-Strauss (1968), the evidence of underlying mentation in social structures, has been called structuralist since it refers to substructural patterns that can be defined algebraically. The rules of the deep structures, as suggested by Chomsky, influence the surface structures.

The reverse, the influence of surface on deep structures—e.g. the idea of psychoanalysis as linguistics applied to the unconscious (Lacan)—is equally valid. In this case the levels of surface and deep could themselves be more appropriately referred to as systems and their intersystemic relationship as structural. The change of one system to another can be seen in the transformation of one culture to another. Inter-systemic relationship could then be referred to as structural, inherently involving cultural differences. Structure and system are dialectical antinomies in conflict.

It is precisely this area of conflict and of transformation that concerns us in our interest in the large group. Rather than a straightforward evolution from biological to social, we detect a radical dialectical clash generating hate, which *has* to be transformed rather than sublimated.

The boundary between conscious and repressed unconscious is formed by the agency of the superego from the internalization of the parents of pre-oedipal construct, e.g. the internal objects of object relations theory. The energy for the superego is derived, it is contended, from the Id, though for us it is the irreversible frustration of anti-Id that provides this energy, a psychic energy transformed from hate. It is inevitable and universal. A crucial transmutation also occurs in the transformation of the guilt derived from the archaic superego into the post-oedipal social shame of the ego ideal.

It is essential to make the distinction between 'internal objects', which are introjected phantoms and therefore things, and external objects, which are people. This distinction is vital since changes in cultural context result isomorphically in structural endopsychic changes in the individual mind—a transformation that is universal. At the same time the two are in a mutually reciprocal relationship to each other. We both socialize our humanity and humanize our social context.

The narcissistic self-to-self, the binary self-to-other (or one-to-one), and the transpersonal or self-to-others represent three distinct structures. The transpersonal structure is specific to the group and is most extensively seen as a socio-cultural manifestation in larger groups. The negotiation of the binary opposition from the digital system of the one-to-one to the analogic tangential analogies of the group network is a primary characteristic of the group process, which we have termed '*lateralization*'.

The development of the network can be blocked when the group 'packs' like a wolf pack (similar to Freud's primal horde), massifies, and establishes a binary type of one-to-one opposition between leader and led. Alternatively, when liberated, the group can individuate through mediation by dialogue, which is tangential and lateral and occurs through the analogies of group association.

In the blocked network there is a dialectic between the powerful but mindless face of the binary follow-my-leader pack, thinking with its cliché-ridden idiom, and the discriminating but small voice complexity of lateralization or Koinonic thinking.

In linguistics a similar process of transformation occurs through re-write rules for the transforming of one sentence into another, from the universal, 'generative', and deep structure to the surface structure. In Chomsky's (1968) words: 'Drama emerges from hidden universal relationships.'

Levi-Strauss's structuralism is said to have been the first systematic attempt to uncover deep universal mental structures (for us subcultural) as overtly manifested in kinship and larger social structures (for us macrocultural). He was the first to adapt Saussurian linguistics to the social sciences, and his ultimate concern was with the unconscious nature of collective phenomena operative in industrial, as well as in tribal, societies.

Semiology has been described as post-structural—a sign occurs when structure and system combine as a unit—an acoustic image with a concept, the signifier with the signified. The sign then is the object, the thing intended is the sound.

Structuralism then is a loosely connected way of viewing theoretical constructs in relationship to the human sciences, viz. Marx in politics and sociology, Saussure and Chomsky in linguistics, Levi-Strauss in anthropology, Freud, Piaget, Lacan, and the Gestalt theorists in psychology. It could be termed 'constructuralism', as distinct from the structures of nature. It relates to culture in its aspect of intellectual development in the relationships between mind and all aspects of the world and is in that sense applied human intelligence. A beehive is therefore, we repeat, not a structure in the structuralist vocabulary since it is instinctive and a manifestation of nature as distinct from intellect, the biological as distinct from the cultural.

Reversing the accepted practice in which free association is taken to be the language of pre-consciousness, of speaking one's mind, Lacan sees psychoanalysis as applied linguistics—that is, language imprinted on what is unconscious and pre-verbal.

This theme of an imposed language can be extended to an imposed culture, language being both a social and a cultural phenomenon. In other words the unconscious system is structured by culture, not only by language. There is an analogy therefore between the vertical diachronic axis of de Saussure and systems, on the one hand, which is processual, historical, time-based, and evolutionary, and the synchronic axis on the other hand, which is momentary and structural, in a frozen static state at any one moment in time, like the state of affairs between moves on a chess game or the still frame out of a moving film.

Each word, like each person, to its very core and by its very nature, depends on its context, i.e. the word 'bad' in

English, which in German means 'bath'. This is a structural, i.e. contextual, phenomenon. All structures are system-based and all systems are structured, but they follow distinct parameters in relationship to each other. Cultures are time-based systems which, through the process of time, become transformed into other systems. For example a patient failed to respond to psychoanalysis in small group therapy, but through the impact of a meeting of 250 people at EST recovered a repressed memory. The change was structural both in the settings and within himself, between his conscious and unconscious systems. Structure is intersystemic.

Existentialism is to do with system, the experience of self. Phenomenological structuralism is to do with context in which existence is qualitatively, continuously, and irreversibly interwoven, the contextual structure.

Thus phenomenological structuralism may be the outcome of a dialectic between these two categories, existence and structure, and concerns intertextuality; above all, it concerns dialogue.

A further example is that of an international congress of over a thousand psychiatric group workers who met to discuss the theme of boundaries. Since the structure of the Congress itself was oligarchic throughout the lecture settings, platforms, panels, and small groups, important cultural issues, and therefore boundaries and structural issues, could not be discussed except as deviant topics, and the main topic concerned internal object relationships. An attempt to introduce broader issues, for instance attitudes to the atom bomb, was ruled out of court as inappropriate to the plenary session: it was indeed inappropriate since the discussion was being orientated towards a panel of eight. By the same token, at this Congress, significant boundaries between small groups could not be discussed. Structuralism was mentioned and dropped, but a vague dissatisfaction with systems thinking was also expressed. The range of topics remained constricted by the very nature of the oligarchyic structure. Polygarchy, a self-evident word, does not exist. In Roget's *Thesaurus*, the antonym of oligarchy is anarchy. So the congress failed to discuss boundaries because the structure itself prohibited it, no doubt through fear of anarchy seen as chaos. Systemically the congress was a success, structurally it was a failure.

Structuralism, therefore, is thought without thinkers, thought revealed socially. It is inter-disciplinary and links anthropology, in particular ethnology or the study of cultures, with linguistics.

Structuralism concerns us in the larger group since systems thinking does not seem to be adequate to explain cultural transformations. For example, in the case of the man we described who had undergone psychoanalysis and group analysis, it was only in the structure of 250 people that he recovered a lost memory, an irreversible structural change, and a transformation between the unconscious and conscious systems. In that instance an extrinsic change from the one-to-one to a one-to-250 resulted in an intrinsic change with marked and permanent clinical improvement. It is this sort of phenomenon that structuralism, in larger groups, is in a position to explore.

As James Anthony stated in his address to the International Congress of Group Analysis in 1980, it is only when the system is altered structurally that a permanent change occurs.

It is the structural implications of the move from the small group to the median group that has stimulated our interest in structuralist theory: it seems to us that culture, in the sense of meta-structure, is a structural phenomenon, in this instance a microstructure. Jean Marie Anzias, in *Clefs pour la Structuralisme* (1967), describes *structure* as *the sense of a system.*

The structuralist debate dominated French intellectual history from 1955 to 1970, so it is not too early—it is, on the contrary, very late—to look at its possible relevance for our purposes. Psychodynamic information provides a mutual deepening of philosophical conjecture, its tenets becoming absorbed into the mainstream of philosophic thought.

Structuralism constitutes a way of thinking that predates and post-dates both existentialism and general systems theory. It explores organization and the co-ordinating and transformational relationship that exists between the steady states of systems. Until the mid-1940s these were seen as structures in terms of levels—e.g. surface, deep, super-structures and infra-structures—and in terms of perspectives and relationships—e.g. synchronic and diachronic, figure and background, '*parole*' and '*langue*'.

The wider implications of the rules of structuralism are distinct from the intrinsic fields of forces within systems. Structuralism sets out to explore extrinsically inter-systemic relationships and the more lasting nature of boundaries between systems. The word 'system' is derived from the Greek, meaning 'to combine' or to 'cause to stand', and it has come to mean a regularly interacting interdependent group of items forming a unified whole under the influence of self-regulating forces, with a tendency towards equilibrium. Structure explores the sense, the means (derived from a word 'to tell'), and therefore the meaning of systems in relation to each other. In *Tristes Tropiques* (1976) Levi-Strauss, 'the father of structuralism', saw structuralism as a method of uncovering deep universal mental structures as latent in social structures.

Gestalt, relativity, field, and systems theory have been claimed as the biggest single shift in thinking since Plato. The cause–effect approach excluded too much. Systems thinking was first described in relationship to biology, subsequently in relationship to engineering. It was then further developed by certain sociologists, e.g. Buckley (1967), who saw systems thinking as a helpful model for the understanding of socio-cultural systems. More recently it has, of course, been widely applied in family therapy.

However, in examining the human sciences, for instance Marxism, psychoanalysis, linguistics, and ethnology, the systems approach has itself proved to be too mechanistic and behavioural, too ceaselessly circular, to do justice to the dynamic and transformational nature of cultural phenomena. For example, a melody, in transposing its key, transposes its structure but not its system; it is in a different scale but in the same mode.

In 1968 Piaget (1971) wrote: 'All the social sciences yield structuralist theories, since, however different they may be, they are all concerned with social groups and subgroups, that is, with self-regulating transformational totalities.' It is questionable whether self-regulation is a distinctive feature of structures; rather, it is intrinsically characteristic of systems, but in fact a structure is 'the seat of transformations from other systems'. It is intersystemic, and therefore it is in no way self-regulating. A social group can be thought of in intrinsic systemic terms, as, to quote Piaget again, 'evidently a whole dynamic being or as a structure open to extrinsic transformations from without'. He writes that a basic fact about groups is that they 'impose all sorts of constructs, norms, rules, that are self-regulating'. How can a construct be imposed and at the same time the system be self-regulating? No! It is crucial to make the distinction between systems (the seat of self-regulation) and structures (the seat of transformation). The same confusion arises over the question of free association and discourse.

The self-system in relationship to the social system is distinct from the self-system in relationship to the group system. It is no longer self-regulatory but open to influence across boundaries, and if these influences become irreversible we are dealing with structural change or transformation. We see this as a cultural process, distinct from the analytic structuralism of Levi-Strauss. Analytic structuralism has its deep structures from which empirical surface structures are derived. Levi-Strauss (1963) suggested that these analytic structures are ultimately logico-mathematical and do not belong to the world of 'fact'. For us this cannot be so since logos is derived from the cultural dimension, and, as culture is a group or mind phenomenon from both levels, it is both global and analytic; this is in keeping with Lacan (1977), who described the analytic as 'imaginaire' and the global as 'real'. It is only when one meets the other in processes of transformation that Lacan's concept of psychoanalysis as applied linguistics can be said to apply inter-systemically—i.e., as a structural phenomenon.

As already mentioned, systems thinking was derived from biological thinking and then from engineering, being first conceived by a biologist and later developed by an engineer, after this it was applied to the psychobiological context of the family. But in the family context it comes into difficulties; there are already three systems at work, namely the self-system, the small group system of the family, and the extrinsic social system of the referee from outer space, or family therapist.

At this point it becomes crucial to look at the situation structurally since systems thinking is proving inadequate for exploring the wider dynamic parameters of mind in relationship to society and culture. Walter Buckley (1967) makes the point that the term 'social' can be adequately applied to the biological organizations of animals and insect species, but in referring to human structures he recommends the term socio-cultural.

Alternatively, we would suggest that, since social is partly biological, organismic, and even mechanical, we should reserve the word culture for the human shapings of nature, society and the universe. The term sociocultural, which Levi-Strauss constantly used, obscures the essential issue, as does the confusion between structure and structuralism. The former term can be applied to the structure of a hive, as we have said, but the latter is a way of thinking and refers to human institutions. We are concerned with the cultivation of cultures, the fashioning of models, and the trans-boundary nature of transformation. When the framework of a transformed cultural structure has been established, the modalities of its subtended systems also become stabilized in steady states. In the larger group it is possible to examine these structures, including the pathology of cultural communities, which, as Freud pointed out, involves not just the neuroses, but the fate of civilization itself.

'Systems' refer therefore to instinctual self-regulatory units; whilst 'structures' refer to transformations and social units in conflict and therefore, by definition, not self-regulatory. Sometimes we are confronted by the razor edge between the libido and hate, the watershed between system and structure, between instinct and culture, between the bio-social and the socio-cultural. One is reminded here of Kant's reference to revolutionary and antonymic thinking as distinct from evolutionary thinking.

The individual members in larger groups are mainly unaware of the substructural patterns that are occurring in terms of constellations of social relationships, as Levi-Strauss has described them. In our larger or 'median' group this level is deliberately cultivated by looking at the macrocultural suprastructures that emerge as transformations from the subcultural infrastructural levels.

The reason we see fast-moving microcultural changes in the median group is the bracketing off of its structure from the social context or macroculture of the outside world and from the inner subculture, with all the focus being placed upon the microcultural patterns of the median group itself.

Levi-Strauss (1963) has expressed interest in the new science of ethnology, which concerns the 'most ancient and most general study of traditional humanism'. He brings together all spheres of human knowledge and suggests that we need to invent new methods. He points out that classical humanism was restricted to the privileged classes in terms of its objectives and the benefits it brought. He suggested that bringing together methods and techniques borrowed from all the sciences could aid us in understanding mankind and bring about a reconciliation of man and nature within a generalized humanism.

It has seemed to us that social anthropology does not clearly differentiate material culture from spiritual culture. It has also seemed to us, in the median group, that the facts of *materia realia* are social rather than cultural, that material society is distinct from mental culture, and that the two are in a dialectical relationship to each other which is composed, decomposed, and recomposed in oppositions and reconciliations. Both Max Weber and Levi-Strauss decry art and deplore its trickery, ignoring its basically creative, fresh, unknown, supernatural (suprastructural) qualities. The wing of a butterfly, Levi-Strauss suggests, is a form of art distinct from the man who contemplates it and conveys his impressions through art. For us, on the other hand, it is the human inner relationship to *realia* that creates culture, idiosyncratic, individualistic, and personal. Levi-Strauss points out that being separated from nature and dissociating consumption from production drains the individual of creative feeling. (What then of mass unemployment through displacement by microelectronics?) But in observing this dislocation he is himself acting culturally. He says that culture must first be inspired by a feeling of deference towards reality; we would suggest, on the contrary, that microculture often clashes with reality. Cultures, though initiated by individuals, concern groups and involve impact, action, and moulding, cultivating, and growing, a matter not of facts and causality but of meaning. Men communicate by symbols, and culture is the cultivation of symbols, the creative growing. The median group creates rapidly growing microcultures, rapidly changing because untroubled by the *realia* of economic and territorial considerations. These changes or transformations refer to translation, to transpositioning, and transculturing, as distinct from transferring.

In the median group we are dealing with ethnology in the pure state, undiluted, and this can be compared with the way that the ethnologists study so-called primitive society in order to get back to the live source. The anthropologist does the same thing through studying cultural formations remote from himself, the more remote the better. But because of his very distance from the remote culture being studied, the ethnologist considers he sees matters 'objectively'. By the same token he loses the value of subjectivity and inter-subjectivity, and on the face of things the experience bears little relationship to himself or his own culture.

Levi-Strauss (1968), however, in describing slavery, does make a distinction between cultural and social phenomena. Slavery enabled cultural development to take place at a rate previously inconceivable. The industrial revolution, involving mechanization through scientific discovery, marks a similar cultural transformation. Egalitarianism, slavery, and industrialization involve distinctively different cultures. These changes in culture are re-structured in a dialectical spiral; what was once a cultural phenomenon becomes institutionalized, 'frozen', established in society, and therefore 'social'. Out of this dialectic new cultures are synthesized. Levi-Strauss considers that ethnology has not received its dues and that we must make up for lost time, 'a dawning awareness, almost a remorse that humanity could have for so long remained alien to itself'.

It is Rousseau (1913) who is said to have been the founder of ethnology, i.e. the study of man in which one must define distinctions in order to discover their characteristics. Between the exteriority of the world and man's interiority lies a vast historical arena of societies and civilizations. Rousseau made the threefold passage of nature to culture, of feeling to knowledge, and of animality to humanity. To us, on the other hand, the individual human is like Pan, he is always dualistic, both animal and human.

As we said, anthropology studies other societies, whilst ethnology studies other cultures. In the median group we hope to study not other, but our own, microcultural developments, our own ethnology.

Levi-Strauss (1968), in stating that 'even the simplest social structure can never be constructed from the biological family made up of a father, mother and their children, but that it always implies a marriage relationship', describes a social reality. We, however, are concerned with cultural realities. Many social groups do, in fact, behave as if they see themselves in terms of the sibling relationship of the biological family or the hierarchical familiocentric culture, e.g. small bureaucratic offices. By the same token, in these groups, sexual relationships are seen as incestuous, and as long as such assumptions are accepted, the groups continue to be neurotogenic and therefore not psychotherapeutic. We have often found this oedipal microculture operating in the median group with almost persecutory intensity, and at such times sexuality is seen as persecuting.

Ethnology is the science of culture as seen from the outside. Perhaps one could make the distinction that while it is social anthropology that sees cultures from the outside, cultural anthropology looks at cultures as experienced from the inside. The median group attempts to look at its own evolving microcultures from inside and to view the surrounding sub- and macrocultures from the outside. It constitutes a phenomenology of culture in the making.

In the median group we have become interested in the constantly changing microcultural patterns that have a freedom and speed not seen in the field of anthropology. This freedom to develop comes from the fact that the members are not directly involved with each other in functional ways, either biologically or socially.

Macro-cultures can prove extremely intransigent. An example of this is described in Turnbull's book, *The Mountain People* (1974). The culture of these people became immutably tied to the iconography of their mountain god and to a hunting structure. They were unable to leave the mountain to adapt to agricultural methods, and the whole tribe literally starved to death, dying for an inappropriate culture. One member left for better circumstances, only to return to her death. Belief systems can be even more compelling than kinship ties.

There is confusion in suggesting, for instance, that society has meaning. The social world has no meaning, though it may have a function. Only the single individual can be said to create and experience meaning, which is the text between individual subtext and social context.

This leads us to the final conclusion: In the same way that psychoanalysis is applied linguistics, larger group therapy (and, in the final resort, citizenship) is applied culturation in which the culture itself and the cultural assumptions are themselves made manifest through dialogue and open to inspection. So if (to quote from the heading of chapter three) only the village idiot can speak his mind, the village code or microculture must itself be idiotic. This reminds us of Foulkes's comment that the neurotic is fixated to a previous small group—namely, that of his family. It is the awareness of cultural assumptions and their relatedness to the 'Conscious' that the median group sets out to explore.

A woman patient who had had an extensive small group experience appeared to have made a complete recovery and was able to tackle her career as a tutor in a small college successfully. She attended the median group and immediately had a relapse, having thought that she had managed to get away from 'all this madness' and develop her career amongst normal people. It then became evident that the madness of the median group symbolized a resurgence of the madness of her parental family from which she had managed to escape. Another new member at the same meeting felt he had to get away as it reminded him too much of the older people in his family, from whom he, too, was trying to escape—something that he had successfully done as an in-patient at the Cassel Hospital. It must partly be assumed, therefore, that this median group was still heavily under the sway of a family microculture.

Our conclusions are, therefore, that:

(A) by the very nature of the increased size of the median group, a greater emphasis is laid on the role played by context and culture;

(B) increased size has the effect of increasing the pressure of frustration on the individual members. We respond to this in one of three ways: (1) by packing, massing, mobbing; (2) by flight or panic; (3) by containing the pressure and expressing it, given sufficient time and space, through dialogue. Frustration of narcissism provokes hate, a psychological condition of mind, which is quite distinct from the physical, biological, instinctive expression of aggression; hate constitutes the mental psychic energy which mobilizes dialogue. Hate (which in Greek also meant grief) then constitutes the basis for psychic energy, which is transformed and expressed in the form of thinking dialogue and learning, as distinct from an instinctual process. (4) This results in the transformation of alienation into the bonding of impersonal fellowship, that is, denizenship of Koinonia; (5) the emphasis on time, place, and consistent structure provides the security and opportunity for exploring the cultural assumptions freely. Through the emphasis on the significance of extended dialogue, or discourse, or 'intertextuality', metastructure, cultural codes, or microcultures become more manifest in the larger setting than in small groups and thereby more open to appropriate transformations. Cultural transformations are more than a manifestation of the processes of systems thinking since they are intersystemic. They do not constitute a self-regulating, spontaneous flow of biological instinctual energies, but involve conflict and differences between systems and are concerned with the negotiating of boundaries, essentially a learning process, from the biological to the psychological, from physical causality to the cognition of meaning.

Conversely, it is not objects but mental structures or concepts that are intrinsic to the mind and only become mobilized when structures and systems integrate. They then take the form of intrinsic endopsychic reality, which, when expressed in the larger group, constitutes cultural reality, neither objectively extrinsic nor subjectively intrinsic but intersubjective.

Dead, fossilized intrinsic structures can only become mobilized if transformed into the extrinsic structures of the group, and then only if the latter becomes mobilized by the system of group dialogue. The endopsychic structure of the superego is a graveyard of abandoned loved objects—abandoned and abandoning—which accumulate in the mind and become, as it were, consolidated in the group itself. These become both objectively seen and subjectively experienced as intersubjective group dialogue.

There is a conspiracy of silence between structuralist and system thinkers. The essence of structuralism lies in the relationship of surface events to deeper levels, which are not self-regulating as systems are but mutually transformational systems, which become structures when the latter relate to each other. Definitions go through many developments, but all seek out hidden universal relations, reconstructing objects in order to manifest the rules of their functioning, amounting to thought without thinkers. This must surely refer to culture. Jean Marie Anzias (1967) suggests: 'It is the discourse that keeps ethnology in touch with linguistics. It is the work of the method itself that speaks the actual language of its object. It is the sense that unveils itself, the sense of a myth or a system.'

Dialogue has to be heard; shape on the other hand has to be seen. The first is a process of system, the latter is a structure. *La parole* is auditory, *la langue* the total visual written language. The first is praxis, the active use over time diachronically, the second exists in static space synchronically. Perhaps it is the use, the translating process of creative hermeneutics, sometimes referred to as post-structural, which is beginning to look at dialogue through time; and not only as binary and oppositional, in the way that Levi-Strauss describes language, but as mediated in the third dimension of dialogue itself. A change of language through dialogue affects a change in myth, metaphor, and culture, demythologizing old texts. Myths are macrocultural structures equivalent to subcultural dreams.

Post-structuralist discussion centres around questions of time and space, social space for instance, class structures, and de-alienation through participation, presumably through dialogue. Discussions concerning intertextuality (in the texts of Chomsky, Levi-Strauss, Sartre, Plato, and Lacan, for instance) reconstruct Western thought, but are only operative in dialogue.

The puritanical dismissal of fads, fashions, salons, intelligentsia, literateurs, student café communes, coffee houses, the analytic couch, etc. are all an attack on dialogue itself. People fear to express their thoughts and therefore fear dialogue. We each have our own personal inner dialogue, our own texts, not shared or revealed, *therefore conscious,* deep, generative, and narcissistically highly charged. But this internal dialogue must be clearly distinguished from dialogue proper since it is only rudimentarily verbal and is between introjects as distinct from people.

Along similar lines, Joel Kovel (1980) wrote: 'Marx and Freud staked out their discoveries on the line between the human and non-human.' For Marx this line was the boundary between value and material substance, for Freud between word presentation and thing presentation. Marx wrote: 'The ideal is nothing but the material world reflected by the human mind.' Both writers focused on mediating the boundary between subject and object, between idealism and practice, between humanization and nature, between the transformation from subject to object (Marx) and from object to subject (Freud). For Marx the human element dropped out as a result of alienation by objectification in terms of 'commodity fetishism'. For Marx this transformation takes place over history, for Freud it takes place over time—'diachronically', to use de Saussure's (1970) term. Freud focused on the emergence of the individual psyche, whilst Marx set aside individual consideration in order to scrutinize the relentless track of dehumanized consumerism.

Both Marx and Freud were involved with the dialectical junction between opposites. For Marx this was the class struggle, for Freud (1933a [1932]) the primary and secondary processes, referred to in structural, i.e. spatial, terms. He described the unconscious crudely as 'an anteroom in which various mental excitations crowd in upon one another, a sort of reception room in which consciousness and pre-consciousness reside. At the threshold is the doorkeeper who censures and denies admittance of these ideas.'

These structures are shaped by the two principles of pleasure and reality. Viewed from the larger group, there is a third principle, the cultural-cum-semantic principle of meaning. Meaning is the 'excluded middle' of the traditional logicians and attains its highest level in dialogue. Neither the material of Marx nor the unconscious of Freud, neither economism nor dream, has dialogue. Freud (1900a) wrote:

> The dream work cannot create conversation in dreams . . . neither does mathematical calculus come in the province of the dream work. The latent thoughts disclose themselves in a distorted form in the manifest dream. The dream work is a kind of model for the formation of neurotic symptoms.

As distinct from neurosis, dialogue is neither a denial nor an affirmation of the pleasure or reality principles, and, like the transitional object and genitality (social and sexual), it faces in two directions. All three—pleasure, reality, and meaning—meet comprehensively in larger group dialogue. Entering the larger group is like entering a dream but with the added dimension of dialogue. The individual mind both structures the situation and is re-structured by it. The dehiscence occasioned by the narcissistic frustration by the setting (the lack) is filled in by the mind mnemically by re-membering. It constitutes a universal deficiency for everyone and confronts the problem of hate by discovering alternatives that are neither analytical nor interpretative.

The basic fault of Balint (Balint & Balint, 1961) relates to a fault in the initial dyadic relationship. Dialogue offers an alternative for the problems that can never be solved dyadically except in the pathology of a psychotic transference. In dialogue space–time, structure-system are reunited and re-constitute the mother–infant dichotomy by a process of transformation. Winnicott (1958) describes the mother as the subject–object; dialogue, on the other hand, is the objective subject—a universal facilitator for the re-activating of splits made tolerable through mutuality. The 'bad' object becomes transformed into the impersonal but human fellowship of Koinonia.

The rules of binary logic have been widely applied to the physical sciences but are too limited for psychology. It is only in the wider context of dialogue that cognition can be approached. Whilst free association and dreams provide 'royal roads' to insight into the unconscious, only dialogue is adequate for the investigation of consciousness (through outsight).

In the multiple lateralizations of dialogue, in the multipersonal network of the matrix, binary syllogistic logic no longer applies since it is based on the one-to-one dyadic relatedness between two people.

Whilst reality has no middle, mind with the unique capacity to separate form from matter, first described by Aristotle, is at the middle per se; and the 'excluded middle' most strikingly reappears in the lateralization of dialogue. It is this area that is explored by phenomenology, existentialism, systems thinking, and structuralism. Until the advent of the psycho-dynamic dimension the uniqueness, the basic and primary nature of this quality of mind was always treated as epiphenomenal. This is no longer the case, and we now have a head-on collision within the ranks of 'scientific thinking'.

It is only the mind that can separate systems from structures, and this in turn concerns us in relation to dialogue in group situations. Here the separation is clearly revealed; dialogue re-constitutes the excluded middle.

The binary, logical, 'excluded middle' syllogism constitutes a split structure that logic, from the earliest tradition of Aristotelianism to the symbolic logic of the present day, has promulgated. It constitutes an underlying infrastructure to scientific thinking and shapes our outlook in the name of science, confining us to our percepts of objects and increasingly excluding our experience as subjects. As Professor E. H. Hutten said, in his paper, 'Self, Group and Resistance', presented to the Fifth European Symposium in Rome in 1981: '[The Greeks,] to whom we owe so much of the unique features of our civilization, notably science, were in fact concerned both with understanding themselves, the subject as well as the object of nature which surrounded them. This has been lost sight of. The tail now shakes the dog.'

In dialogue there is not the division between unconscious and conscious that occurs in the individual mind, since what is unconscious cannot be defined unless it be conscious to someone. Similarly, in the multi-dimensional tangential analogic associations of dialogue, contradictions live happily side by side, enabling developments to take place intellectually and emotionally in a manner that could not possibly occur if people's comments were based on dyadic traditional binary logic. There is an absence of negation, which favours the process of unfolding. Aristotle had to formulate philosophy out of ordinary everyday human speech; dialogue is coined in everyday language, and it translates, transforms, personalizes, and in general negotiates syntheses. The phenomenon, of group associations acting as interpretations, already noted by Foulkes, is seen even more clearly in the larger groups, and permits a process of expansion in which interpretations are arrived at in a rounded fashion through dialogue itself. Expansion of dialogue in the group is morphogenically and isomorphically connected with the expansion of individual consciousness; the larger group offers us through dialogue the opportunity of knowing more about consciousness. Group structures affect the way we think.

Freud talked of the unconscious but did not refer to the conscious; in fact in 'The Outline of Psychoanalysis' (1920g) he wrote: 'There is no need to characterise what we call a "conscious"; it is the same as the consciousness of philosophers and of everyday opinion. Everything psychical is in our view the unconscious.' And later: 'This reminds us that consciousness in general is a highly fugitive state. What is conscious is conscious only for a moment.' He added that the quality of consciousness is derived from the work of the function of speech.

It is clear to us that the avoidance of a definitive consciousness is totally unacceptable in approaching any larger group work: culture, consciousness, dialogue, and context are all intermeshed and so cannot be relegated to simple philosophy or everyday opinion. For us the conscious is a matter for primary consideration, not only in the interest of science but also in the interest of humanity. If we are to survive hate, we have no alternative but to transform hate into the endopsychic or mental energy of consciousness. The drive to think rests on the capacity to transform hate into psychic energy expressed in terms of mind.

Freud considered that culture served the purpose of protecting human beings against nature and also of regulating the relations of human beings amongst themselves. Alas! If only this were so! Culture does not by any means protect us against nature since it often destroys nature, nor does it automatically regulate relationships since it often destroys them, too. We believe that civilization is not built on the renunciation of instinctual gratifications but on a successful transformation of the inevitable anti-instinct of fury: there is no question at all of renunciation of instinct, but there is an imperative necessity to handle hate.

The matter can be schematized:

The unconscious + dialogue + the conscious + culture.

The mind is handling the hated object and in order to prevent its destruction reflects the object as an introject and divides it into the two aspects of structure and system. The structure is transformed into the superego structure of abandoned, and therefore hated, loved objects, whilst system transforms hate into psychic energy.

'Nervous or psychical energy occurs in two forms; one freely mobile and another, by comparison, "bound"' (Freud, 1940a [1938]). The psychological function of consciousness consists in raising the passage of the id to a higher dynamic level, perhaps by transforming freely mobile energies into bound energy. Freud uses the term 'psychical intensity' or 'cathexis' as equivalent to psychic energy. He goes on to say: 'A portion of the external world has at least partially been abandoned as an object and has instead by identification been taken into the ego and thus became an integral part of the internal world. This new psychical agency continues to carry on the functions which have hitherto been performed by people (the abandoned objects in the external world); it observes the ego.' By splitting the psychic into two parts, in this instance structure and system, we become involved with object relations theory.

People in groups are constantly engaged in ascertaining personal individual meaning in relation to the wider sometimes universal impersonal symbols of the group. In external reality no moment can be repeated; in psychic reality repetition occurs constantly. Boundaries both block and facilitate access to consciousness.

So illusion may bring satisfaction, but this occurs only when there is no external equivalent available. The supremacy of the reality principle is a misconception of reality since reality is of two kinds, psycho-social and material. Neither can be 'supreme'—they continuously intermesh. Freud (1940a [1938]) wrote: 'With the introduction of the reality principle, one species of thought activity was split off, it was kept free from reality testing and remained subject to the pleasure principle alone. This activity is fantasising.' He appears to have disregarded fantasy's essential role of selecting through recognition what is pleasurable. Splitting off fantasy from external reality in order to establish an introject capable of imprinting and carrying information from other times and places is essential to an organism's separate identity, its separate process of organ-ization. However, as Freud pointed out in the last lines of *The Interpretation of Dreams* (1900a): 'A day dream is a text to be deciphered; psychical reality is a particular form of existence which is not to be confused with material reality.'

Foulkes' (Foulkes & Anthony, 1957) central construct of localization, which originally provoked his interest in groups, the mapping of personal matrices against the group or social matrix, is the group's equivalent of searching, seeking, testing; and recognizing the function of personal fantasizing becomes much clearer. The repressing quality of the superego, which has been lifted intra-personally and projected inter-personally onto the group, provides us with the amplifying quality that is so characteristic of the group approach.

Dialogue, then, like dreams, often appears disconnected, accepting the most violent contradictions without objection and disregarding knowledge that carries great weight in other situations. Symbolism, as Freud pointed out, is not peculiar to dreams (for us subcultural) but is characteristic of unconscious ideation in folklore, popular myths, legends, linguistic ideas, proverbial wisdom and current jokes (for us macrocultural), all of which is subject to scrutiny by dialogue.

Structuralism is distinct from phenomenology and existentialism, since the latter, in studying experience without postulating underlying process, rejects the unconscious and metapsychological. The phenomenologist's and existentialist's experience cannot be experienced from the outside but is formulated from the subject's point of view. Phenomena are the appearances of things as we perceive them; metaphysics is concerned with actual things in themselves.

Structuralism does for existentialism and systems thinking what Kant did for empiricism and rationalism. Phenomenological structuralism looks at the self-regulating intrinsic system of existence as influenced extrinsically by other equally valid systems. A family can be seen as a structure isomorphically influenced by the system of the social context in which it exists. The significance of this is far-reaching if we consider that 'objects' are always both systemic and structural, as distinct from 'introjects', which are structures capable of being both out of time and out of place. The mind can conceive of fantasies or ideas that can never exist in the percepts of objects in time and space. In this sense the mind is active.

Hume began the *Treatise of Human Nature* with the discovery that it was the activity of the mind rather than the nature of its contents that accounted for all the puzzling features of empirical knowledge. This insight was exploited by Kant and has influenced subsequent studies of language habits. By the same token this activity is also characteristic of dialogue and culture and of the meshing of dialogue, culture, and mind, given an appropriate facilitating structure.

Noam Chomsky, in *Syntactic Structures* (1957) outlined a generative grammar with philosophical and psychological implications for the relationship between language and human mind. He described how deep universal rules or grammar or structures can generate an infinitude of surface structures via a set of transformational rules, as the Chinese script has for centuries held together all the different dialects of China.

Eleven years later, Chomsky followed up *Syntactic Structures* with *Language and Mind* (1968), in which he pointed out that 'with the early 1950s most active theoretical minds turned to the problem of how an essentially closed body of technique could be applied to some new domain say to the analysis of connected discourse or the other cultural phenomena beyond language'. The study of mind or mental structures is not simply a question of quantity or more of the same, of the S–R psycholinguists. Rather, it is a question of a qualitative change in complexity introducing 'the creative aspect of language use', the distinctively human ability to express new thoughts within the framework of an instituted language not formulable in terms of behaviour and the interaction of physical bodies, nor of the most complex automata. He thereby postulated an entirely new principle: in Cartesian terms, that of a second substance whose essence is thought alongside a body. He wrote: 'I think it is correct to state that the study of properties in organization of mind was prematurely abandoned in part on quite spurious grounds in favour of a so-called scientific attitude.'

The sixteenth-century Spanish physician Juan Huarte, in his study on the nature of human intelligence, quoted by Chomsky (1968), pointed out that the word for intelligence, '*ingenio*', has the same Latin root as 'engender', to 'generate'. Huarte believed that one may discern two generative powers in man, one common with the beasts and the plants and the other part of a spiritual substance. Ingenio is a generative power. The mind has three aspects; the first that of sense or perception, the second that of cognition and rearrangement, the third that of creativity. Huarte deplored the severe disability caused by restricting the human mind to the first aspect of empiricist principles, reducing people to 'eunuchs, incapable of generating', and recommended the use of language as an index of the creative human intelligence.

It is illuminating to read of Ludwig Wittgenstein's struggles while he was writing both his *Tractatus*, published in 1921, and his *Philosophical Investigations*, published in 1953, two years after his death.

In the *Tractatus*, his aim was to set a limit to the expression of thoughts: 'The whole sense of the book might be summed up in the following words: *what can be said at all can be said clearly, and what we cannot talk about we must pass over in silence.*' (We should like to comment here that this cannot possibly be said of dialogue.)

However, he did make it clear that the *Tractatus* consisted of two parts: the one he was able to present at that time, and a second part, which had not been written, the crucial part, left out, as in a Chinese painting with a 'significant silence'. He considered that communication had two functions, the one to expand, the other to compress, and he pointed out that the German word for poetry, *Dichtung*, is related to *dichten*, which means to compress.

At the turn of the century there was a general feeling amongst linguists that the German language had become too flowery, and that what was needed was a pruning by a purist mathematization. This corresponded to a reductive approach towards the speculative sloppiness of metaphysical philosophers generally. It was exemplified by Moore and Russell's logical atomism in the best of British tradition and furthered by Wittgenstein, their brilliant student, during his pre-World-War-I years at Cambridge, part of which he spent in a hut which he had built himself in the mountains in Norway. The *Tractatus* was written when he was a P.O.W. in the hands of the Italians. It was finally published in 1921, after numerous rejections.

The logical paradox of Russell and others, the modern logical procedure of formulating categories or classes, replaced the excluded middle of syllogistic logic. (It is worth noting parenthetically that the Freudian unconscious mind does not acknowledge paradox since it does not follow the laws of classical logic, nor does it recognize contradiction, e.g. in the unconscious opposites are the same—black may mean white.) Whilst it is impossible for the mind to imagine spatial objects outside space and temporal objects outside time, it is possible to imagine space outside time (treating past events as if they were present) as well as time outside space (temporizing by establishing matter as eternal). Time is systemic and moves continuously, whilst space is structural, and never moves.

In the *Tractatus* the structure of language is determined by the structure of reality, and the world is composed of objects arranged as facts: the atomic independent fact of elementary proposition bears a direct, mirror-like relationship to the world—reflecting without distorting. Factual atomic propositions are well formed, scientific, and meaningful. Anything else is a pseudo-proposition and is meaningless. Language can legitimately reflect the indwelling structure of the external world but can also produce propositions that are neither legitimate nor meaningful.

However, the main point of *Tractatus* was deceptively underplayed—namely, the concept that a proposition is a picture that cannot describe itself in words, cannot be said, and can only be shown. Attempts to show what is valuable as distinct from what is logical are metaphorical—i.e., symbols, ethics, aesthetics, religion, the cultural dimension. Wittgenstein himself called this, in a later correspondence, the unwritten but more important half of the *Tractatus*, and it shows how far removed Wittgenstein was from logical positivism.

Perhaps the essence of the matter lies in the humanizing process he underwent as a result of six years as a teacher, between 1920 and 1926, in a children's school in the Austrian mountain village of Trattenbach. During this time he became interested in the work of the philosopher Karl Bühler, the chief theoretician of the School Movement stemming from Vienna. Bühler's child psychology was related to Gestalt psychology and subsequently greatly influenced Piaget. Gestalt psychologists were radically opposed to positivism, which was seen as a physical approach that related to the materialism of Marxism; they were also opposed to associationism, reductionism, behaviourism, and logical atomism. Bühler considered that theory-making and organization were basic functions of the human mind, which is capable of 'imageless thought'. Thoughts have an intentional aspect due to the fact that the elements of thinking are 'wholes', i.e. totalizations. Words are arbitrary conventions and only meaningful in relationship to each other; therefore atomism, and elementarism, gave way to conventionalism, contextualism, or configurationism, and the idea was introduced that people and their ideas are similar or different in relationship to background.

Wittgenstein's experience with the parents of the children he taught brought him slap up against the rigid cultural protocols and the highly structured and limited outlooks of the local farming community, who attempted to run him out of the village. The adult disapproval of his unconventional approach and homosexuality contrasted with the response of the children themselves, who became enthralled by his inspired teaching and with whom he was extremely popular. The same thing was to occur again with his students in Cambridge.

In the *Philosophical Investigations* Wittgenstein (1953) declared that the *Tractatus* contained 'grave mistakes'. Atomic propositions are not needed for meaningful communication and therefore the legitimacy of claims is irrelevant; it is usage that is primary and not final analysis; a sentence does not have to have a definite sense; a concept can be 'blurred'; precision in particular cases is relative to context. He stressed a need for a detailed examination, not of words but of ordinary language, opening up to multi-determinism, to 'multi-farious relations' and to 'complicated networks'; to be over-exact was simply silly. In fact, he made a volte-face; basic laws of logic were not basic but conventionally determined by usage. His external realism had given way to radical subjectivism, to a belief that people interacted with their environment rather than with the world, that human language is projection of the human mind rather than a picture of the world. He described two sorts of grammar: (1) the surface grammar concerning the way in which a particular word is used in the construction of a particular utterance, and (2) a depth grammar concerning the meaning or point within the form of life in which that word plays some role. It is essential to recognize where different grammars are getting mixed up; in order to avoid category mistakes, important utterances must not be divorced from their proper context. He wrote: 'I shall also call the whole consisting of language and the actions into which it is woven, the "language" game' (which is what we see as dialogue). He, however, explored 'socially fixed language games', whereas we are interested in the constant flux of dialogue in order to discover and question the unfixed meaning and appropriateness of differing cultural assumptions. For example, it is vital to differentiate physical from mental concepts, such as 'my nerves are bad; they need a tonic'. The language of the mental, Wittgenstein wrote, is not reducible to the language of the physical.

This whole matter is constantly seen in larger groups, where the interplay between individuals (e.g. the narcissistic, self-referential, impervious 'windowless monads' of Leibniz) plays a vital role in the generating of hate. The issues at stake here are the development and change of conceptual frameworks, which Plato, Spinosa, Hume, Kant, and Russell saw as the fundamental role of philosophy, i.e. to undertake a criticism of fundamental categories. It is this that has more recently given rise to semiology, the science of cultural values.

So Wittgenstein finally allowed for mutual incomprehension. 'One human being can be a complete enigma to another' (*Philosophical Investigations*)—a far cry from: 'What can be said at all can be said clearly, and what we cannot talk about we must pass over in silence' (*Tractatus*).

The philosopher who does most justice to our purposeful approach to large group dialogue is Hegel. In much the same way as Freud maintained that dreams have meaning, Hegel's central belief was that history has meaning and is not simply a nihilistic hotch-potch of one thing after another, of chance permutations and blind forces, of no ultimate purpose beyond the myriad purposes of countless individuals; it is not 'a tale told by an idiot, full of sound and fury, signifying nothing' (quoted by Peter Singer, 1983).

For Hegel, history has purpose, direction and destination. 'The history of the world is none other than the progress of the consciousness of freedom.' 'Man is destined to be free.' In the ancient Oriental world, the only free individual was the ruler; in the Chinese state the family came to the fore, still based on the paternal management of the Emperor; after that came the caste system of India as devised by the Persians. When the Persian fleet was destroyed by the Greek fleet at the epic battle of Salamia, the despotic oriental world gave way to the Greek city states, where some men were free but not all men (since there was slavery). This gave rise to the 'Man know thyself!' of Apollo and to the free untrammelled enquiry of Socrates in dialogue, which, in fact, often meant duologue and dialectic. Reason, not social custom, became a revolutionary force, though it was opposed by the Athenian state as too independent. Finally came Christianity, opposed to slavery, and also to the oracles with their reliance on chance happenings of the natural world, replacing morality with spiritual love and individual conscience. As Hegel put it: 'Man's existence centres in his head.' 'Thought ought to be given spiritual reality.' 'There will be perfect harmony between the free choices of individuals and the needs of society as a whole.'

Hegel's *Geist* included both individual mind and group mind. 'I' is simply a thing that thinks. History is the development of mind and freedom, a journey towards forms of consciousness that increasingly grasp reality, cultivating 'absolute knowledge'. Mind, not matter, is the ultimate reality. For Hegel the mind was the instrument and medium for regarding reality, or truth. For us the larger group can become an extended instrument for so doing if developed correctly through the medium of dialogue. Hegel saw the development of consciousness as a necessary one. For us it is not gratifying, nor is it reality, but it has the quality of meaning.

Hegel's play on the multiple meanings of the German *meinen* is relevant to us—belief, intention, meaning, opinion, and surely 'mynde', vote, or mind.

Sense-certainty gives rise to self-consciousness in the move towards absolute knowledge, but self-consciousness cannot exist in isolation and can only evolve in consciousness of the other, and for us this is plural—'the others'. It is interesting to note that Hegel maintains that the relationship between self-consciousness and the external object is in the best tradition of a love–hate relationship that comes to the surface in the form of desire. Self-consciousness needs the external object in order to exist yet feels limited by it and wishes to destroy it—a typical Hegelian dialectic. In relating to each other in this ambiguous way, identities would become destroyed, only being preserved by evolving a master–slave relationship of mutual need, which replaces independence with hierarchy. For us this exemplifies the typical binary totalization of true or false syllogistic logic which the Koinonic lateralization by dialogue transforms into the analog of the multipersonal group, unimpeded by coercion.

Hegel insists that knowledge is only knowledge if it can be communicated—therefore consciousness develops into consciousnesses; individual minds exist together, or they do not exist at all—a social universal theory of mind.

The greatest of all Hegel's discoveries was that of the dialectic method of logic. Dialogue is an extension of the dialectic method, multifaceted as distinct from triadic. Traditional logic is form without content and tells us nothing about the content of the actual world. The classic example is equivalent to algebraic equations that proceed syllogistically. A syllogism is Aristotle's most important construct in logic—it is an argument consisting of three parts: a major premise, a minor premise, and a conclusion.

A is *B*

X is *A*

Therefore *X* is *B*

Leibniz wrote that he considered 'the invention of the form of syllogisms one of the most beautiful and also one of the most important made by the human mind'. And Kant: 'Fallacious and misleading arguments are most easily detected if set out in correct syllogistic form.'

But for Hegel the conclusion does not turn back on itself but proceeds to a third form, which is distinct from *A* or *B* along the lines of the dialectic of thesis, antithesis, synthesis. For example, if we mix the colours yellow and blue, we have green, which is neither yellow nor blue.

For Kant there was thesis and antithesis, which he called antinomies, but for Hegel there was a sense of proceeding continuously and spirally through successive theses and antitheses to syntheses, which then became the new theses and gave his philosophy a dynamic quality. He wrote: 'The essence of matter is "gravity", the essence of "mind" is "freedom".' Reality is inherently self-contradictory. Bertrand Russell, quoting Heraclites, said: 'Nevertheless there would be no unity if there were no opposites.' He added: 'It is the opposite which is good for us.' 'This doctrine', said Russell, 'contains the germ of Hegel's philosophy, which proceeds by the synthesizing of opposites'.

For Hegel the ultimate reality is mind idea-ism; reality is constituted by mind, but mind at first does not know this. It is the intellect that systematizes the raw structural information of the senses. Kant's 'things in themselves' are unknowable.

Some commentators claim that Hegel's dialectics have produced an alternative to all previous forms of logic and have therefore superseded traditional syllogistic logic. He himself regarded dialectic as a simple rhythm and thought that dancing to it demands no great skill. This is in contradistinction to Marx's concept of a primary infrastructure of materialism and economism and to Freud's concept of the underlying structure as primarily biologically determined and masked by thought. 'Of philosophy', Freud (1916–17) wrote, 'we have nothing to expect'; of art he said (1933a [1932]): 'Art is almost always harmless and beneficent—it does not seek to be anything else but an illusion. Philosophy is a derivation of paranoia and religion of hysteria.'

Our experience supports Hegel. We see the matrix taking shape as microcultures under the influence of dialogue, and in time these microcultures come to influence human individual thinking. For us consciousness is essentially a cultural matter, in which culture is on a dialectical level with matter, a polarization between 'physical' reductive analysis on the one hand and totalized psychological cognition on the other. Humans are essentially psychosomatic. Neurosis is essentially the confusion arising from psyche being treated somatically and soma being interpreted psychically.

In dialogue, which is of the mind, there is a constant multifaceted individuation taking place, in the round, intersubjectively, and multipersonally. There is freedom, as distinct from the reified processes of incorporation, and identification, the primitive defenses of splitting, valency, bonding, and the dyadic personalization of syllogistic logic.

The characteristics of the psychoanalytic experience are its non-sensorial quality. For us the large group is like mind, an apparatus for thinking, and is cultivated by cultivating hate, transforming it into endopsychic energy and cathected socio-cultural structures. We try to develop in the group the culture, attitudes, and structures that Bion asks of the analyst, namely, a state of discovery. 'Unknowable reality' in the Kantian sense can only become known through its transformations. For Bion one of the outstanding features of the psychotic personality is the intolerance of frustration, which, together with a predominance of destructive impulses, manifests itself as violent fragmenting hatred of internal and external reality. For us in the large group it is more direct: hate is simply untransformed mental energy, which is by its very nature destructured as distinct from destructive. The structuring is a transformational linking. For us there is no such thing as disturbance of thinking, no such thing as concrete thinking, merely a failure in transformation of psychic or mental energy into thought, i.e. symbolization, abstraction, reflection.

We agree with Bion that all needed objects are bad objects in that they generate frustration.

Self is derived from a word meaning possession. Unlike Bion, who considers tolerance of frustration to be an innate factor, we believe it is not the tolerance of hate but its transformation into psychic energy that is crucial, and this takes place not by splitting the good from the bad but by splitting the frustrating or bad object as an alternative to destroying it externally. This is effected by internalizing not the object but a reflection of the bad objects split into two, namely the form or structure of abandoned objects within the impregnable superego structure, which becomes systematically mobilized into psychic energy. Externally matter or objects never exist 'bare' but are informed; internally the mind rearranges matters, not only to preserve them from attack but also to extend this information. This is not logical but phenomeno-logical. In groups (of minds) this process is further creatively elaborated through dialogue.

The human being differs from animals in being both natural (animal) and human (artificial). The human being philosophizes. In ecology we need to start not by cultivating nature but by cultivating humanity.

As has already been mentioned, the Freudian family prototype is the horde, a family writ large, contradicting the view put forward 40 years previously by Engels in *The Origin of the Family, Private Property and the State* (1884). 'The animal family and primitive human society are incompatible.' 'Famulus means a household slave and familiar signifies the totality of slaves belonging to one individual.' 'For a horde to arise the family ties must have been loosened' . . . 'at its inception the collective feeling of the horde can have no greater enemy than the collective feeling of the family.'

It is our experience that, whilst the small group focuses on the family patterns, the large group symbolizes the deeper, unverbalizable, more primitive structures of the unconscious (one specific example being the biting impulse). It actively creates an alternative symbolic system of dialogue which is not instinctive but has to be learnt via the milk of Koinonic dialogue. Eventually there is no loss of individual distinctiveness since each contribution, each vote, each mind is individually voiced—not in chorus but uniquely—a task that 'would appear to be as formidable to the adult as the relationship with the breast appears to be to the infant' (Bion, 1962).

In this age of 'technical brilliance but cultural barbarity' the problem is in no way even remotely technological. It is purely and entirely cultural. We are involved in the monstrous struggle between destructiveness and dialogue, between cannibalism and creativity.

Language interposes itself between man and external reality and is a tool for thinking, the most elaborate realization of this intermediary sphere. In dialogue, tension arises between the discussion and content and the non-discursive connotation of the intended meaning. Symptoms represent an unsuccessful attempt to link the non-discursive with discourse. And therapy, amongst other things, in the dialogue of the larger group, arises when an articulate translation occurs between the already established structure of the group's culture and the on-going system of dialogue.

The prime quality of language is that it is trans-individual 'collective consciousness' (Durkheim, 1972); it is handed down culturally, and the culture is the primary carrier of collective memory. Language is therefore the most immediate record of unconscious fantasies, of pre-consciousness, and of collective motives. Everyday mythology is encased in language which is essentially vulgar and profane and provides a greater continuity than does myth, connecting us with pre-historic ages. It has been suggested by Freud that not only disposition but contents can be inherited. To us this would be primarily a cultural transmission. Little surprise therefore that the psychoanalytic technique carries with it a moral philosophy, which involves a whole cultural movement. It has rightly been said that man cannot see things in themselves but can only see their meaning, so that whilst expression is a primary function of the body, communication is a primary function of the mind. We have already referred to the observation by Thass Thienemann (1968) that in English the words 'brother' and 'sister' have not had a common name such as the word 'sibling', until recently; no doubt they were felt to be too disparate to be spoken or associated together.

In brief, language and dialogue are an archaic heritage transmitted through the individual. As a collective unconscious structure, etymology offers us a supreme method for exploring personal, unconscious fantasies in relationship to the culture of the whole community. There can be little surprise, therefore, that descriptive linguistics is not interested in etymology any more than behaviourism is concerned with dreams. They are both structural approaches per se which leave out the dynamic systems approach existing in the whole of the situation. Transliteration for the behaviourist does not exist.

CHAPTER SIX

Ecological perspectives

The role of numbers in structure and the influence of numbers in shaping, blocking, or facilitating dialogue

There are certain crucial numbers that have been recurring throughout history—the *one* of rhetoric, the *two* of duologue, the *three* of the dialectical triad, and the *eight* of the family, the oligarchy, and the small group. These constitute a 'natural number', and so does the *twenty*-to-*thirty* of the social group, which demands dialogue for purposes of learning to handle itself. Five hundred has been suggested as the largest natural social unit in which every individual can form some personal relationships with the whole group: This appears to have been the optimum number for villages in all parts of the world over the last 10,000 years.

The next numerical turning point begins at 5,000 and goes up to 10,000. Here we have tribal units of several villages and the beginnings of cities. Beyond 100,000 the ills of megalopolis begin.

Kirkpatrick Sale, in his book *The Human Scale* (1980), talks of *parthenothanitos,* the death of culture. He tells us that the Parthenon will have totally crumbled within the next half-generation, dissolved by droplets of sulphuric acid in the air as a result of pollution. He sees this as a symbol of the human condition.

The Human Scale is a book about immediacy, mediation, and dialogue. Before we do anything, we must learn how to talk to each other. The median group offers itself as a medium that is universally available; one that each one of us could set up to facilitate our handling of these cultural conflicts. Instead of breaking off relationships, we need to cultivate them. The voice of the masses must be heard before it is too late.

The journalist Jill Tweedie wrote in *The Guardian,* 9 July 1981:

> A human scale is the key. Many human ills and evils are intimately linked to number. Certain inner behavioural mechanisms enable us to recognize our conduct and our sense of worth but these mechanisms break down once the size of our communities grows too large and have to be replaced by mechanisms imposed from the outside with varying degrees of force and varying results of individual apathy, alienation, violence and chaos. Overwhelmed by numbers, we lose the human scale and begin to commit the inhuman crimes that now threaten our planet.

She is referring to Richard Leakey's (1981) book, *The Making of Mankind,* and the archaeological evidence that the early hunter/gatherer bands contained about thirty members. To this day in certain African tribes every member's voice is heard in making tribal decisions. It was only after settlement began, with the emerging of agriculture, herds, and property ownership, that hierarchy evolved and individual voices became drowned. The original human scale has vanished.

Tweedie asks whether it is possible to apply this human scale to all existing structures without diluting political beliefs. She finds a paradox between the power of large numbers and this essential quality of democracy and sees 'the Luddites as protesting not against the machine but the power of the machine to disrupt essentially human culture and relatedness'.

For us the reactivating of dialogue reinstates the vast power of polylogue, the power of people talking freely and audibly in the lateralized non-mechanical situation. The wider surface of the median group appears to provide the deeper levels with greater coherency, to permit the structuring of the underlying biological system by dialogue.

The problem is how to move freely from one structure to another, how to sustain transformations appropriately. The biggest leap takes place from nature to culture—that is, from the small to the median group. The small group is the transitional object between individual dyad or triad on the one hand and the family on the other. The median group lies in a no-man's land between family and society.

Sale (1980) writes that larger groups have the problem of humanizing, i.e. individualizing, the massification of giantism. What occurs is a social split between structure and system. This can produce an unbridgeable gap with no interim steppingstone, no cultural transitional object. Lewis Mumford has suggested that the breakdown of civilization occurs as a result of a failure to reach an organic solution to the problems of quantity. The small unit has always been the repository of civilization. Leviathanism is ecologically disastrous, logistically unworkable. The failure of so many international conferences must be attributed to problems of structure.

The oligopoly of vast conglomerates is ruinous to quality. Bureaucratic structures become uprooted, leading to personal irresponsibility and impersonal authoritarianism. When bureaucracy reaches a certain size, power becomes almost automatically resistant to any will, including the elected will of the people, and Koinonia is lost. In fact, bureaux are small family-like groups, and there can be a biologically instinctive resistance against expansion. In group-analytic history, we have Bion and Rickman's attempt to establish a large group at Northfield Military Hospital—a field experiment that produced a different culture from that of the military; it was closed down after six weeks.

The split between big state ventures and community interests can only be approached through the traditional intermediary of medium-sized groups.

The hunter/gatherer bands of pre-historic times are thought to have numbered thirty and to have been linked to larger tribal units of 500 concerned with mate selection and large enough to provide an adequate gene pool. From Australian data, we know that tribes speaking the same dialect also number about 500. Gregarious primates live in herds ranging from 100 to 700 and averaging 500. Gordon Rattray Taylor considers 500 to be the natural largest social unit in which every individual can be aware of a majority of the other individuals and their relationship to himself.

After 500, the next significant number, 5,000 to 10,000 people speaking the same language and sharing the same currency, uniting the tribal 'units' of several villages, was typical of the beginnings of almost all early cities. In the fifteenth century London, for instance, numbered 4,000 to 10,000. These two numbers (500 and 5,000) have become known as the 'magic ranges' providing the basis for communities and for direct democracy.

A recent conclusion is that no city should be larger than 100,000, since in smaller cities there is a far higher rate of cultural participation. Above this number the *ills of megalopolis* begin.

Exhaustive studies have been made of the effect of size in neighbourhood groups and workplace democracies, with the conclusion that there is an optimal size beyond which no self-governing human unit should grow. In many civilizations, as in many institutions, there has been a movement towards smaller units. Examples are found in Greek city states, mediaeval municipalities, Swiss cantons, the old New England settlements, Dinka villages, Sweden and Norway, the British Empire, solar energy communitarianism, psychiatric units, the German principalities prior to the unification of the German states. Modern Greece, based on small-scale settlements, still has the lowest crime rate in Europe; the United States, with its massive structures, has the highest crime rate in the Western World.

If we regard the merits of democracy as axiomatic and accept John Stuart Mill's dictum: 'The government is one in which the whole people participate and cannot take place in a community exceeding a small single town', then dialogue as such takes on a crucial significance. The cradle of direct democracy was Greece, where the average city and the rural surroundings seldom encompassed more than 10,000 people; 5,000 was the optimal number for direct participation.

In the Swiss mountain cantons the principal governing body covering a population averaging 2,000 to 3,000 is an assembly of 500, meeting once a month; this has been described as the ideal in a direct democracy. Again we have the figure of 500. It is clear that it is only in smaller units that people become politically active.

Along the same lines, Eric Trist, in an address delivered in Melbourne, described how organizational theory has developed since the Second World War. Passing from single organizations or microsystems, there has been increasing interest in the macrosystem, the field as a whole. With the realization that single organizations could no longer be treated as closed systems came an increasing emphasis on the 'task environment', on negotiating the 'social slag-heap', with a move towards a pluralistic society as distinct from bureaucratic control. This field he calls 'organisational ecology' as distinct from bureaucracy, negotiated order based on collaboration rather than competition. 'We need to stop the flight into either personal paralysis or interpersonal discord' and to introduce a learning network. 'These interface relationships are as basic to systems of organizational ecology as superior–subordinate relations are to bureaucratic organisations', so we have significant organizational ecology versus bureaucratic despair, self-regulation of the parts versus external regulation from above; appreciation and judgements of value as well as of facts.

Eric Trist goes on to say that, in an era where production is no longer the central problem and where market mechanisms are no longer self-regulative, this interface level of social organization is, 'a desert which needs to be brought under cultivation'. He describes an experiment known as the Jamestown Model, in which management and labour, in a number of failing plants, were invited to meet regularly, encouraged by a young and charismatic mayor. This initiative proved successful despite an initial year of stormy meetings, and eventually it led to a process of continuous adaptive planning and the establishment of a system of public learning. 'The hope for the future lies in the creation of an active society.'

Trist refers to a third type of organizational domain (the first two being bureaucratic and ecological). This domain was established during the 1960s by the youth movement; it was a-programmatic, non-political, leaderless, informal, and fluid, with key figures passing in and out. The aim was a revolutionary change in values and lifestyles operating through culture rather than structure, the culture of rock music, drugs, Eastern philosophy, and communal living. This culture operated through information and the information-based technology of modern communication, viz. records, tapes, videos, radios, television, cars, and air travel carrying a serious message concerning our need to de-programme ourselves from bureaucracy. This combination of culture and technology can work without formal structure, moving away from bureaucracy towards principles of organizational ecology. This involves a re-centring and a basic shift of culture, a figure-ground reversal away from the boundaries of single organizations with their formal roles, a cultivation of the skills of the 'boundary spanner', of 'a network man rather than an organization man', and therefore a shift away from the now inappropriate Protestant work ethic. He sees organizational ecology as a movement away from bureaucracy and towards culture, brought about by the microelectronic revolution and conditions of contextual turbulence. 'Organisation, democracy and bureaucracies will be in for a surprise.'

Trist concludes by stressing that organizational ecology allows for the study of inter-organizational relations, for regular meetings of thirty to forty members, which are more cultural, less structured, more interdependent, giving coherence to the desert area of society between the micro and the macro system. Being fashioned on ecological and democratic rather than bureaucratic and totalitarian lines, such meetings can provide a means to negotiate a safe passage from an industrial to a post-industrial order. For us the essential key to the whole problem lies in the architecturing of regular meetings of the relevant citizen of that domain, meetings of between thirty and forty people.

It is of interest to read that Levi-Strauss, in his 'Reflections of Liberty' (1977), examines the ecology of freedom, pointing out that 'life in society promotes the biological individual to a dignity of another order'. He points to the confusion between recognition of the private sphere of personal freedom and the demands of social life. Speaking of societies where the political institutions are extremely simple, he writes:

> Such societies vary in size between forty and two hundred and fifty members. When the population falls below the minimum the society in question sooner or later disappears; when it exceeds the maximum, the society divides. It appears as if two groups of forty to two hundred and fifty members are viable, whereas a single group of four hundred to five hundred is not.

This he calls 'optimum population levels'.

> There might be a way of verifying experimentally the existence of a need, possibly shared by the whole of mankind, to live in small communities which would not prevent them from uniting if one of them should be threatened from outside.

Aristotle once warned us: 'To the size of state there is a limit, as there is to other things, plants, animals and implements. The great city is not to be confounded with a populous one' (quoted by Leopold Kohr, 1957).

Today marks the end of an era with the beginning of widespread significant change in cultural values. In this it seems that people are ahead of the politicians, despite accusations of simplistic naivety. People today are better educated than at any time in history and are preparing to dispense with the measurability of matter in favour of meaning. Matter is simply pinched-up pieces of energy, which require information to establish any meaning, and when this fails, apathy, indifference, violence, and violation follow. We are confronted by an imperative need for thinking and minding.

Despite the increase in sophistication and education over the last fifty years, following the increase in wealth engendered by the industrial revolution, there remains at present an appalling cultural failure to use our wealth in such a way as to benefit humanity as a whole. The post-industrial revolution, which brought about political and economic imperialism, is being questioned by the culture of the young: the state of the nation is not simply an economic phenomenon, it is a cultural expression of the penumbra of peace-loving 'lazy' nations, neither left nor right, accompanied by an abandonment of the work ethic. There is a growing realization that once organizations grow beyond a certain size, active participation turns into negative passivity, e.g. bureaucracy. In small office oligarchies there is a hiatus on one side of which are the small groups and on the other giantism. It is the connection between these two sides that needs to be established.

The conclusion of Robert Dahl and Edward Tufte's *Size and Democracy* (1973) was that there is only one cause behind all forms of social misery: that is, the problem of size. This problem was also taken up by Leopold Kohr in *The Breakdown of Nations* (1957). He considered the cultural theory of social mirroring and recommended a structural approach.

On the other hand, in conducting a medium-sized group, we find that size itself is not the only problem; there is also the group mindlessness which fails to link individual with group mind, i.e. culture. It is not the structures as such that are at fault but the dehumanized emptiness, the loss of a living system of dialogue, which can potentially relate structure to system.

The word 'separate' is derived from *se paré,* to engender, to produce a child, to hatch, to wean, to make ready. Alvin Toffler (1980) talks of the new psycho-sphere, a new civilization of the 'prosumer' (both producer and consumer). Simple-minded 'yes or no' rules no longer apply. We are in need of more sophisticated polling methods with more deliberation and discussion, with an increase in adult education and involvement over important issues.

In the mid-1970s in Sweden 80,000 people took part in the formulation of a national energy policy for solar, nuclear, and geothermal energy; they were able to arrive at recommendations that produced devolution of power away from giant bureaucracies, an emphasis on rather than a dismissal of intelligence, and a concern with civic action relating to untapped resources. (Typical, of course, is the untapped information and resources of the nursing staff in mental hospitals in relationship to the patients.)

The first wave Toffler describes is the rise of agriculture. Originally, he reminds us again, most humans lived in small wandering groups, hunter/gatherers in small tribes of about 30 people in which the first sign of culture appeared in the form of agriculture. The second wave is still with us in the form of industrialization, but at the same time there is a growing tendency towards ecological degradation. The third wave of civilization, which began, he suggests, in the 1950s, could heal the historic breach between producer and consumer (the alienation of Marx and the anomie of Durkheim), giving rise to the prosumer economics of tomorrow. 'It could turn out to be the first truly humane civilization in recorded history.'

James Stevens Curl, writer and town-planning consultant, has studied the seating structure of governing bodies throughout history and throughout the world:

> As far as we know only the semicircle has been used in governing bodies rather than the full circle; dialogue is therefore unlikely to occur other than dispute. Dialogue is made impossible by the very nature of architectural arrangements which create and harangue captive audiences. This is particularly marked in modern assemblies, where there is a rostrum for the president. The Politburo meetings of the Soviets are particularly intimidating for those on the floor because the audience is faced by ranks of the bosses on a podium; a condition of vulnerability and inferiority of the majority is produced by the very architectural plan.

In a personal communication, Curl wrote:

> When the Palace of Westminster was engulfed in flames in 1834 a competition was held between 10 designs; the scheme that was finally built was by Giles Barry and Augustus Pugin in the event that both the House of

> Lords and the House of Commons were firmly rectangular as was proper to the Gothic style. Arguments about restructuring the plan of the House of Commons after the Second World War damage raised once again proposals to adopt a semi-circle but these were resisted.

It was considered important to retain the traditional parliamentary pattern in which Government and Opposition confront each other on parallel benches, separated by two sword lengths plus one yard.

Churchill is said to have remarked at the time: 'We shape our buildings, and thereafter they shape us.'

In conducting a medium-sized group we are suggesting that a circular plan without a podium or pedestal is the structure that favours the group-centred, as distinct from the leader-centred, approach. Curl himself has his doubts about such a structure. He writes that 'debating in the round became circular and collective murder replacing collective responsibility; by its very shape it was unable to pinpoint a position of responsibility and there was no one place where defensible space in debate could be held by those of like mind'. The circular plan became the instrument of the Reign of Terror in the French Revolution, and he regards this as the ultimate plan for avoiding personal responsibility.

Our experience suggests otherwise. We have noted that, given time and opportunity for dialogue to develop, without goal or task or personal leadership, a culture does in due course evolve which is democratically highly responsible. Until the culture of dialogue is established and learnt through experience, over considerable time spans, the participant members are not in a position to deal with goals and tasks and leadership, let alone with governing in a politically sophisticated way.

Postscript

The median group applies Foulkesian principles, coupled with the face-to-face multipersonal primary group—'the nursery of human nature'—operationally.

The characteristics brought about by increase in size can be listed as follows:

- a generating of envy, hate, and fear occasioned by the frustrations of this anti-incest setting (anxiety is a word derived from *angere*, to strangle);
- transformation of hate into psychic energy via dialogue; the emerging of gratitude;
- exercise of thinking and mind (*mynde* = vote); learning how to talk; discursiveness;
- a goldmine of information;
- the evolving of a wide range of microcultural springboards

(not only Bion's four); multi-lectical as distinct from dialectical;

- outsight into the surrounding cultures outside, into the superstructure;
- emerging of a principle of meaning (in addition to reality and pleasure);
- expansion of consciousness (versus 'shrinking');
- the development of a symbolic order, conceptual and abstract thinking;
- transposition as distinct from transference;
- a large container for powerful emotions;
- pulling away from inappropriate transpositions, e.g. breast, oedipal, family, materialistic (mater), tribal, and other infantilizing and trivializing models that 'play ludo on a chessboard'; evolving of levelling and lateralization and flattening of hierarchy of all time, giving rise to over-bureaucratization (the word *infans* means 'not speaking');
- the establishment of Koinonia (Greek passion for the State as distinct from love of family);
- a suitable soil for the cultivation of the individual, the idio culture, the juggler ('better a clown than a clone') as distinct from massification;
- the humanizing of society as distinct from the socializing of the individual;
- a de-mythologizing process of inappropriate social dreams;
- distancing from the social network and an increased capacity to approach the alternative non-person space of the universal, e.g. death ('in divine things you should be occupied intellectually' [Eckhart]);
- increased capacity to handle diversity and cultural clashing;

- increased capacity to handle separation anxiety;
- increased capacity to treat the traumatic neuroses as distinct from psychoneuroses.
- Koinonia is equivalent to Ian Suttie's (1988) companionship.

Spiral course of introjected, projected, reintrojected, and reprojected objects via the larger group matrix

I.	II.	III.	IV.
Introjection of the bad object into the mind.	Projection into the larger group structure.	Re-introjection of the miniculture becomes reconstituted in the mind.	Re-projection.

Frustration by external objects (*'ananke'* [Freud, 1917]) results in introjection of bad objects to prevent destruction of 'minding'.	A. The larger group takes over the function of the superego, which projectively identifies with it.	A. This larger group miniculture as metastructure or meaning becomes reintrojected as the ego-syntonic ego-ideal. (Where superego was, there shall ego be.)	This recycles the next level of the spiral, reconstituting the suprastructure of the social macroculture towards an increasing humanization. The springboard of the evolving group miniculture (specific to the larger group) enables distancing when both subculture and macroculture come under observation.
External reality. The image of the hated object is split into: A. The primitive impregnable superego, a mausoleum of frustrating objects. B. Free-floating unbound hate, a subcultural, subconscious nightmare without dialogue.	B. Hate becomes bound in dialogue. The subculture associated with sphincter morality, oral sadism (biting), in particular pregenital impulses, become transformed into a self-regulating system of neutralized endopsychic energy, which gradually takes on a minicultural meaning.	B. Dialogue has reshaped the subculture (e.g. attitudes to money). Consciousness expands and ranges from insight to outsight, achieving an affiliative Koinonic miniculture of impersonal fellowship.	

The psychoanalytic, the small-group, and the large-group settings

	SYSTEM *(Diachronic, evolving in time*				
	Structure (Context)	**Energy**	**Process (Text)**	**Content**	**Meta-structure, Miniculture (Sub-text, or meaning)**
I.	*Psychoanalytic* (Two person) No context Relational Dyadic	*Libidinal* Desire and gratification Pleasure Principle	*Free Association*	*Transference* Intrapersonal and binary, 'digital', 'vertical' thinking	*Psycho-biological* Egocentric Pregenital Narcissistic Subcultural

STRUCTURE (*Synchronic, static in space*)					
II.	*Small Group* (8 people) Oligarchic Hierarchic	*Anti-libidinal* Frustration and hate— oedipal Reality Principle	*Group Association*	*Transposition* Inter-personal discursive group matrix	*Biosocial* Familiocentric Oedipal Macrocultural
III.	*Large Group* (20 people or more) Affiliative Polygarchic	*Socio-cultural* Mental or endopsychic energy Meaning Principle	*Dialogue*	*Transformation* Transpersonal 'analogic' tangential social matrix 'lateral' thinking	*Socio-cultural* Sociocentric Genital organization Post-pubertal, 'Two-faced' Minicultural

Conclusion: Pathological cultures arise whenever confusion between the three structural levels occurs (i.e. between I, II, or III). For example, when a large group is treated as a family or a small group as a transference situation, or a large group as a two-person relationship (horde or pack), or a two-person as a large group ('Hypnosis is a group of two' [Freud]).

THE THREE CULTURES

The emerging Self mediates and is mediated by all three cultural contexts, three aspects of a whole that can be intermeshed by the actual praxis of dialogue

BIOCULTURE	SOCIOCULTURE	IDIOCULTURE
	Frequently based upon the family and tribal subculture, the most powerful and primary hierarchy of all time, but also the most inappropriate.	*From 'idio' (to make one's own), e.g. idiom, idiosyncrasy; 'only the village idiot speaks his mind'. Personal identity. Unique, original, therefore creative; the generative order.*
SUBCULTURE. Of the inner world, from the unconscious mind; e.g. dreams, symbolic images, 'objects', sphincter morality, Kleinian cosmology, the Oedipus complex, the family and tribe, primary process thinking, 'the imaginary' (Lacan).	MACROCULTURE. Of society, usually regressed to the subculture of a small-group psychology; familial, bureaucratic, oligarchic, involving stereotyped cliché thinking, rôle-playing, non-discursive, conformist, tribal. Language as such (*la langue*), e.g. 'speaking six languages with	MICROCULTURE. 'Existential' idios in dialogue evolving small cultural springboards from which to view other cultures, arriving eventually at the impersonal fellowship of Koinonia, which transforms the frustration and hate into mental energy and is a source of mind, of

	nothing to say'. Power structure, social machinery, anti-libidinal, anti-incestuous, generating but structuring frustration and rage by convention and hierarchy socioculturally.	demythologizing thought, misinterpreted by the tribal and family subculture as exile. Dialogue is systemic as distinct from structural; it circulates, a process of self-regulation that lays down structures in the form of microcultures.
MATERIAL REALITY. (*Mater* = mother). Non-verbal ('No conversation in dreams' [Freud]). Non-discursive, physiological, psychosomatic, reified, relates by identification, by fusion.	SOCIAL REALITY. 'Objective', often treated as 'reality', 'numerate'. Like the superego, it 'recapitulates the historical institutions of mankind', e.g. tribalism. There is both a social *unconscious* (e.g. myths that are the equivalent of social dreams) and a social *consciousness*, which establishes ideologies that can be either appropriate of 'false'.	SYMBOLIC REALITY. Analogic, discursive symbolization by words; learning to talk to each other. 'Subjectivity' with expansion of consciousness ('The work of the function of speech' [Freud]). Free speech, *la parôle* ('In place of biting and devouring the object' [Abraham, 1924]). Metaphor is not the fact. (*'Le non du père, c'est le nom du père'* [Lacan]). Characterized by levelling, lateralized, affiliative, non-hierarchical communication, mutuality; the symbolic order, which extends to the cosmic.

BIOCULTURE	SOCIOCULTURE	**IDIOCULTURE**
INSTINCTUALIZATION. Libidinal.	SOCIALIZATION. Socializes the instinctual.	**HUMANIZATION. Humanizes the social and creates psychic energy (enthusiasm). Also humanizes the cosmic.**
PLEASURE PRINCIPLE. Mindless power. Equivalent to id.	'REALITY' PRINCIPLE. 'Humanoids'; appearance of being human, robotic, institutionalized. 'Hardening of the oughteries.' Equivalent to superego.	**PRINCIPLE OF MEANING A third principle, that of individual experience. Powerless mind. Equivalent to Ego.**

METHODS

Our approach to larger groups is based on adopting principles similar to those that Dr. S. H. Foulkes, the Founder of Group Analytic Psychotherapy, applied to small groups and has subsequently been furthered by Dr. P. B. de Maré, et al.

(a) A group of about 20 people meets in a circle for one and half hours on a weekly basis over an extended period of time.

(b) There is no defined topic, agenda or task other than learning to talk to each other.

(c) The convenor is non-directive and aims to facilitate dialogue, pointing out when attitudes and cultural assumptions are impeding its free flow.

It is hoped that systematic observations and application of these methods in different settings will deepen our understanding of social and cultural factors—specific comparative and transcultural—relevant to many current organizational, national and international problems.

AIMS OF THE SECTION

i. TO BRING TOGETHER AND CREATE A FORUM FOR PEOPLE WHO ARE INTERESTED IN LARGE GROUPS.

ii. TO ENCOURAGE THE APPLICATION OF SIMILAR LARGE GROUPS IN A VARIETY OF SETTINGS.

iii. TO PROVIDE SUPPORT, INFORMATION, EXPERIENCE AND TRAINING FOR POTENTIAL LARGE GROUP CONVENORS.

iv. TO PUBLISH RELEVANT FINDINGS.

v. TO ACT AS A REFERRAL AGENCY FOR LARGE GROUP CONVENORS.

vi. ULTIMATELY TO HELP HUMANISE OUR SOCIO-CULTURAL CONTEXTS THROUGH AN UNDERSTANDING OF DIALOGUE AND CULTURE.

The Section meets on Tuesdays at 8.15 p.m. at 1, Daleham Gardens, London, NW3 5BY (Tel: 01-431 2693). Those interested (which includes guests, associate and full members of the Society, students and graduates of the Institute of Group Analysis) are invited to contact the Secretary.

A charge of £47 per term of 10 meetings is currently being made.

THE LARGE GROUP SECTION

OF THE

GROUP-ANALYTIC SOCIETY

(London)

1986

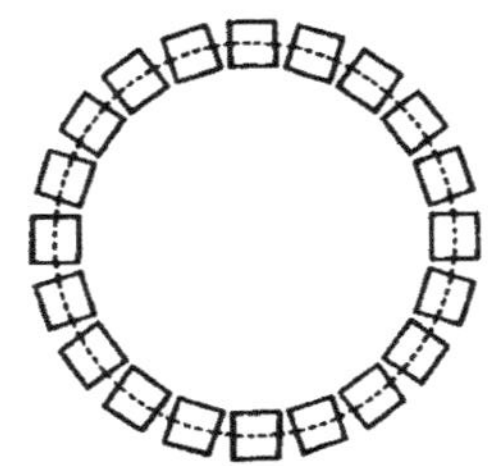

1, DALEHAM GARDENS, LONDON, NW3 5BY

Tel. No. 01-431 2693

INTRODUCTION

Group-Analysis has been described as a way of understanding group processes in both Small and Large Groups.

The Large Group Section comprises Members, Associate Members of the Group-Analytic Society, and visitors who are interested in furthering the development of an understanding of Large Groups, of 20 members and upwards, convened along Foulkesian lines.

The decision to establish this section arose from the growing interest in larger groups started by meetings set up by the Institute of Group Analysis in May 1984 for training purposes.

BACKGROUND

Everybody has experience of larger groups. They are important to everyone in all aspects of life. Yet as social phenomena they remain, operationally speaking, unexplored.

The flow of communication in larger settings is of primary importance, but only too often people experience large groups as intimidating, inhibiting or violent, which impedes this flow, and the development of Koinonia.

There is evidence to suggest that through dialogue in large groups, micro-cultures evolve which enable us to examine cultural assumptions and myths which would otherwise remain in the collective unconscious.

The first step is to provide a setting in which people can learn how to talk to each other, whether they be in treatment, training, industry, politics, etc.

PRINCIPLES

It is through dialogue in the Large Group acting as a springboard that cultures can be examined.

In the Large Group, we move outside the Kleinian and Oedipal mythology—beyond the personal and the familial—to enter the post-Oedipal exile of the social domain in which we can more adequately observe our cultural assumptions. Our aim is not so much to socialise the individual as to humanise society. This is in contrast to Small Groups in which the context is often couched in family culture terms.

The large group diary

Records of large group meetings

Samples of the brief jottings made after the weekly meetings of the Second Large Group, co-convened by Pat de Maré and Robin Piper between 14 January and 17 December 1977.

SECOND LARGE GROUP

14 January 1977
Bickenhall Mansions
First meeting

[28 attended]

Despite the uncomfortable conditions at the new venue, there was a feeling of goodwill similar to last year. Thirty people attended. Unfortunately two members were not able to stay throughout. Jason had to leave at ten, having arrived at nine-thirty. The pressure of the six members from the first large group seemed to be a highly important factor in the linking and culture-carrying—this particularly with regard to the persecutory anxiety and survival fears of newcomers, who were sensitive to the question of who knew whom. Nell in particular, in a typically Midland and abrasive manner, pointed out that Pat had told her that most of the members were in the helping professions and that there would also be a few 'patients'. She said this accusingly, as if she were being attacked or excluded as a 'patient'.

The group could not settle the punctuality problem, and the conflict then began to centre around the polarity of smokers versus non-smokers. We were questioning how decisions could be arrived at, but interpretations were made by Robin, Serge, and Jake to the effect that this debate might concern more the smokescreen—i.e., are we to survive with each other? Jason suggested we were learning to structure ourselves.

Tom began to destroy this intelligent comment, but others intervened and said they found this valuable; that we are agreeable to being organized; that we, the elementals, as it were, were not obliterated by structure. This also in reply to the attack by Nell that we were up in the sky, that she was free-floating, but this was not confirmed by others. In fact, she is a solidly built young lady, very down-to-earth, and it was suggested that she had landed in the basement. This by Robin, which provoked a defensive anxiety from Nell. Another girl said that in fact she was a parachutist, and Serge told Nell she was blowing his mind. Basil, who is highly intelligent and fluent and manages to activate people to talk more freely, said he had certainly come here as a patient. Jake wondered whether there was any hidden agenda, and Robin said that coping with Tom was our main agenda; this provoked considerable laughter, and several jumped to Tom's defence. Tom, incidentally, had formed a blocking system with Indus, and the impression is that he is much less rigid this year. For instance, he suddenly introduced a memory of French letters falling onto his basement in response to the opening of the window in this stuffy basement room (Bickenhall being a basement room), and he was completely as a loss when asked why he had mentioned this. Pat suggested that there is a good atmosphere when people are able to make sudden inconsequential remarks.

The question of agenda: it was suggested this centred around the matter of attendance. The main resistance seems to take the form of simply not turning up. The next point on the agenda might concern whether or not we meet outside, slanting our attitude one way or the other. Serge was emphatic that this was a form of socializing, which he sees as part of becoming a citizen. Pat, on the other hand, pointed out that we might equally well decide to become less social and more thoughtful, that is, cultural. But culture and social are frequently anti-thetical and are not synonymous. Shaun, the Irish priest, supported not meeting outside the group so that people could express and experience their minds more sensitively and elementally, experientially, without being impeded by social considerations. Angela (from last year) said that she had never joined a pub group and felt excluded, and that if there were a pub meeting this year she would certainly attend. Robin felt that the group last year had been a harmonizing experience.

The group ended in good spirits, and Pat felt that people had not treated him with the suspicion of last year. The atmosphere was definitely friendlier, more encouraging and receptive, almost fraternal, Koinonic. He expressed a certain fear that in some ways this could be spoilt. The young and intelligent contingent were very much in evidence.

Robin has been reading Levi-Strauss's *Triste Tropique* (1976) and was particularly struck by his reference to power in primitive societies being dependent on the capacity to be generous. For instance in 1560 the definition of a chief was 'he who unites or joins together'. Four hundred years later, Levi-Strauss discovered, the definition had remained completely unaltered. If, as is likely, the chief represents the consensus of a group, we might consider that the atmosphere of a therapeutic group could be supportive and that people could at least be serious, united, and linked. Levi-Strauss states that

> certain data taken in conjunction with other evidence contradicts the old sociological theory temporarily revised by psychoanalysis, according to which the prototype of the primitive chief was a symbolic father, so that the elementary forms of the state were a development of the family. We have seen that, underlying the most rudimentary form of power, there is an essential feature which is something new by comparison with biological phenomena; this new element is consent. Power originates in consent and is bounded by it. Apparently unilateral relationships, such as those characteristic of gerontocracy, autocracy or any other form of government, can arise in groups with an already complex structure. Political relationships boil down to a kind of arbitration between, on the one hand, the ability and authority of the chief, and, on the other hand, the size, cohesion and goodwill of the group. These various factors exert a reciprocal influence on each other.

This makes the idea of reciprocity a fundamental attribute of power. The chief has power, but he must be generous. The equivalent in the large group, reciprocity, giving, and receiving, would seem to revolve around dialogue.

26 January 1977

[41 attended]

Pat was feeling very remorseful about being heavy on Edward and Davina. He did not even recognize that Edward was present.

The meeting began oppressively, with many complaints about the structure of the group in Bickenhall Mansions. The room was too small, and alternative accommodation was discussed. Pat was glad to see that Gregory and Ian had come, and several other new faces. The matter of a closing date for the group was mentioned. Pat brought up the matter of Edward being missing. Edward then spoke up (he was then sitting exactly opposite Pat), saying that Pat had been a bit heavy in suggesting that the structure was being criticized since Pat was the convener. The fact of Pat refusing leadership was also seen as his hangup; Elizabeth said Pat had been talking about primal hordes being irrelevant over 20 years ago. Pat suggested that it had taken 20 years to get the large group going, and it was proving that the primal horde myth was a misguided attempt to impose a family-type structure onto a large group that could not possibly be a nuclear family, and therefore such a Leviathan construct merely distorted this as yet unknown and unexplored potential of the large group. Dialogue in the large group might help to resolve the kind of problem one came up against in over-bureaucratized institutions.

Some people were saying that they were bored. Perhaps a manifestation of anti-horde leader response and a fear of the horde itself—a horde that could lead either to violence or panic.

Tom then expressed quite heatedly the objection he felt at people's comments about himself. He seemed to be provoking a scapegoat response. People attacked him rather than Pat.

The second part of the evening arose out of the first, in the sense that there was a feeling of greater ease, people spoke more freely, and Pat sat down on the floor. People were doing this, giving up their seats to those who were already on the floor, and Pat found he could participate more freely on the level, as it were. Gregory took Pat's seat. Hilda, a rather aggressive older woman, considered that the contributions were insignificant and meaningless, and Jason followed this up by saying it was like cocktail-party talk. Somebody said, 'Some cocktail!'

Hilda brought back the topic of Pat's role, and Pat suggested it was not food we were short of but air. People had mentioned devouring him—and that being close to each other was dangerous. Jason said that Pat should answer the question of his leadership. He suggested he already had done so. Hilda felt she was not making any mark. Shaun said he had to speak as last week he had felt he was losing his identity because he had not spoken at all. He said people were making a split between emotion and contact on the one hand and thinking on the other, and this annoyed him—a pseudo-sincerity type of emotional response.

Basil spoke freely, but he did not care to feel as if he was a patient being observed or that he was being discussed as an interesting 'case'.

The third part of the evening developed with Ian saying that people had mentioned their fear of silence, and he attended greater meetings where silence was primary. The person who spoke finally spoke as from the spirit of God and this was equivalent to the primal horde leader or Shaman as distinct from the free exchange of dialogue.

Iris spoke for the first time. She said she normally spoke in social gatherings such as cocktail parties, but here it was different, speaking was frightening; even though she was generally silent, she had participated in listening and found the meetings interesting, and she felt that being an observer had made her apologize, and she knew how uneasy this made people feel. She spoke loudly and clearly, and she was introduced to Ian, as they both travel to Salisbury. Andy spoke more and looked happier. Most of the members had spoken.

3 February 1977
Fourth meeting of 1977

[36 attended]

There was a feeling of absentees, as the group seemed much smaller. Neither Jason nor Basil turned up. Diana wrote, bidding goodbye to the group, which she felt she could not really manage, owing to other commitments. She sent her best wishes, saying that she had found the group friendly but had not noticed that any themes had developed as yet.

Pat mentioned that we were still having difficulties over accommodation, and the continued discontent over the crowded circumstances had seemed unbearable last week, though less so this week owing to the five absentees. It was said that there had been something hostile and aggressive last week despite the jocularity, and again there was a feeling that there was some sort of dangerous aggressivity around. Probably Basil had felt it again as he objected to feeling a patient amongst professionals who observed him. Gregory linked the group to a lifeboat at sea, with people being pushed over the side or jumping out.

Jacob mentioned the 'fragility' of the group. The boat was leaky, relationships were occurring or not occurring in an insecure context. There was some boredom. Cecil, a bearded, intelligent young man, was yawning.

It was pointed out by Robin that the ambivalence over the structure of the group was related to the feelings about Pat not organizing things properly. Rajah suggested we remove the bookcases. Pat said he would try to arrange this.

Pat recalled his sharpness of last week to the older woman who was not present at this meeting, who had seen the meeting as amateurish and had clobbered the young generally. In fact, she never returned. Jason had said it was like a cocktail party, but his somewhat arrogant approach had been questioned.

Ian recommended silences recalling Quaker meetings and wondered whether this was a Shaman type of approach, which transcended group dialogue.

Joanna mentioned her collision in a car and described it with quite noticeable release of affect with tearfulness. She pointed out her scars, and Jacob drew attention to Joe's birthmark, linking this to his own birthmark, which is his Jewishness. Suddenly Celina, who is also Jewish, changed the course of the conversation to a rude attack on Gregory, saying that he was blocking her view by his large back and rocking backwards and forwards. Gregory is half-black African.

Serge mentioned the crushed conditions and that there was insufficient space to express himself. Jacob responded by saying that Serge's smoking was an irritant to him, and Gregory said he felt he had been attacked because he was black. The topic of blemishes was elaborated and the differentiation between inner blemishes and outer observable blemishes. Karim, a young Swedish social worker, said she felt blemished because of her Swedish accent.

Pat suggested people felt an enforced intimacy as a result of the closeness, that the 'context' within which relationships take place is extremely important. Rajah, who is black (from Ceylon), said the English were masochists and enjoyed discomfort. Eventually the topic arrived at the concept of deviance—can you show your blemishes, or deviance, and still retain Koinonia, which is probably equivalent to a kind of consensus, or affirmation.

Robin made the distinction between aggression and hostility, and Gregory said it was the way Colina spoke, not what she said. Pat thought that hostility implies enmity, and aggression is the driving power of mind and also of dialogue.

The question of a firm structure again arose. People were asked for a show of hands, and the majority—at least 25—were happy to go on as we were, provided no new members joined. Pat asked whether people would choose this context had they known it to be 'a black hole', as Kapi called it; there was clearly an indication that they would not choose this situation. Pat suggested the confusion of the seating, with people getting up and exchanging chairs with cushions, was obviously contra-indicated and said he would see how better accommodation could be arranged. He felt really dismayed, as the meetings had started off so positively and outgoingly.

9 February 1977

[33 attended]

The group started in very muted tones. Colina said she had slipped in the bath and cracked her skull and hurt her shoulder and back, and she connected this with her guilt about last week's display of aggression against Gregory. At the previous meeting she had come from a minor fracas with visitors using her bath.

Gregory said he had been angry for three days but felt better as a result and mentioned Robin's distinction between hostility and aggression. Pat suggested Colina's aggression was capricious and gratuitous and unusual for her personality as a whole, and he had felt afraid of spoiling the group by being unintentionally damaging, as if the large group provoked aggression such as 'lynching' or panic reactions. Robin mentioned that the group made people behave atypically. Gregory and Rajah began talking about the racial problems (they are both black).

We then went over to the new accommodation—a Welsh Hall in Chiltern Street, around the corner. Several commented that we were going through the bowels or uterine passage.

The large circle was experienced as a very marked difference from the hotch-potch of Bickenhall. Pat felt that it clarified the large group structure in a very distinguishable framework of a circle where everybody could see everybody, and that the dilemma of 'I' versus 'the rest' was abundantly manifest. The impression was that it was cooler and less cosy, but that it was easier to think aloud without being muffled. There was less muddle and therefore the racialist issue, for instance, became more clearly formulated. Also, the new structure was enabling in the sense of containing the aggression and vexations of the spirit in a firmer framework, so that formulation and thought processes were less muddled, as Andy pointed out, less gladiatorial and more dialectic. Even the comments between Gregory, Rajah, and Angela became more pointed and less heated. Indeed the impression was that the capricious, mercurial aggression had to find a rationalization, in this instance through the medium of racialism, on which Rajah was insistent, and he kept ramming it home so that Angela burst out and shouted that she was fed up with the topic. The Northern Irish contingent also made their contribution; Tom started grilling a woman teacher from Northern Ireland to such an extent that it became an inquisition, and, indeed, he laughed at Gregory's paranoia and said that Gregory is like a grizzly bear, as Jack had said.

Nell said she called everyone by nicknames: Rajah was Hari Krishna; Jacob was Rubin, which he took badly, and started teasing her. Some suggested Rubens and everybody laughed, since Nell is voluptuous in a Hogarthian sense.

The finale was the passing round of a list of names in order to contact those who were not present and needed to be informed of the new address. Somehow the fact that we were an entity in a circle made the situation more coherent. However, Iris protested, and another joined her, that they wished to be back at Bickenhall provoking a capricious destructiveness. The question is how to channel it and how to resolve inappropriate rationalization, such as racialism.

16 February 1977

[34 attended]

A good consolidated atmosphere in the new premises, roomy and quiet, with a large circle, which gave the feeling of very much being an entity.

It proved to be a good meeting. People questioned the relevance of the racialism of last week and elaborated on other ways of feeling isolated that were even worse than belonging to a minority group. For instance Jillian felt she was really French and was somehow odd and different; Andy said, even though he was English, he felt totally isolated. Angela said her outburst was because she felt she had become involved with the close exchange between Gregory and Jack. Gregory seemed calmer and said he felt relieved after last week's racist argument. Angela said how insecure she had felt as a girl in a Public Boys' School, where her father was a housemaster. Rajah said he always felt vaguely uneasy and indicated he was always afraid of gratuitous, unexpected aggression and was frightened of loss of personal identity; he speaks very softly. Most large groups caused unhappy experiences with loss of identity and made people feel capriciously aggressive; loss of identity was equivalent to being killed psychically and therefore made people feel murderous and damaging. Neurosis could be viewed as a splinter left by some large group experience in the past.

Tom had made an attempt to speak against the Methodist atmosphere in the hall where we were meeting and said he had experienced this in Northern Ireland. He blocked and stammered and said this always happened when he got close to speaking about things that really mattered to him and came to a halt as if he had got too close to his identity to dare to voice it.

The theme of wild, mindless aggression was continued—the capricious nature of it, for instance, racialism and mob violence. Several people described large group experiences that had contributed to their fears and antipathy and alienation in large groups generally.

The atmosphere was far friendlier, so much so that the question was raised that good experiences do not prepare you for the world and should therefore be avoided. Joanna flirted with Joe. It was noticed that three people who had not attended last week felt strangely out of the meeting until they had begun to speak.

(1) Bad previous large group experiences result in repression and inability to participate in any large group subsequently, e.g. Angela and the boys' school experience; (2) the splinter theory; (3) the identity and death issues.

23 February 1977

[36 attended]

Basil turned up and apologized and said he would have to be irregular since he had, as a result of the first meetings, decided to try and take his musicology degree at the Guild Hall and had to attend a lecture.

One of the girls said she almost did not come since she had been to the funeral of a man friend of 42, and she felt she could not tell this to the large group. But she saw their faces, and they were friendly, and she decided to come, and indeed they were friendly.

Basil too was struck by the improvement in the atmosphere.

Andy elaborated on last week's group, that he felt he had nothing to give, not even a minority to belong to, even though he was English, and he dated it back to the atmosphere in his family. Lionel pointed out that he said all this with a strange wry sense of humour.

There was some confusion over the family feeling at home and the dimension of personal friendship. Surely Andy had friends, and the large group dimension, as Pat pointed out, was a confusion. We were talking of the atmosphere of Koinonia of the large group, which still had to be discovered and was characteristic of large rather than small groups. Hedi said the first feeling of this she had had was when she first arrived in London as a refugee; she felt free for the first time, and even though she had first gone to Rome on leaving Germany, London was the place she adored, where she was free of her critical aunts. This alienation she felt both in Rome and in Germany.

Mention was made of the large group being too cramped, so Pat suggested people form a proper circle, which meant an increased spread; people had to speak louder but could see each other better. This curiously improved the atmosphere, and people asked to have the heat turned off.

Pat suggested that in Andy's irony, which is a word meaning 'dissembling' (dissembling what, I suppose, is the question), the timbre of his voice showed anger. He replied that he never understood when Pat was being intellectual, which caused a laugh. Joanna said she never saw the group as a group but as a collection of separate individuals, as if she feared seeing them as a collective. The word 'mob' was mentioned, and the Irish woman described how difficult it was for her in Northern Ireland last week, where she felt she had at least five nationalities.

Joanna was frightened of the mindless mob because of her experiences in Germany, but she would not assent to this suggestion as she saw all groups as the same, all being equally persecutory.

In the middle of this a cat started mewing, which caused a general laugh. Pat's comments were also laughed at, and later Pat felt violated by this.

Jacob and Karin returned to the death of a friend, a subject that had been dropped, sad news avoided, looking at the problems of the group itself, and elaborated on feelings of loneliness, which no doubt was a response of the large group feeling rather as a violent mob or as a panicking crowd.

Later, after the meeting, it was said that there had been too much verbiage. On the other hand, Anna, who brought this subject up, said she had not dared to talk of the mob experience that she had had in Germany and was encouraged to do so next time.

2 March 1977

Eighth meeting

[35 attended]

Rowena, who had not been present at the previous meeting, launched an attack on the heartlessness and patronizing approach of Jacob towards Nell, especially the comments that had been made by others at previous meetings. Andy, too, was questioned about his not understanding words as a way of putting people down.

The seven old members of the large group of last year were brought to task. Serge said he often wanted the old large group, and this comment was resented. Robin said it

is easier to hang onto history than onto the present reality, and Basil said his family had made a great impression on him, more than any other subsequent group. Colina said she was relieved to see Joanna was still here, looking more together and less scared. Had she resented revealing things about her past? Joanna said yes, but she could not remember what she had said. Finally she mentioned she could never see any group as a group.

Deirdre said she knew what it was to be shunned, which was what Joanna said she felt; her friends in South Africa had recently boycotted her after her boy had been sentenced to ten years for pamphleteering. There was a shocked silence. Someone said they had wondered why she had always looked so sad, and then two people, the first a woman, responded that if this was the first time Deirdre had felt alienated in her life, she was lucky, as on the whole she gave the appearance of being rather conventional. Jason started talking about Sartre, Lorca, and George Orwell, and of *1984*. Both were attacked for avoiding the obviously strong feelings of sadness, and Joe said he was fed up and did not understand all the jargon that was being used. Jacob replied Joe had a fetish about jargon. Pat encouraged Heather to say what she felt this group was about. Tom did not feel identified with the old group. Serge was called diabolical, as he had been a member of the old group.

Conclusion: Pat made a longish statement that the family, good or bad, might for many people be the only situation where they felt they existed. To establish existence in the new group was experienced as an ordeal entailing hard work, a long haul.

One interesting point was that Pat found the place he normally favoured had been taken by Hedi, so having walked round the circle he found a place next to Rajah. Otherwise he felt that the power points might become unbalanced. For instance, sitting next to Robin or Hedi or

Gregory was too loaded. Also, certain people were interested sexually in each other; Joanna next to Joe who attracted her, and Jillian wanted to be introduced to Rajah but was too shy.

9 March 1977

[35 attended]

The themes were as follows:

1. Jargon was discussed; alienation versus annihilation. Last week David had felt clobbered when Pat asked why we should have to talk only one bloody language—the common language 'yes' as distinct from 'no'.
2. Someone said we had talked closer to ourselves, less intellectually last week, particularly Tom, despite the presence of jargon.
3. The question of what we talked about was discussed; matters intimate, triggering off seesawing, and loving, were mentioned. Davina produced a dream of being in a boat.
4. A confusion between group Koinonia and the personal one-to-one love.
5. Confusion between alienation and annihilation; indeed, people might enjoy alienation as freedom, provided it did not lead to annihilation.
6. Serge was again attacked for his ironical sense of humour, and he elaborated, discussing themes of the 1960s and the time when humour ran riot. He was scoffed at personally for being of the 1960s, but of course in one way or another we are all dated.
7. Confusion between relating to people and relating to ideas, of sharing between people and the sharing of

ideas, the confusion between leading ideas and leaders. The tendency in the present climate to promote the personal aspects and demote ideas as intellectual.

8. The question of transitional object was raised by Robin. The large group is a transitional object. This idea was scorned by Jan, but Heather mentioned that a transitional object was the presence of the love object in absentia.
9. Then Pat suggested that objects, fantasies, and ideas were all transitional objects away from people, and steppingstones towards a cultural dimension, cultivating individuation.
10. That sexual intercourse and procreation are cultural phenomena, delivering, as it were, genitality from pre-genitality, which is natural, biological, and incestuous.
11. Surreptitiously covered pairing is occurring, with considerable secretiveness. At the moment the conflict is between group and pairing and is paramount. The polarization between belonging to the large group, Koinonia (the large group par excellence is imperiously cohesive), and the demands of the individual. By the same token fear of loss of identity is equally compelling; the individual is of prime consideration; therefore pairing must take place to produce another individual—affirmation by another recognizably personal individual is love and a cultural phenomenon.
12. Therefore the large group inexorably stimulates erotic desires and equally inexorably obliterates and annihilates. Alienation is essential in the face of a threat of annihilation. A compromise is arrived at; everyone behaves like a glorified film star. The word 'cultus' means care for adoration. Ritual is a temporal containing structure that holds ungovernable

> emotions; one might say that ritual bridges panic and turns it into more manageable fear. Absence of structure, ritual can result in panic. One suggestion was that panic was an unspeakable sexual hunger; unspeakable is equivalent to there being no context.

Joanna had described herself as deformed by her refugee experiences and did not wish to reveal her deformity and, in Robin's words, discover the new group in which she could reform. Deform took on the meaning of being crippled.

16 March 1977

Ninth Meeting

[36 attended]

The meeting was in the Welsh Chapel adjacent to the hall we normally use. Surprisingly very little comment, probably because of the fairly structured circle, i.e. the circle can be transplanted. The theme was, in Robin's words, 'bonding'. It seems there are two sorts of bonding: (1) transpersonal, which is contextual, and (2) dyadic, or personal and relational between two people. The atmosphere of the large group is still preoccupied with the family scene, and the dyadic bonding is regarded as forbidden because it is incestuous. Theme 2 was Davina's envy of Rowena as Pat's mate in the group of last year's seven members.

Celia referred to overall envy of anyone in relationship to Pat as a Hemingway character, leading to young, cruel, intelligent men followers, unable to inseminate ideas except homosexually. Men have the intellect, women the feeling. No hetero dissemination except with homosexual virgins. The suggestion was made that Pat should take a week off; there were references to Hemingway, homosexuality, and suicide.

An impression of homework done during the interim week which has to be voiced before the group can proceed, e.g. Rowena referred to an attack she had received from Heather, the massive projection of envy that relates to Rowena's white, privileged, Jewish South African antecedents. She felt paralysed by collective envy.

Obviously Rowena saw the voice of Heather as the vox populi: unless challenged, it appears as a collective will and mind. How to distinguish between one and the crowd through dialogue as a learning process? Dialogue is contingent on feedback; a comeback to the challenge must continuously be met by re-encounter. No let-up. Existential parts cannot be obliterated, alienated—must be spoken to, otherwise it becomes annihilation.

Robin brought out the vital issue and distinction between (1) rehearsing neurotic regression, and (2) creative genitality. At present the rehearsal is that we are a family group writ large, therefore one-to-one bonding is forbidden in favour of massified group bonding.

Aggression is inevitable as a secondary response to the frustration of the one-to-one bonding.

Therefore we have this contextual transpositional rehearsal of family, imposed and imprinted onto the large group. As a spell, it is spellbinding—break the spell, and the one-to-one is born. Mindless aggressivity remains the hallmark of larger groups at this point of development. Equally held holy deadlock can emerge in the single bonding, almost as a primitive response of the massified bonding.

The fear of love being present was raised. The future theme, perhaps, will concern competitive feelings between young women and old men, and young men and older women.

The change has changed the unbelief of the group by irrelevant and lengthy statements. Tom has lost some of his incongruity. Rowena no longer brings her bongos, the tribal drum. She is perhaps a bit more deeply emotionally involved and less posturizing.

Irene shows evidence of jealous feelings that this group has for previous groups—for instance, jealousy of those who had been active in the 1960s and also, in this group, jealousy of the seven old members.

23 March 1977

[33 attended]

Pat was away with flu. Only a few knew that he would be away as he had only contacted three members. There was silence and then a rather troubled atmosphere. A lot of discussion about Pat: how much did he create the idea of this large group; are people coming to the large group because of him or because of the group itself?

Joanna said she could not think or see or hear and related this to being put on the train that contained the Jewish children emigrating from Germany. Anna mentioned that she, too, had been evacuated from Germany.

Robin was attacked because he seemed to feel he had to instil theory in comments about the large group. Betty mentioned that Pat and Robin had given a lecture on the Introductory Course. Robin revealed that Pat and he were writing a book together.

Simon mentioned Pandora's box. Was the lid off? Would things get out of control? Joe was upset about their writing a book.

Dialogue between Anna and Joanna, sharing their private nightmare of Germany. Only those who had experienced it could really share this with them. Joanna mentioned her overall guilt about survival and the implications of being Jewish as well as German. A nation had come together against her. Davina panicked at Pat not being there.

30 March 1977

[34 people attended]

Pat had received three cards and felt highly embarrassed at this friendliness; being loved is an embarrassing thing, much to be desired but so humiliating if withdrawn suddenly—devastating, as Joanna had felt it.

The Easter break, the unpaid membership, and the question of our moving permanently to the Chapel were discussed. People seemed more confident, less prickly. Heather observed that Rajah looked depressed. Pat said he could not think of this group in a state of mindlessness and accused Heather of being punitive. She became quite apologetic. Then Rajah said he felt a sense of loss, of remorse and sadness at having to share Pat. The theme was the different roles in relationship to Pat, particularly the special role of Robin and Pat, who were writing a book. Objections to reporting were made, and to the dual role of Robin being both a member and an observer. Jack mentioned we were all in a dual role.

Pat wanted to clarify the matter of 'report'. Last year many people had written in *Group Analysis* about the large group, but it seemed only reasonable that any writing he submitted should be first seen by the members.

Basil said he felt personally very jealous of Robin and Pat's relationships and wanted to plunge a dagger into Robin. The suggestion of Pat and Robin being in a homosexual relationship was mooted, and Basil said why not, what is wrong with homosexuality?

It was suggested that Robin was disgracing Pat in the primal horde struggle. A very interesting point was raised by Andy, who said he hated the coldness of the middle class. Pat wondered whether his forgotten childhood memories—up to the age of five in a slum, followed by a removal to Harrow—made him feel culture-less.

20 April 1977

[30 attended]

Rather slow in turning up, and it was the first meeting after a three-week Easter break.

(1) A certain dread of re-starting was expressed, like prison, police force, or school, or a clique, yet reassuring friendly shining faces dispelled this in actuality, to everyone's relief. (2) There seems to have been some mourning going on—Tom's father had died, the topic of father's dying and the need for father's blessing and benediction, and (3) splitting between the convenor as father in the group as a totality. People having difficulties in participation 'conforming to a group if they hadn't received a blessing for their right to individuate and still remain a member'. Freedom of identity, shades of prison doors closing were mentioned, versus the forum. The primal horde is a massified and coercive group, which one does not wish to get lost in.

Joanna and Anna talked again of their German experiences (they had both been refugees in the 1930s) and the time slip problem, Joanna speaking as if these years still existed in the present and as if she had never received the blessing of the social contexts since. There was an experience of psychic death as distinct from physical: for instance, Godfrey said that he had actually experienced physical drowning. The physical dying he described, as did

Tom, as not being frightening. Tom wept, and this indicated the sort of trusting basic alternative that seems to be prevailing. Andy finds it impossible to move from the relational personal father family model, which for him was very unhappy, and he still sees the large group as alien, as an alien family.

Jason started trivializing by intellectualizing about death and then was encouraged to talk about his LSD death and panic experiences.

Psychic Death without blessing or without negotiation, freedom and exile interplay with each other. Massification. Two forms of death. Massification versus exile, unless the group dimension is encountered and taken fully into account, evolved as a mutual negotiation through dialogue or discourse.

The climate underpinning the large group has certainly emerged into a nurturing atmosphere for the moment. Gregory said he no longer felt scared of Pat and had become less blistering and rather warmer. Pat felt the need to turn Anna back to her mob experiences in which she had to say '*Heil Hitler*'. As it is, she wears a continuous smile of denial.

27 April 1977

[34 attended]

People had felt moved positively and negatively by last week's group, which had talked of death and blessing. A problem complicating the situation was that the hall is now only available at 9:10 p.m. instead of at 9:00 p.m. Rajah, Jason, and Simon were missing. Joe and Basil turned up. Blessing was talked about, its implication and rites of passage, self-blessing, father-blessing, mother-blessing. All blessings of separation—the Jewish Sabbath, which the father ends with 'Thank God I was not born a woman'. The separation is from the family. People felt this discussion was intellectual compared to the meatiness of last week. The fact that the large group does not give blessing but initiates by religion and ritual was discussed.

Andy had an outburst against middle-class intellectuals, rituals, and Christian judgement. God was discussed. Particularly, he felt God was used by the middle class against the working class. It was pointed out that it was not just his problem but that of the whole group. Basil said his father was a shit. Andy said that his father was a very crushed being, which did not help matters, and that he could not possibly have called his father a shit as he felt so sorry for him. It was the fact that Basil was middle-class and therefore his father had not suffered in the basic way that Andy's very impoverished father had that made it easier for him to be in that sense freer in his feelings of hostility towards his father.

4 May 1977

[30 attended]

The meeting had a feeling of fulsomeness. The theme of class was again brought up. Joe suddenly got up and walked smartly out of the meeting (never to return). The beginning of the meeting was not helped by having to gather outside the hall because of the meditation class, which is now being held in the hall prior to our gathering. Jason said that Joe had told him that he was going to announce that he was leaving, and meetings were not doing anything for him. The impression was that he found the ticklish topic of class distinctions too awkward to deal with.

Paddy, who had missed the last two weeks, also said it was all too intellectual, as did Jason (of all people); others, on the other hand, particularly the more sophisticated, felt strongly that class is a very highly charged topic. Tom started shouting violently at Jason, and Jacob added fuel to the conflict by recommending emotive responses as being more real than thoughtfulness and supporting his emotion against intellectualization. Pat suggested that he talk of himself rather than what we should be doing, and several members said they felt that neither Paddy nor Jason appreciated how deeply and intimately they felt about the things they were talking about.

Pat felt (1) that neither Paddy nor Jason could be quite honest about class and had to gloss over the problem. Jason's Eton and Magdalen education vs. his present job as night porter, where he wears Wellingtons and denims and looks really extremely impoverished (rolls his own cigarettes and that sort of thing), was a form of inverted snobbery perhaps, or a defence against the aggression that lies all around us over inequality. (2) Aggression is ill tolerated by the group as a whole at this stage. (3) Fighting father, father's death and blessing, and fighting the group and group leader therefore seem to be linked. (4) A personalization, a form of regressed rage to avoid the potency of an authentic working class who share ideas and learn to think and use minds, instead of defending against intellectualization—the 'collective conscious mind', as it were.

11 May 1977

[35 attended]

Outside the hall people were mentioning a certain apprehension after last week's meeting. Pat felt the apprehension and also a fear that nobody would turn up. However, the meeting was well attended, but Joe and his colleague left a message with Davina that they were not coming again. She said she thought Joe was disturbed, and both felt as much rejected by the group as rejecting it, and she was surprised when Joanna felt she had herself been rejected. Pat had said to Davina before the meeting that he would be glad to see Joe to talk about things.

People continued to talk about death and also felt that the absent members were treated as if they had died. Also, Basil and Jacob had not turned up. In some ways the group seemed to be able to group-associate more easily without Jacob's obfuscations. The theme seemed to be of a Kleinian nature, balanced between the depressive anxiety of this week and the persecution of last week.

Rowena said she still mourned the large group of last year and felt she was not allowed to voice this, as the rest resented it and resorted to persecuting those who did.

Ian felt you could not mourn a group but only a person. Shaun said you could feel sad and nostalgic about a past group and that this nostalgia enables loss to become more acceptable. Pat agreed that sadness and nostalgia transformed depression into something less frozen and more expressable. Heather said she envied people the privilege of being able to mourn and be sad. She felt nothing about her parents' death since she felt nothing about them in any case.

Several people resented her use of the word privilege and led back to the topic of privileged people and classes. Andy said he felt people would not accept that he saw his own father as underprivileged, and when questioned about the word he said 'poor, misfortunate, and unlucky'.

Andy said he had started working at the age of 12 and appeared to support the notion of every man for himself, as he had obviously done. He saw life as the luck of the game. Pat asked what he had meant when he said he understood Joanna. At this point he said he had been born as 'from London', and Celia asked from where, but this was not clarified, obviously avoided, and the group simply did not seem to want to know.

Gregory mentioned an incredible experience in a troop ship nearing Trinidad, when he discovered that those whom he had regarded as being his friends increasingly began to ostracize him (despite his public-school education) because of his being part Negro.

Jason stepped in dismissively with his rather contrived explanations.

The dimension of social awareness that some people entirely lack (let us say Koinonia, the group collectivity) is entirely distinct from the cosiness of friendship and personal relationships and the family ethos. Koinonia, one might say, seems to be a sort of impersonal friendliness.

Jason continued to obfuscate about this discrepancy; in fact, a scene seems to be developing in which consistent mindful thinking can only emerge against a background that has been acknowleged for better or for worse and cannot occur when there is dishonesty—particularly when this is apparently unconscious.

In the large group there is enormous mind potency and potential, an enormous area of consciousness, of knowing things with others. It is the individual who is only partially conscious. It takes the large group, in extended dialogue, to achieve fuller consciousness, 'consciousness raising'.

Rajah said there is a privileged group in this large group, namely the pub group. He felt out of it and did not wish to belong, and he pointed out that in a small group he attended subgrouping had ruined the therapy.

The theme is that the small group lends itself to reflecting a family constellation by the nature of its size; on the other hand, the large group lends itself to being socially orientated; it is representative of social structure, but in this social structure sex is not taboo. The Foulkesian principle of not meeting outside the group is not applicable to the large group in structural terms. Indeed, it is often impossible. In terms of content it becomes a major issue that has to be sorted out in the course of dialogue in the large group itself, rather than being a part of the established proceedings from the beginning. For instance, people did not wish to hear what Rajah was saying, they almost shouted him down, and this gave rise to a widely shared dialogue about the pub groups. Gregory insisted that in any case he must have a drink, and there were only 20 minutes in which to do so.

It seems that we are really treating context in the large group, 'outsight', a social form of insight. The object, the raison d'être of the large group, its modus vivendi, is to develop this social dimension and social insight or outsight. Personal insight has constantly to be in dialectical relation with social insight.

Some people are academic geniuses but socially inept. Others, like the 'genius without arms', for instance, Andy, are personally underprivileged, untutored, but socially perspicacious and sophisticated; they have the power of anger and force but not the strength and the skill of academic information and dialogue.

18 May 1977

[29 attended]

The smallest attendance yet, and an immensely intensive discussion about various forms of death. Heather wept (after declaring she had no feelings for her parents) in describing how horrible the ritual was of their being burnt at their cremation. Andy was extremely witty, to the effect that 'they' would get him, even at the moment of death. After this there was a lengthy discussion, which included Joanna describing her depression. Some members questioned whether people were avoiding the difficulties of living, including sexuality, which after the act made Jacob feel very much alone and encapsulated.

Serge brought up the matter of boundaries, of fears of loss of control, life and death, madness, going over the edge. Andy and others mentioned their LSD treatment. Pat suggested the group was also discussing its own boundaries here and in the pub groups. About the pub group, which had been mentioned last time, no decision had been reached, although pros and cons had been discussed.

Serge described his problems with Prue of last year's group, having lived with her and finally separated from her last week, and his feelings of depression and panic.

Andy said there was no close intimacy, generosity, or relatedness in the group, and he objected to Pat pointing out that a relationship takes place in a context. He objected to this and said that at present the climate of the group was antipathetic to intimate relationships: these took place in the pub.

The theme seems to be that people seek relationships in the group. Joanna felt rejected by Joe, who had left, as if the whole group had rejected her, confusing the two distinct categories. Andy also confuses context with relationship. Joanna kept talking of moving to another contextual situation, both in relationship to the pub and in relationship to the large group. Her cultural migration from Germany might be addressed if she could migrate with the group, as it were, without losing her cultural identity.

25 May 1977

Eighteenth meeting

[32 attended]

It was opened by Ian pointing out to Karen the question of her not wanting to come. You can choose your large group, but you cannot choose the family you are born into. You come to the large group because of choice and equally well you can get away, though someone mentioned the fact that payment is in advance and that this constricts freedom to get away.

The theme is that choice is an active procedure and relates to shooting consciousness at reality 'internationally'. The missing members were mentioned. This further relates to context. One has to burst through to contact context or the environment. It seems this is the long haul. The honeymoon is over. Several people have been depressed (oppressed) by the work of the group.

Sexual contact via the pub group has not been discussed, despite the fact that many people go to the pub. Depression and guilt over forbidden contacts was introduced.

Jillian and Joanna talked freely, and Joanna stated she was frightened of the group's envy and considered that chronologically she belonged to an age she did not feel, namely, the old-age group. Nevertheless she is seductive and attractive; she is averse to declaring attraction and denies it by joining the oldsters, ending by asking somebody to give her a cigarette. Two young men leapt forward.

Jillian said she envied those who had been educated like her brother. Serge said he was fascinated by her 'dead pan'. Lois said Serge also had a dead pan in the form of a permanent smile. This rather blocked Serge as a sort of non-comment, so that he got back to Jillian, who suddenly smiled broadly at him with flashing teeth.

Rowena said the group was envious of creativity and procreativity, and it seemed here that original 'culturally creative and fresh' comments often got blocked by social clichés, for instance those of Lois. Two of the members are expecting their wives to give birth shortly. A long discussion of the pros and cons of university education then took place. Megan said she had been to university and this had blocked her natural 'curiosity'. Andy continued his envious attack, saying that it was O.K. for those who had had the advantages of university to speak so disparagingly of education, but this was definitely a 'have or have not' situation.

Andy himself had spent many years at an art college, and this had apparently destroyed his creativity, but it was a bad college. Two members said so were their universities.

A clear differentiation was gradually emerging between the deadening social effects of institutions versus people's creative potentials. Ian mentioned that, in the past, large lecture situations had caused him to panic, but this was no longer the case. This group is now the ordeal; other groups are like chickenfeed.

This group is now a behavioural bombshell. This is the place we reached last year, where people cannot stand the pace, the pain, the commitment, the uphill grind of the long haul, the sweat, the sisyphus nature, the watershed. Last year we had to write to people to try to encourage them to sweat their way through. The fallout has begun, and the honeymoon is over. What began as a narcissistic quest, as a game, a curio, as a sort of joke, as Pat's folly, as his own narcissistic ego trip, has got beneath the skin of others, has become a pressgang; worse still, an existential choice confronts us, a crucial issue, survival of self versus the narcissistic wounding at the hands of the group, persecutory panic versus depressive anxiety and work. Blood has been shed.

The balance is between choice and non-choice, between family and friendship. Payment is a token of friendship. We are blood brothers whether we like it or not, but we can now choose.

Pat suggested that creativity and curiosity were related, that we were curious about each other personally. Will procreation lead to a stillbirth, asked Robin.

This large group is the university we are arguing about. Is it to become an academic desert, or is it to become a cultural, creative oasis? People continue to avoid the large group and elaborate about the universities. Serge uttered a crie de coeur about his incredible experiences at Essex university in the 1960s, where the structure, in order to create a cultural climate, became totally chaotic and disappeared altogether—i.e., the duality of context and creativity had not been contained and had become boundary-less. Serge had freaked out. He mentioned that several of his friends had also broken down. The fear of chaos, which also exists in this large group, seems to have provoked several people to block with social clichés and sniggers. Nadia made a creative point, which was blocked by trivializations.

Subsequently, two days later, Robin and Pat got together and discussed the structure of the individual's internal dialogue that can be altered by the extended dialogue of the group, where the two encounter each other in the intercourse of discourse. Sexual dyadic relationships either occur as isolated structures or can be expressed in the open structure of the large group. For example, let us say, in a group of thirty, all members may meet in the pub or in couples elsewhere; but this may never be discussed, and thus the dyadic relationship may never become manifest, and therefore it will be generated in a private, as distinct from a public, context. This privacy takes on an intimate oppressive nature, which may very well be experienced by the individual as depressing or frightening and take the form of guilt, because the lines of communications are blocked and unshared.

To predicate means to assert, logically to declare publicly, affirm, also to complete the meaning of a popular or linking verb; also something that is affirmed or denied of the subject in a proposition in logic, e.g. 'paper is white', whiteness is the predicate (the process of re-structuring is what we call culture—for instance, agriculture).

Eros and language mesh at every point. We touch here one of the most important but least understood areas of biological and social existence. Intercourse and discourse—popular and population—they arise from the life need of the ego to reach out and comprehend, in the two vital senses of 'understanding' and 'containment', another human being. Sex is a profoundly semantic act—that is, it occurs in an ongoing cultural context. Like language, it is subject to the shaping force of society. Rules of proceeding and accumulated precedent occur.

We are, however, as large group therapists, concerned with the continuous restructuring of accumulated precedents, a permanent dialogue. This restructuring, reculturing, is a creative not to say procreative process, which can easily be stunted by a rigid social culture.

1 June 1977

Nineteenth meeting

[28 attended]

A very fraught meeting. It was noticeable that there had been a fall in attendances. Davina was not there.

Ian started by saying he felt Gregory was unnegotiable in the way he adamantly insisted on going to the pub. A discussion followed of the pros and cons. Joanna said freely that she wanted to apologize to Gregory, but he responded somewhat cruelly and rejectingly. Joanna's over-apologetic attitude was noted, as if this were an excuse to try to make contact. Gradually the idea of one-to-one relationships emerged, with their possible sexual connotations; the attendance was low today because the meeting last week continued so late as to prevent people going to the pub afterwards.

The exclusiveness and excludingness of those who had dropped out was also discussed. Andy's meeting with Serge was also mentioned, to do with the interest and the purchase of a painting by Serge. Basil said this was not relevant to the group, which annoyed people, as they were obviously curious. But the laughter made it difficult for Andy to be heard; he suddenly became extremely annoyed and refused to go on. Basil said Andy was behaving in a nagging way, like a spoilt child. People objected, and Gregory confronted Basil for missing the point, as if he were being condescending. Basil got very angry and said he had explained that he could not help missing meetings, and he marched out shouting, never to return. He had already said he did not need the group to interfere with his social life, and that he saw the pub group as part of social life. He did not wish to join it. Gregory was obviously badgering, bullying, and provoking him. The pros and cons of David's behaviour were discussed, and it was very similar to Andy's and the anxiety of missing members. Pat decided he would write to these missing members. Something similar had occurred last year. Basil's going was a considerable loss to the group.

Ian made an interesting statement to the effect that the large group needed to retain its diversification and that the pub meeting was a natural feature.

Megan noted that people seemed to be feeling a shortage of supply of some unrecognized need. Pat pointed out that there was a marked shortage of women: only eleven were present, and several had dropped out, particularly this evening. The absence of several attractive, nubile, and reproductive women was referred to—for instance Davina, Rachel, Iris, and Celia. They had all missed two meetings. Louise, Nadia, Betty, Jacqueline, and Allison had all become irregular in their attendance. There had been a lot of male tension between Andy, Gregory, Basil, and Serge. Only four men were missing. The theme of the group seemed to be about thunderbolts, and certainly Andy, Gregory, and PB had all been fairly unpleasantly aggressive.

8 June 1977

Twentieth meeting

[29 attended]

Fraught, difficult, but productive group, starting off in a cheerful manner but rapidly becoming tensed up again. Pat found himself preoccupied with the fact that several were absent, particularly the younger men, and even more so the 'nubile' women. Allison is also still absent and Andy, too, was missing. Joanna started off by discussing the oppressiveness of the one-to-one situation and referred to the primal scene. Robin went on to say that he felt people were preoccupied with Pat's and his relationship and the writing of this book, particularly with the feel of the favourite child.

Jacob attacked Robin pretty heatedly in a one-to-one engagement, Robin saying that he felt stabbed in the back, and Jacob saying he stabbed facing him. Serge, who was between them, suddenly removed himself, first to the floor and then to the opposite side of the circle. Jacob and Robin then turned their chairs and faced each other. Nadia asked if she might be allowed to hear what they were saying to each other, as they spoke softly so as to exclude the rest. Several people said they felt excluded, and Rajah launched a diatribe against the one-to-one, saying they were avoiding the presence of the large group, which is what he is interested in. *So a dilemma was reached between the duologue of the one-to-one and the dialogue of the group, mutually exclusive, as if separated by a stone wall.* Robin continued the theme of the loss of the reproductive women, which somewhat annoyed Angela and Joanna, who felt that their creativity had been belittled, confusing procreativity with creativity.

Pat pointed out that the massive nature or climate of this group seemed definitely hostile to the primal scene couple, the procreating between Pat and Robin, and it was because of this that the nubile women and some younger men had left. References indicating castration fantasies were fairly openly voiced.

Jason felt he could not mention his unclear private ideas, in the climate of this group. He felt he was either the favourite son or damned, whereas what he wanted to become was simply ordinary. That is why he had been working as a night porter; in fact, he had been educated at Eton and Oxford and has a beatnik appearance, wearing Wellingtons and denims and rolling his cigarettes.

Pat, Davina, and others pointed out that being ordinary was in fact creative, and this did not have to be a breathtaking intellectualization but could be very earthy.

There was further mention by Celia of Hemingway and of the group in the chapel when several of the younger women had sat together in a sort of chorus. Celia found she was shivering, and it was suggested the younger women were frightened of the older ones. Celia considered the non-reproductive older women had become the creative thinkers—'insemination'.

Subsequently it was suggested that there was a pronounced homosexual element, and in fact there were eight young men seated together, with Davina sitting in the middle.

The main theme continues to concern the dilemma of the procreative one-to-one in the middle of the large group context. Neither of these systems appears to wish to relate to the other.

Pat saw the presence of two types: The first were the people who seemed to be opening themselves, as if saying 'yes', and the second were the people who constantly appeared to be saying 'no'. Obviously this subject is likely to be taken up next week.

16 June 1977

[33 attended]

The atmosphere seemed more secure, fuller, and more confident. Several people who had been missing—Alison, Rowena, and Jacqueline, for instance—were there.

Gregory said after moving two chairs that it would place him either next to Davina or next to Ian, that it would be either a homosexual or a heterosexual choice. He makes comments of this kind, which are rather crude and, in a curious way, irrelevant, off the point, and he appears to be tied up with a wish almost to violate the more delicate thoughtful processes that are taking place in the group.

The scene of last week was discussed again, Rajah saying he had fantasied the scene between Jacob, Robin, and Serge as having been set up deliberately, by arrangement. Pat suggested that he had felt quite persecuted by the one-to-one relationship that is as a primal scene because the group still sees itself as a primal family group.

The more vulnerable young women had left because of the feeling that both creative and procreative relationships were not part of the present climate in the group, and much was said of the homosexuality between the men. Rowena had mentioned this the last time she had been present, three meetings ago.

Angela and Joanna felt the older women were being used as padding in the group. Joanna felt persecuted by the younger women; she felt as if she were cannon fodder.

Heather went on to say she had spent the day invigilating children, mainly black, for the CSE. She felt in a false position, as they obviously would have no job to go to and she was accepting a salary.

Gregory came down on her, suggesting she was really being racist, and Pat felt he had to protect her. He pointed out that she was as much a victim as the children, in a total setting that was persecuting all of them.

The question of sado-masochism arose, Joanna saying she feared she might be shot in the back. Serge endorsed this, saying he felt fearful of being stabbed in the back himself, that he had been depressed, and that he felt too depressed and exhausted to be the sadistic devil he normally was. His diabolical smile was referred to. He said he wanted to be sadistic to women; Heather also was accused of being sadistic.

Rowena said she felt masochistic and hated it, described a man living at her shared property who kept storing up his milk bottles—there were something like two thousand of them in the house.

The only way to deal with anger as distinct from being masochistic was to become a terrorist, and Robin felt he had been terrorized by last week's experience. Rowena said she had not been able to face the group over the previous two sessions.

The meeting finished with Pat saying that the one-to-one seemed to be a clobbering relationship—Gregory with Basil, or Gregory and Ian, or Geoffrey and Heather. Gregory said Pat was clobbering him, and Pat replied that this is where we are—in fact, we were in the middle of a bad primal scene, before murdering each other. Andy put it that he was being kicked up the arse, and he felt it was a good thing that Serge was able to say how ill and depressed he felt.

Godfrey thought the atmosphere was surprisingly more 'mature' since he had been attending three weeks ago, and for the first time he spoke clearly and could be heard.

Megan talked her way through a violent panic attack, and Pat referred to her, pointing out that in such a sado-masochistic scene kindness and understanding are regarded as signs of masochistic weakness; to be intelligent and kind and to link up is construed as weakness and wishy-washy. Neither Megan nor Rowena could bear their masochism. They hate it in themselves, and Serge cannot bear his sadism, which therefore makes him depressed and inert.

Certain themes seem to have arisen in the group. One is the politico-socio culture structure, the private versus public polarization. Second, that of the primal family, as though the large group were a primal horde; this is an attempt to make a family out of the large group. Third, the large group is treated as a breast, good and bad, with splitting. Father social and spiritual, Mother natural, material as distinct from spiritual (*mater*). Fourth, there is the splitting of gender in the same person. Birth and death are split: psychic death through fear of psychic birth by projecting these into the physical body. Homosexuality puts the denied psychic gender into the body, the mind being hermaphroditic in the sense that the infant is born having to relate to two parents in two different gender fashions. Loyalty to the group and the bonding of the one-to-one splitting takes place between these two, between bonding and loyalty.

Conclusion. The oral breast relationship towards the primal scene seems to be showing itself. All these splits are over and above or below the ostensible higher levels of dialogue, which is the group's spiritual aspect, the oedipal primal scene, which concerns genitality, and the Kleinian–oral level, which concerns the materialistic or maternal. These three levels are (1) intelligence: bad viz. cold and persecutory versus emotional, which, however aggressive or destructive, is regarded as good, warm, real, empathetic and becomes idealized, as distinct from the persecuting coldness intelligence. (2) The one-to-one clobbering: bad, persecuting, primal scene; bonding, on the other hand, concerns affection, love, kindness, goodness, and idealization.

Thought processes stuck in a continuum of a treacly sweet climate of bonding versus an atmosphere of hostile anxiety. In the bonding everyone says 'yes'. In an atmosphere of hostility and persecution everyone says 'no' and becomes involved in blocking. (3) The third category seems to be the sado-masochistic split. Can Rowena and Megan integrate these without succumbing to the horror and terror of the opposite—Serge's masochism, Megan's and Rowena's sadism? To do so would result in depression, so Serge's masochism and Rowena's and Megan's sadism is repressed and unrecognized. Until these are recognized, therefore, sadness, depression, remorse, wisdom, and maturity cannot supervene with their concomitant sense of greater reality.

23 June 1977

[31 attended]

Jacqueline told us that her father had at long last died. Nell handled the situation well, getting Jacqueline to talk freely, which made her cry. Heather went on to talk of the death of a child of a friend and of the latter's hypo-manic denial of sadness. Jason talked of his friend, who is in danger of suicide. Serge talked of a friend at work, a woman who had committed suicide in a most bizarre manner, and Robin of another instance of suicide.

Previously to this theme, Joanna had said how worried she had been by last week's meeting; she felt that Pat had clobbered the older women, including herself, and had sided with the younger women, the nubile ones, and the older women were just put in to fill up the numbers. She said that Pat had made it clear that it was the young procreative and creative who had it all, the others might as well be dead—'fodder', as she called it. Pat said in fact he had made distinctions, that not being procreative is not in any way similar to not being creative, and this was not just applied to the younger women.

Theme: a mix-up between the themes of procreative–creative and sexual. Doreen felt threatened by the heaviness of Robin and Pat writing a book. Jacqueline had some ideas about distributing Smarties, this being extremely helpful for young suicidal girls who could carry Smarties around with them and take one whenever they felt impulsively suicidal, which apparently had a relieving effect.

The theme is possibly to do with the double-bind of sexuality. If you cannot be sexual, you might as well commit suicide, yet sexuality is forbidden in the group in its present climate.

The alternative is to be creative or to have friends, both being interpreted as being homosexual.

Jacob, whose wife has had a baby, walked out, and Basil went after him; it turned out he was, in fact, only going to the lavatory, which occasioned a laugh.

Later Gregory walked out, and one felt that Heather, who was weeping, was wailing on behalf of the whole group but in an histrionic manner.

The atmosphere was such that it was said we should not, in the circumstances, go to the pub. Several, not many, did go, and apparently the atmosphere was convivial. Tom turned up at the last minute, saying he had been delayed and that he had knocked one of his pupils off his bicycle. He came, despite the lateness, because he feared Jacqueline's father had probably died.

Andy, during Jacqueline's grief, made a very humourous joke, which occasioned a gust of laughter, to the effect that it would take a helluva lot of Smarties to commit suicide.

The theme was unbridled sexuality versus suicide if you do not get it, and therefore depressing topics were given priority. For instance, while Joanna was saying how miserable she had been last week, Jack had rejected her in the pub. On the other hand, he looked into the middle distance and seemed to be rather ashamed, as if he had been pressurized into responding by the social atmosphere of the group, whilst in fact the culture is highly experimental, ad libbing and flirtatious, with an almost spontaneous coquettishness and free thinking.

The oedipal pattern of older women and younger men, the older women winning, the younger women and the older men. So Pat and Hanna cannot get it. Pippa and Robin, only Hannah and Dick. Pat and Peter, Pat with Rosemary, Pat with Megan. So Pat felt he could not encourage Megan to say what she had tried to say, as he would be accused of going for the younger women, as usual. The theme then is that the large group is anti-sexual. Joanna could be openly seen to flirt with Jack, who looks guilty and oppressed—an open secret which is observed and enjoyed but not stated.

The light touch of cultural genitality becomes the heaviness of the socially structured, of creativity on the one hand versus clichés and institutionalization on the other.

Biological versus social structures—i.e., the biological individual is the thesis versus the antithesis of social structure; the synthesis results in culture, the praxis of this is dialogue, and this continues as a sort of spiral.

Several people seemed to be involved with distinct mood swings: Rachel, Joanna, and Serge, Ian, Heather, and Andy. People changing, as it were, from the schizoid to the depressive position. Is there a danger of people being driven into the depressive position? Pat found himself wondering whether this was a real risk.

29 June 1977

[29 attended]

Ian introduced the matter of his colleague having committed suicide at university, of his father's suicide, and of his own depression, triggered off by a similar situation to his colleague, who had been working in a unit that was being slowly run down in favour of another, which was being developed in the same faculty.

People asked after Jason's friend, but Jason was not present. Jeremy said he had heard from him, that he had returned safely.

People asked after Gregory, who precisely at that moment appeared at the door slightly drunk.

Iris said she was interested to know more about Lionel's father's suicide, that this was more relevant than Pat's questions about Ian's department.

The theme of suicide continued. Gregory asked what was the opposite of suicide? Pat suggested sex. Gregory was encouraged to look at his physical rather than his racial problems, and he described how his life had been ruined by the very severe accident in a goldmine in South Africa, when he had been paralysed from his neck downwards. He wept bitterly in describing this event. Jacob tried to comfort him and held him with his arms round his shoulders. Nell was angry and asked Pat or Robin why they did not comfort him. Pat suggested that it would be more appropriate if she herself did so; she replied she had felt too inhibited.

After this there was a long preamble about Gregory and 'race', with many people taking part. On several occasions Pat tried to get a word in edgeways; eventually he was successful and commented that it was not race that was the difficult fact to acknowledge, but the fact that Greg is a 'cripple' and the ways that this affects him in the large group and in the outside world; he thought that the general nature of his anger could not be put down or attributed solely to the fact of race. Greg then spoke very movingly about how he had been a talented sportsman, and when working as a geologist he had been blown up and had lost the use of his legs. He eventually went into medicine and trained as a doctor. During the period of great emotion in the group, Jacob had offered Gregory a handkerchief; after this had finished Pat was accused by Nell of not really caring about anybody else in the group, asking who seems to care most for people in the group. Last week, when Gregory left the group, it was Rosemary who went out to show him some comfort.

The issue of friendship versus genitality was brought up. In what ways is one able to show friendship, particularly to someone of the same sex, but also to someone of the opposite sex, without the comfort/friendship being sexualized?

The concept of values and value judgements being made about each other—are they constructive, and what form do they take? Are they part of a hierarchical cult or of a cultural nature that is being constantly viewed in the large group setting?

Geoffrey asked how Pat was feeling. Pat said he was glad that something of this nature could happen in the large group setting and that boundaries of trust were in consequence being opened up.

6 July 1977

[21 attended]

Joanna read out a statement about her sexuality and how threatened she felt, particularly by the younger women who, she felt, wanted to kill her—particularly Davina.

Jillian said she had in fact not just flirted with people, but had slept on three occasions with Rajah; this was a disappointing experience, she said. Rajah was absent, and Robin said he had heard he was coming, but also that Rajah had told him he had gangrene of his left arm. Everyone laughed, as though it was a punishment brought upon him by Jillian.

Both statements were extremely honest and provoked varied responses. Megan commended Joanna highly; Jason said Jillian was an exhibitionist; Andy said Jason would not allow either thought or emotion, which he called exhibitionism. Jason mixed up talking about sex with the actual action of sex, and Serge was impressed by Jillian's honesty. Heather was absolutely furious with Iris and threatened to murder her. Jillian stood up well to the attack.

Rosemary's fury verged on the paranoid. She was frightened and worried that the group would be overheard talking about sex through the open windows and that it would give the group a bad name. So she got up to make sure no one was there, then closed the windows. Rowena felt similarly but was less worried about it all.

Subsequently Jacob changed the subject to the death of a pigeon, which had knocked against the window of his car, and Zinova softened the clash between Heather and Jillian by saying she longed for Wednesdays and hated Sundays, which was half-way between. Sunday was the day her husband had died. She said she was a good deal older than most people and felt that friendship was more important than sexuality.

Andy said he liked her and said he, too, felt a need for warmth and ordinary friendship.

The theme seemed to be suicide and sex again, in which sex is punished by death. Death, at any rate, is more respectable.

In fact Rajah is in hospital for investigation for rheumatoid arthritis, and Joanna said she had subsequently developed jaw ache from speaking. This stopped her from talking more, but her joint troubles were mentioned, and articulation seems to be a theme.

13 July 1977

[29 attended]

The meeting opened with comments from Nell about her holiday in Hastings. She had been away during the previous meeting, and she had had a dream of having a machine-gun, and of being redirected at a railway point; she had been attempting to make approaches to Gregory and Pat, and this was the reason she had been so angry through fear of rejection; the machine-gun was not really hers.

Rajah's absence was mentioned, and Pat explained that he was in hospital possibly with rheumatoid arthritis, though in fact it turned out that he had developed a small ganglion in his wrist. Incidentally, the old-fashioned method of treating ganglion had been to thump it with the family Bible.

The theme now seemed to be sex and life, but Jason continued to support Heather's aggression. However, she is clearly in a minority, and people questioned why she turned up late. Nell told her immediately she arrived that she had been talked about.

20 July 1977

[29 attended]

Jillian spoke very fully and coherently about the break of the oncoming August holiday; this, coupled with a fulsome description of the nihilistic depression of Joanna, of staying in bed, of Zinova's mourning, and of Ian recommending that one should try and burst through depressions through books and art, saying that his childhood had been very bad, and depression had to be combatted. He had come very much to life when he had been evacuated during the war with people who were considerably more cultured. Pierre said depression, in his case, gave way to creativity, like gestation. Heather became friendly with Jillian. The theme seems to be that there is a negative transposition of being confronted by mindlessness on the one hand, which is equivalent to barrenness and destructiveness and nihilism, as distinct from creativity and dialogue on the other. The dialogue is like a sounding-board: broad themes emerge in a manner that is well-defined and clear—nothing hazy, nothing opaque. For instance, suicide, sex, and death, punishment, persecution, and time and space—these themes serve in the large group to bring about changes. Rajah, Joanna, and Paula have all been ill, but there have also been changes for the better, in the sense that Nadia, Robin, Serge, and Angela have all made positive changes in their job situations. Those who contributed most would seem to have been Gregory, Iris, Heather, Andy, Serge, Nellie, Angela, Nadia, and Basil.

27 July 1977

[22 attended]

Pat announced the death of Paula the previous Friday as a result of a tumour on the brain; she had died during an operation. This came after Jack saying he dreaded coming to this last meeting. Nadia said she would be happy to survive this last meeting, with the gap of the August holiday, and added she had recently landed an extremely good job in her career as a lecturer. Jason and other members were not present, and it became clear that Pat had criticized him too much and that therefore he now dropped out. Pat tried to explain that it was not people but leading ideas that mattered to him, and that the split between social clichés and cultural thinking was for him the most interesting area, where the greatest conflicts took place; he felt that it was the prerogative of the large group unhampered by the usual social and institutional implications that had allowed cultural thinking to become more evident, more mobile.

The large group dwells on death in a manner that could not be seen in individual or small groups as a recurring theme.

Dyadic relationships occur as head-on collisions, often with the conductor; pairing takes place, and people cannot participate. It is not customary to stand up to the conductor, so the loser withdraws, thereby weakening the large group itself and incidentally the conductor and his 'offspring'. Prue and Serge, Rajah and Jillian, Pat and Robin, Joanna and Jack are examples of important one-to-one relationships. Jillian, Joanna, and Megan succeeded in forming a powerful 'junta'. Megan is showing increasingly what a strong personality she really has, and she talked her way through a panic that has been presenting a major symptom for her. She felt small and wanted to fall off the chair; in fact, she is a tall, strongly built young woman, Welsh, powerful, bending over backwards to deny her strength and beauty.

Holiday break of five weeks. During this time Pat had sent a circular to all members of the group saying: 'To the Members of the Large Group, 8th August 1977. Following the August holiday the next meeting will take place at 9.00 p.m. on Wednesday 7th September in the Welsh Hall as usual. The last meeting will be on November 30th, so there remain thirteen more meetings.'

7 September 1977
First meeting after the holiday

[28 attended]

A positive and cheerful atmosphere prevailed. The circular Pat had sent out was not mentioned. The previous year he had written to the members at about the same time. The meetings have become a real marathon, and tensions at times seem overwhelming. Resistance takes the form of dropping out. In fairness to each other and to the total experience, members are asked to do their utmost to continue their attendances, otherwise we shall never know.

In fact, the last meetings proved crucial in the resolution of the often harrowing and 'long-haul' nature of the whole experience, and this year has been as intensive as last year, if not more so. It is clear that time and place are essential factors to assimilate these events, and therefore it is important that people maintain their regular attendance, as indeed they did last year.

Rajah was again present, after having been away from the group for the operation on a ganglion on his right wrist, which had been variously interpreted as cancer, gangrene, rheumatoid arthritis, and tuberculosis; amputation and death had been invoked in fantasy. It was associated with Paula's death; as mentioned, she had in fact died under anaesthetic of a cerebral tumour, which had been diagnosed as a cyst. Rajah still could not see that his participation had been stopped altogether and that it had had possibly psychosomatic implications. He mentioned appendicitis as being impossible as an example of a psychosomatic phenomenon. He was given a warm welcome.

The whole matter of groups that could not tolerate bonding in the one-to-one friendship or sexual meetings was raised by Lionel and others, including Heather. Some welcome these associations, but the culture of the group is one that does not so far encourage one-to-one relationships. Therefore scapegoating of Iris continues but not quite as vociferously. Heather is still very persecuted and resentful of Iris, who seems to be the only one who can stand up to her, even though she herself is intimidated. 'I'll smash your face in. Shut up!', Heather shouts. There seems to be a flagellation of Iris. The theme is that the group culture is still very hierarchical, puritannical, persecutory. Idealism swings into persecution. When it is idealistic, it gives the appearance of good intentions and of a spurious liberalism. On the other hand, Heather is vitriolic. Iris also turned on Lionel, who, despite insight and valuable comments, appears in some people's eyes as a voyeur who punishes Jillian, whom he accuses of exhibitionism when he had in fact invited her to talk; in other words, he has a pretty punishing nature. It was in fact an exciting meeting, since there seemed to be for the first time the beginnings of 'Koinonia', with less bickering and less puritanism. The culture is perhaps beginning to admit the discussion of sexuality, as if the possibility of genitality can be mentioned in a friendly atmosphere; the atmosphere in the past could not allow people together in the one-to-one relationship.

The theme is to do with bonding between people of the same sex, and a flight that punishes heterogenital sexuality. Bad heterogenital relationships are beginning to be regarded more favourably than good homosexual ones. The Joanna–Jillian and Megan alliance is seen as a threat by a homosexual male because of his 'older ugly sisters', as he called them. Many in fact cannot stand the clash between Jillian and Heather, but Serge derives, he says, a fiendish, sadistic pleasure from witnessing their quarrelling. The *big question* is whether the whole group is in a state of sadistic voyeurism and passive participation, and whether it can be allowed to proceed as the group ethos is still that of a family hierarchy, and Koinonia is still unacceptable. How to alter the culture, in fact, from the family to an affiliative Koinonia?

Rajah expresses terror, which to him looked like the memories of his LSD nightmare of a cobra snake, hanging like a sort of umbrella over his head and causing him panic. This was a treatment he had received in 1968 and therefore provoked 'therapeutic sympathy'; he was well able to elicit sympathy from the group, which he feared would exile him. He was pale and clearly very frightened, positively agitated, though he denied it. Pat suggested he was in fact in a panic. The large group had met again, and it was more a matter of coping with the group culture as a possible threat, at which point Heather launched her attack, representing in caricature, one might say, the sadistic superego.

14 September 1977

[30 attended]

It started with a discussion of the 'fishwives'—Heather's and Jillian's quarrel of last week. Basil and Gregory argued. Gregory saw it as fishwives, Basil saw the friendly alliance of Joanna and Jillian as a threat, as it reminded him of his sisters. The whole group took up the themes of the Jillian-and-Heather confrontation, Megan saying she did not like seeing Jillian being told she must not say what she was thinking, but did not in fact mention that it was Heather who had said this. It reminded her of her own family . . . and Heather said it also reminded her of hers, and thereafter seveal people questioned Heather, gently comforting her, and she burst into tears, apologizing for last week.

Esther and Joanna said they had been frightened by Heather's violence.

Previously Greg had told Basil that he did not like him and would not give a reason. It seemed increasingly clear to Pat that neither love nor friendship was permitted, and Megan said it was because it was a family as distinct from a free and easy social context or culture. The two themes of love and friendship—love being genital intercourse, therefore heterosexual, and friendship basically agenderized between man and man or woman and woman, creative as distinct from procreative. The theme being that friendship as much as love encounters difficulties, perhaps not repression but non-recognition, or is distorted by being sexualized and termed homosexual. Equally, love is often attenuated into 'can't we be friends?'

Greg abuses friendship by an alcoholic type of bonhommie or camaraderie, which he calls friendship. The great thing was that the group took up the responsibility of love and friendship. Ian could not admit last week that there was a person—could admit that he was not having a love affair, but he could not admit that he was having a very stimulating friendship with a man with whom he was walking on the Yorkshire moors; this would be misinterpreted as sexual, whereas for him it was an exciting, creative, thought-provoking friendship. What had occurred in the atmosphere in the large group in the meantime?

21 September 1977

[23 attended]

Pat was unwell so was away. The issue of Jewishness was very much the topic and whether to come to the group or not, as tomorrow was the Day of Atonement.

Angela said she was feeling less happy and had been feeling like this over the past few weeks but had been unable to say this in the large group. Hanna was also feeling less and less integrated and sane and was very worried about this.

The issues seemed to be, first, sexuality versus the family, and, secondly, conformity or estrangement and difference versus conflict.

An extremely interesting incident occurred between Basil and Greg; they crossed the centre of the group and embraced each other and kissed. Greg said later that he did not really like Basil. Basil retorted that he had been thinking of not coming this evening as he had had dinner with Jewish family members and this had put him off the idea of attending the group. Yet in some ways he was happy to be here. Angela can support Heather's abuse; she recognizes Heather's persecutory anxiety over love; she can be friendly towards those who are anti love; she cannot be friendly towards those who support the love theme. She has yet to learn of a Koinonia that promotes love and therefore resolves paranoia; this results in a skewing, or a twisted approach to straight thinking (that nice things are nice) and a tendency towards the tragic schizoid thinking (that it is the good impulses themselves that are bad), the basis also of the puritan ethic.

28 September 1977

[Only 22 attended]

But the atmosphere was of a serious, thoughtful, enquiring nature. Pat had been off last week with a cold, and Joanna had been attacked generally. She had stuck her neck out, but she seemed remarkably unruffled. Pat had been accused of supporting 'love' and neglecting other factors, but he felt he had been misunderstood, and it was the friendship–love polarization that had to be looked at, that love needed Koinonia in the atmosphere or culture of the context.

A heavy meeting. Pat accused of being more oppressive this year. A quiet, but intensely serious meeting. Some felt that the large group did nothing for them. Eric did not realize he did a lot for the group, and others found it an intensely earnest meeting. Pat, in particular, felt he was interested in how much he had learnt at the meeting. Jacob played games, rather like Greg, because he had never had friendship; neither Alan nor Greg had had the experience of friendship.

5 October 1977

[29 attended]

This, on the contrary, was a very cohesive meeting, intellectually speaking. The love and friendship theme. Greg, Basil, Megan, and Andy, who is absent, are all frightened of friendship, but Pat managed to get through Jacob's defensiveness by pointing out how people felt friendly towards him and towards Andy but those particular people, like Jacob, found it difficult to respond.

Lionel made the point that love was a one-to-one exclusive relationship and that friendship could be shared and could lead to Koinonia and was not exclusive.

Love and friendship could be in a polarized dialectical relationship, but not necessarily, and they could also be mutually supportive. It could be either homo gender or hetero gender, and reciprocal, mutual, complementary.

Joanna revealed that for the first time she could tolerate alienation, rejection, clobbering, and persecution by the entire group and survive—indeed, even remain friendly. This provoked immediate laughter.

Basil read out his letter to Pat accusing Pat of homophobia, but obviously very few people had any inkling of Pat's attempt to relate genital to genitalia, anger with definition, i.e. the frustration by love of sexuality results in an attempt to think, but is still largely left in the form of hate and anger. Therefore Pat said with kind regard in love, but not in friendship.

In the same vein Rajah is now like Jacob, in a baleful state of mind; having been frustrated in sex, he now seeks to express anger as a form of vitality. He says that the group lacks vitality and that this is Pat's responsibility; neither he, nor Basil, nor Jacob—all highly intelligent people—agree to use their thoughts, their minds, their understanding, but prefer to regress to a state of resentment, which at present renders them vaguely impervious to any approaches, particularly approaches from Pat. This could be a transference phenomenon. Perhaps Basil, Greg, Rajah, Jack, Andy, Serge, and Angela all have particular problems in a lack of friendship with their fathers. This then becomes pregenitally sexualized, or distorted in such manifestations as phoney relationships, bonhommie, camaraderie or gamesmanship, not to be confused with sportsmanship.

Greg gave a magnificent description of his wish to establish relationships with a woman who 'was not damaged', which was misinterpreted as looking for a male woman. Basil asked why he could not imagine a man or a boy as a woman, since he appeared to see women as men, which was a grossly simplistic statement. Pat suggested that we are all psychically hermaphroditic.

[Next two meeting reports missing]

24 October 1977

[23 attended]

Discussion about matters to do with hysterectomy and menopause.

Robin asked Davina why she was looking so unhappy. She then revealed that she had just undergone an abortion, which, in fact, turned out to be a miscarriage prior to the actual operation and the foetus was dead. She described her suffering, and Pat felt vibrations of concern on his behalf, having missed last week being on holiday in Crete. Robin directed the group's attention to Colina, saying her car had broken down and she was having considerable trouble with her periods and the menopause. This gave rise to an extensive discussion to do with hysterectomy. Davina described her suffering and said how grateful she had been to Greg who had visited her in hospital.

From there a gradual shift to male chauvinism emerged. Megan and Joanna accusing Greg of brutalization, which the men laughed at in a somewhat chauvinistic way. But it became clear that Greg has to denigrate what is precious to him as he feels he is inhabiting a friendless world that would destroy open expression of love, his insulting tenderness and attentions being a disguise, like that of a naughty boy. Jillian said that she feels that she is not in dialogue, but in competition with all other speakers.

2 November 1977

[26 attended]

This started very desultorily, with only about 10 members, but fairly quickly rose to 26. The topic was the family and the helpfulness of the extended family in distancing and reaching assessments about that family or particular members in that family.

The atmosphere of the large group was surprisingly friendly and relaxed. Celia talked of her divorced parents who had met at her own home for the first time in 10 years with some of her friends, and why she had been missing from the previous meeting in both senses, but had been surprised at the ease with which she had coped with these tensions. She felt that she was, in a strange way, helped by her friends who live with her in a sort of commune.

Nadia spoke freely of her mother, her paranoia, her aggression, and her mother's physical violence. This persecuted picture of the really disturbed bad mother was countering the idealized image of the mother preserved by relations. There was no one for Sandra to turn to except her father; her older sister, for instance, had spent four years in a mental hospital, being a very aggressive and limited personality. Nadia, who was a very 'nice' child, coped by sublimating and almost achieved a First in Philosophy at Oxford but was pipped at the post by a paranoid breakdown when she identified her tutor with her mother. She recalled the manner in which her mother had destroyed her written school work and her books during her childhood. This was the first time that Sandra spoke so fully about her mother, and this is in contrast to the time several weeks ago when she forbade Pat to mention any of these problems with her mother.

Rajah talked about his father and how he had rebelled by having a large photo of Stalin above his bed and had bought Marxist writings instead of buying school books in defiance.

Megan talked of her parents, and Jillian said that her extended family had been great and some compensation for her own wealthy parents, who had neglected her and her brother. She did not know, and it was necessary to know, who her extended family was. She did not know them personally, but only as 'presences'.

Shaun talked of his family. When his mother died, he was surprised that his father was so popular, when in fact he had expected more appreciation to have been expressed of his dead and highly idealized mother, who was indeed a very idealized figure in the village.

The theme seems to be that there is a family relationship, particularly in regard to the mother–child relationship. This occurs in the extended family or in a social circle, for instance the village. If the surrounding extended family, equivalent in the situation here to the large group, is able to support the child's misgivings about its mother or close nuclear family members, this is a valued cycle for further future development and independence—for instance, Jillian's extended family. But if not, then, as in the case of Megan or Nadia or Shaun, the large group or extended family is sensed as being disapproving, and a disapproving atmosphere makes the child feel his thoughts are wrong or bad. Megan for instance: her mind actually blanks out if she has to confront a personality who is powerful, and this sometimes occurs with Pat and with Greg. It was here that Jillian brought in the comment that she is never in dialogue but always in competition with other speakers.

People commented on the friendliness of the large group this week. Cairns could not believe it was happening and felt the aggression, or in Shaun's terminology, hate, was being displaced and projected into all this talk about mothers and families and external groups and onto the extended kin or social life of a village.

Pat's feeling was that people were beginning to develop a sense of Koinonia by the sublimation of hate, possibly in response to the interpretation last week.

Greg's sensational story about having his dog put down, in his talk of the tears of his children, of the dog biting his wife, and of the vet telling him it was a matter almost of the dog reflecting his own domination in the family.

Only the large group is varied enough to allow for the projection of (1) extended family or (2) a social circle of friends. So we have the permutations of (a) the one-to-one relationship, (b) one to the small group (family) and (c) one to the extended family and to the circle of friends, such as a village, which is equivalent perhaps to the dimension the large group is exploring.

9 November 1977

[26 attended]

A cohesive, friendly atmosphere. Serge began to explain why his utterances had been so sporadic recently, that he had lost his attempts to pose, he had become depressed, and he was constantly seeing Prue; he was also undergoing psychoanalysis and was sticking to his present job, which was longer than he had ever been able to tolerate before. He began to weep, talking about remembering Prue sitting there cross-legged on the floor in last year's group. There was a holding and gentle containing silence.

Greg came across, kissed him, looking embarrassed, and then later Rachel said she knew how Serge felt, and they kissed each other. They had both been in last year's group together, and in a strange way seemed to have arrived at a similar level of depression and recognized it in each other. Surprisingly good feeling in the group was experienced, and Serge then said he felt sad that he could not accept Pat's invitation to the pub at the meeting before last; he had felt friendly but too much so, and this was now being looked at in his individual psychoanalysis. He felt he was identifying too much with Pat but that he felt truly friendly towards him. There seemed to be a gradual, if somewhat grudging feeling of an increasingly friendly atmosphere in the group, impersonal yet friendly, and Basil insisted that we must decide about the meetings for the next year, what people, where, when, and so on. We finally arrived at an agreement to continue in this Welsh Hall at the same time on Wednesdays, some members considering attending a third year.

17 November 1977

[25 attended]
[Some members—Rachel, Andy, Alison, Davina and Jacob—attend irregularly.]

Anna returned in a happier and friendlier state and discussed her feelings about the loss of her husband. I formed the impression that the group is helping her to become more sociable, and she revealed she attends a writing class and enjoys writing humorously. The atmosphere between her and the rest of the group was suddenly friendlier and more cheerful, but she still felt some alienation.

The question of art forms and communication was discussed; Sandra's writing and Anna's in particular. Anna found it gave considerable pleasure. Pierre was producing films for television, and said he almost experienced a panic, a gut-ache, when he finished anything and was grossly disappointed at the discrepancy between what he wanted and what his team finally produced.

Serge said he had felt immensely helped by being able to express sadness in the group last week and that the group was able to hold him.

Pat suggested the object of the group was to create a medium in which people could freely express their own personal creative wishes and experience a sense of liberation. Joanna asked why Jack had become alienated. She had felt and shown her attraction, and he had rejected her. He said he felt she was trapping him sexually. I suggested he linked friendship and sex together, so from his point of view friendship and love are linked. To get away sexually also implied loss of love, fear of closeness, etc. Robin pointed out the need for pairing, friendship, pairing to withstand the impact of the large group in isolation of being one only, and one can add to this also that the atmosphere of the group as a whole could change from a suspicious, persecuting one to one in which there was an overall sense of Koinonia.

24 November 1977

[32 attended]

The atmosphere was powerful. Ian said he was hurt that he had not been consulted and informed about next year's times. Greg said he had been hurt by Joanna. Joanna said she was put down again by Greg, and so she had retaliated by clobbering him. The group retaliated and returned the clobbering of Joanna, who said she had felt violated by the words of last week: 'fuck' and 'pissed' had been used when she had tried to broach a personal matter between herself and Jack.

The theme seemed to be that the cultural was again anti-personal and anti-sexual and that people refused to understand what Joanna was saying. So Pat threw it back at them and suggested we look at the degree of understanding that we had rather than denying any understanding. Pat asked if anyone had heard what Joanna had described. The group began to pick up communications as if they had been on a watershed that had been going towards scapegoating and mob law as distinct from dialogue and understanding. The silent ones spoke now, like a sort of Greek chorus. Pat was able to interpret to people that when they became more personal, they got hurt by the mob culture and then became ashamed of their hurt. They then feared to reveal their wounds for fear of mob law and violence, which would be directed against them in a primitive, punitive way, and so tended to become silent or invisible by dropping out every other meeting. Malcolm had opened the meeting by saying he had missed the meeting when the time and place next year had to be decided, and he felt hurt that no one had informed him.

Megan said she talked completely differently when Pat was not there, and Pat suggested that, of all the people in the group, he, by nature of his status as convener, could hurt people most in a primitive, primal horde-type of response.

It seems to Pat that the primal stuff of the group is hate, the result of the frustrated love of an exclusive one-to-one relationship, perhaps unconsciously with Pat, or with someone else, and less unconscious in that case.

Several events made Pat feel he was involved: (1) Pat sat between Joanna and Angela; (2) Jillian made an ambiguous comment about missing the session with him as her car broke down, saying she could not talk about love with Pat when she meant she could not talk with Pat about love; (3) Davina was offended that Pat had not written to her, as he had to others, when she was absent, that a message to second-best Robin was not enough; (4) Megan's comment about knowing Pat in a small group elsewhere was mentioned.

Feelings about the group ending—if we lost love for Pat, we would not pay, was one theme. Rajah said he felt the large group was hostile, and Jacqueline said that people were warding off love since the group was closing, and Pat was using his primal horde leader power to support the personal revelations of individuals who were being punitively scapegoated. Personal statements seem to isolate.

REFERENCES AND BIBLIOGRAPHY

Abraham, K. (1927). The influence of oral eroticism on character formation. In: *Selected Papers of Karl Abraham*. London: Hogarth Press. [Reprinted 1979, London: Karnac Books.]

Anzias, J. M. (1967). *Clefs pour la structuralisme*. Paris: Editions Seghers.

Balint, M., & Balint, E. (1961). *Psychotherapeutic Techniques in Medicine*. London: Tavistock.

Behr, H. (1985). Editorial. *Group Analysis, 17,* No. 2.

Belbin, M. (1981). *Management Teams*. Oxford: Heinemann.

Bion, W. (1961). *Experiences in Groups*. London: Tavistock.

———. (1962). *Learning from Experience*. London: Heinemann Medical. [Reprinted 1984, London: Karnac Books.]

———. (1967). *Second Thoughts*. London: Heinemann Medical. [Reprinted 1984, London: Karnac Books.]

Buckley, W. (1967). *Sociology and Modern Systems Theory*. Englewood Cliffs, NJ: Prentice Hall.

Chomsky, N. (1957). *Syntactic Structures*. The Hague: Mouton.

———. (1968). *Language and Mind*. New York: Harcourt, Brace & World.

Curry, A. (1967). A critique and appraisal of selective literature on large therapeutic groups. *International Journal of Group Psychotherapy, 17,* No. 4.

Dahl, R., & Tufte, E. (1973). *Size and Democracy.* Stanford, CA: Stanford University Press.

de Maré, P. (1966). Some theoretical concepts in group-analytic psychotherapy. In: *International Handbook of Group Psychotherapy.* New York: Philosophical Library.

______. (1972). *Perspectives in Group Psychotherapy.* London: George Allen & Unwin.

______. (1985). The Ninth Foulkes Annual Lecture: 'Large group perspectives.' *Group Analysis, 18* (2).

______. (1989). *The History of Large Group Phenomena.* New York: Brunner Mazel.

______. (1990). The development of the median group. *Group Analysis, 23.*

de Maré, P., & Kreeger, L. (1974). *Introduction to Group Treatments in Psychiatry.* London: Butterworth.

de Saussure, F. (1970). *Course in General Linguistics.* London: Fontana.

Durkheim, E. (1972). *Selected Writings.* Cambridge: Cambridge University Press.

Duverger, M. (1972). *The Study of Politics.* London: Nelson.

Edelson, M. (1970). *Sociotherapy and Psychotherapy.* Chicago, IL: University of Chicago Press.

Ezriel, H. (1950). The psychoanalytic approach to group treatment. *British Journal of Medical Psychology, 22.*

Fairbairn, R. (1952). *Psychoanalytic Studies of the Personality.* London: Routledge & Kegan Paul.

Fenichel, O. (1945). *The Psychoanalytic Theory of Neurosis.* London: Routledge & Kegan Paul.

Foulkes, S. H. (1948). *An Introduction to Group Analytic Psychotherapy.* London: Heinemann Medical. [Reprinted 1983, London: Karnac Books.]

______. (1964). *Therapeutic Group Analysis.* London: Allen & Unwin. [Reprinted 1984, London: Karnac Books.]

______. (1975). *Group Analytic Psychotherapy: Method and Principles.* London: Gordon & Breach. [Reprinted 1986, London: Karnac Books.]

Foulkes, S. H., & Anthony, J. (1957). *Group Psychotherapy: The*

Psychoanalytic Approach. Harmondsworth, Middlesex: Penguin Books. [Reprinted 1984, London: Karnac Books.]

Fraser, W. (1890–1915). *The Golden Bough*. London: Macmillan.

Freire, P. (1972). *Pedagogy of the Oppressed*. Harmondsworth, Middlesex: Penguin.

Freud, S. (1900a). *The Interpretation of Dreams. Standard Edition, 4–5*.

_______. (1912–13). *Totem and Taboo. Standard Edition, 13*.

_______. (1916–17). *Introductory Lectures on Psycho-Analysis. Standard Edition, 15–16*.

_______. (1917e [1915]). Mourning and melancholia. *Standard Edition, 14*.

_______. (1920g). *Beyond the Pleasure Principle. Standard Edition, 18*.

_______. (1921c). *Group Psychology and the Analysis of the Ego. Standard Edition, 18*.

_______. (1930a [1929]). *Civilization and Its Discontents. Standard Edition, 21*.

_______. (1933a [1932]). *New Introductory Lectures on Psycho-Analysis. Standard Edition, 22*.

_______. (1940a [1938]). *An Outline of Psycho-Analysis. Standard Edition, 23*.

Gerth, H. H., & Mills, C. Wright (eds.) (1946). *From Max Weber*. New York: Oxford University Press.

James, C. (1982). *The Individual and the Group*. New York: Plenum.

Jones, E. (1953). *Sigmund Freud: Life and Work*. London: Hogarth.

Kernberg, O. (1980). *Internal World and External Reality: Object Relations Theory Applied*. New York: Jason Aronson.

Klein, M. (1948). *Contributions to Psychoanalysis 1921–45*. London: Hogarth.

Kohr, L. (1957). *The Breakdown of Nations*. London: South Place Ethical Society.

Kovel, J. (1980). *New Directions in Psycho-History*. Lexington, MA: Lexington Books.

Kreeger, L. (ed.) (1975). *The Large Group*. London: Constable.

Kybal, Elba Gomez del Rey de (1987). *Some Strategies for Effective Decision-Making*. A Report on the Proceedings of the Fourth Nomos Seminar, Bretton Woods, New Hampshire,

26–30 May 1987. Cambridge, MA: Center for International Affairs, Harvard University.

Lacan, J. (1977). *Ecrits: A Selection.* London: Tavistock.

Langer, S. (1967). *Mind: An Essay on Human Feeling.* Baltimore, MD: Johns Hopkins University Press.

Leakey, R. (1981). *The Making of Mankind.* London: Michael Joseph.

Levinson, D. (1978). *Seasons of a Man's Life.* New York: Knopf.

Levi-Strauss, C. (1968). *Structural Anthropology.* London: Allen Lane.

———. (1977). Reflections on liberty. *New Society,* 6 May.

———. (1976). *Tristes tropiques.* Harmondsworth, Middlesex: Penguin.

McDougall, W. (1920). *The Group Mind.* New York: Putnams.

Marshall, T. H. (1963). *Sociology at the Crossroads.* London.

Morowritz (1968). *Energy Flow in Biology.* New York: Academic Press.

Mumford, L. (1938). *The Culture of Cities.* London: Secker & Warburg.

Neumann, E. (1954). *The Origins and History of Consciousness.* Princeton, NJ: Bollingen. [Reprinted 1989, London: Karnac Books.]

Piaget, J. (1971). *Structuralism.* London: Routledge & Kegan Paul.

Pines, M. (1982). Reflections on mirroring. *Group Analysis, 15,* No. 1.

Rice, A. K. (1965). *Learning for Leadership.* London: Tavistock.

Ricoeur, P. (1981). *Hermeneutics and the Human Sciences.* Cambridge: Cambridge University Press.

Roberts, J. P. (1982). Foulkes' concept of the matrix. *Group Analysis, 15,* No. 2.

Rycroft, C. (1979). *The Innocence of Dreams.* Oxford: Oxford University Press.

Sahlins, M. (1959). *The Use and Abuse of Biology.* London: Tavistock.

Sale, K. (1980). *The Human Scale.* London: Secker & Warburg.

Schindler, W. (1980). *Die analytische Gruppen Theorie nach dem Familien Modell.* Munich: Reinhardt.

Singer, P. (1980). *Hegel.* Oxford: Oxford University Press.

Skinner, B. F. (1971). *The Design of a Culture Beyond Freedom and Dignity*. New York: Knopf.

Springman, R. (1974). The large group. *International Journal of Group Psychotherapy, 20,* No. 2.

Stride, M. (1977). *Group Analysis, 10.*

———. (1978). *Group Analysis, 11.*

Thienemann, T. (1968). *The Interpretation of Language*. New York: Jason Aronson.

Toffler, A. (1980). *The Third Wave*. New York: William Morrow.

Turnbull, C. (1974). *The Mountain People*. London: Picador.

Turner, V. (1969). *The Ritual Process*. London: Routledge & Kegan Paul.

Turquet, P. (1975). Threats to identity in the large group. In: L. Kreeger (ed.), *The Large Group*. London: Constable.

Weber, M. (1946). In: H. H. Gerth & C. Wright Mills (eds.), *From Max Weber*. New York: Oxford University Press.

Wilden, A. (1968). *The Language of the Self.* Baltimore, MD: Johns Hopkins University Press.

Winnicott, D. W. (1958). *Through Paediatrics to Psychoanalysis*. London: Tavistock.

Wollheim, R. (1979). The cabinet of Dr. Lacan. *New York Review,* 25 January.

Worsley, P. (1982). *Marx and Marxism*. London: Tavistock.

INDEX

Adler, A., 95
ananke, 62
Andersen, H. C., 33
anomie, in large group, 78
Anthony, J., 25, 31, 51, 77, 105, 132
Anzias, J. M., 5, 132, 142
Aristotle, 1, 41, 145, 146, 158
  list of fallacies of, 84
  logic unknown to, 83
  on matter vs. form, 113
  on Prior Analytics, 73

Balint, E., 145
Balint, M., 145
Barry, G., 174
Barthes, R., 82
Behr, H., 14, 15
Benaim, ix
Bertalanffy, L. Von, 107
Bierer, J., 95
Bion, W. R., ix, xiv, 26, 39, 84, 113, 161, 177
  on basic assumption cultures, 79
  on beta and alpha elements, 127
  and large group, 168
  on objects and frustration, 160
  on psychotic personality, 160
  on toleration of frustration, 108, 126
Blake, W., 26, 113
British Association of Psychotherapists, x
Buckley, W., 133, 135
Bühler, K., 154
Buddha, 79

Cambridge University, 152, 154

Center of International Affairs, Harvard, xv–xvi
Chomsky, N., 39–40, 82, 129, 130
  on intelligence, 66–67
  on intertextuality, 143
  on language and thought, 65–66, 150–151
  on rules of structures, 128
Churchill, W., 175
citizenship:
  and Koinonia, 86
  and large group, 11
civilization, 148
  and dialogue, 60–61
Clark, D., 95
communication, function of mind, 57
content, of median groups, 27–31
cultural context, of larger group, 10
culture, 148
  and context, 32
  and Koinonia, 75–106
Curl, J. S., 174, 175
Curry, A., 97

Dahl, R., 173
Dali, S., 54
Darwin, C., xiv
deep structures, 49–51
de Maré, E., 75
de Maré, P., ix–x, xiv–xviii, 12, 13, 14, 79, 189
de Saussure, F., 66, 82, 91, 129, 130, 144
dialectic, meaning of, 41–42
dialogue, 4, 40–74
  affected by structure, 6
  disconnectedness of, 149–150
  and hate, 60, 108
  and individuation, 159–160
  and minicultures in large group, 19
  need to learn, 17, 26
  and polylogue, 167
  promoted by circular formations, 6
  promotes Koinonia, 4, 5
  properties of, 46–47
  tangential and analogic, 17
  way to Koinonia, 4
Durkheim, E., 57, 76, 78, 82, 118, 119, 162, 174
Duverger, M., 99

ecology, 165–175
Edelson, M., 97
Einstein, A., 65
Engels, 6, 43, 114, 161
Erickson, E., 95
ethnology, 136–139
eutropelia, 30
excluded middle, 145–146
Ezriel, H., 35, 79

Fairbairn, W. R. D., 33, 120, 122, 123
  Central Ego of, 111
fellowship, 89
Fenichel, O., 36
Ferrer, V., 86, 87
Fichte, 43
Forizs, 79
Foucault, M., 82, 125
Foulkes, S. H. ix, 4, 9
  on aggressive energies, 77
  construct of localization of, 149
  dialectical approach of, 83

on ego training, 31
on free-floating discussion, 15, 51, 65
on group
associations as interpretations, 70, 147
matrix, 16, 95, 98, 103, 126
therapy for citizenship, 11
Group Analytic Society (London), founding by, 12
group-analytic principles of, 4, 9, 82, 97
group-analytic approach of, 3
on localization, 149
matrix of, 79
on neurotic fixations, 105, 127, 140
on non-transference aspects of groups, 35
on treatment of group, 25
Fraser, W., 28
free association, 4
freedom, ecology of, 171
Freire, P., 40, 112, 113
Freud, S., xviii, 7, 54, 72, 82, 130, 143
on *ananke*, 30
on civilization, 61
and culture, 29
on conscious, 147
on conversation
and dreams, 38, 70, 144
and the unconscious, 20
on dreams, 156
and conversation, 38, 70, 144
on duality of instincts, 76, 111
on forms of energy, 148
on horde
as family, 6
mentality, 108
primal, 11, 129, 161
psychology, 28
on identification, 112
on inherited contents, 162
on large groups, 114
on love vs. culture, 110–111
on mind, 45
on Narcissistic disorders and relationships, 27
on object relationships, 109
on pathological cultural communities, 12, 31
on philosophy, 159
on psychical reality, 149
on reality principle, 149
on sleep, 71
on taboo, 105–106
on unconscious mind, 36, 118
Fromm, E., 95

genitality, 80
Gerth, H. H., 82
Green Alliance, xiii, xv
group:
Analytic Practice, ix
Analytic Society (London), ix, xi, xiv, 12, 14
association, 4
size of, increase in, 9–21

Halliwick Hospital, ix, x
Harvard University, xv, xix
hate:
and *ananke*, 62
anti-instinct, 77
and dialogue, 60, 83, 108

and endopsychic energy, 114, 125, 160–161
and frustrated instinct, 124
and the large group, 18, 126, 155
and the median group, 29–30
and mind, 117, 120
primal, and large groups, 114
provoked by frustration of narcissism, 141
Hegel, G. W. F., 42, 58, 103, 108, 115, 159
on dialectic logic, 158
on history, 156–157
on knowledge, 158
Heidegger, M., 5
Heraclites, 159
hermeneutics, 72–73
Herodotus, 1
Horney, K., 95
Hospital for Sick Children, Great Ormond Street, x
Huarte, J., 66, 151
Hume, D., 150, 155
Hutten, E. H., 57, 118, 146
Huxley, A., 43

Illich, I., 61
Institute of Family Therapy, 12
Institute of Group Analysis, ix, x, xix, 12, 69
introjection, 120

Jacobs, D., xix
James, C., 109
Jones, E., 46
Jones, M., 87, 95

Kahn, J. H., xi
Kant, I., 42, 43, 102, 103, 136, 150, 155, 158, 159
Kelman, H., xix
Kernberg, O., 124
Klein, M., 30, 31, 54, 123
on hate, 123
Kohr, L., 172, 173
Koinonia, xvi, 157, 161
and affiliation, 92
and citizenship, 33, 86
definition, 1–2, 4
and *eutropelia,* 30
fellowship, 4, 17, 18, 26, 39, 45, 76, 83, 88, 141, 145
group matrix, 45
passion for State, 178
transformation of frustration, 27
Koinonic dialogue, 161
Koinonic thinking, lateralization, 129, 157-158
Kovel, J., 143
Kreeger, L., ix, 12, 13, 97, 98
Kybal, E. G., xvi

Lacan, J., 82, 84, 125
on 'analytic' and 'global', 135
on deep structures, 128
on dialogue, 52, 59, 60
and hate, 51
on human discourse, 49
on intertextuality, 143
on language, 115–116
on psychic energy as drive, 45
on psychoanalysis as applied linguistics, 130
on 'real', 62

on sexuality and symbolism, 53
on thought and language, 48
on unconscious structured like language, 127
Langer, S., 5, 45, 46, 47, 59
language:
and dialogue, 44, 48, 55
quality of, 57
as tool for thinking, 56, 162
large group:
diary, 189–249
establishment of, 9–15
features of, 15–16, 93
foundation of, 12
and hate, 18
vs. therapeutic communities, 101–102
Large Group Section, aims of, 14
larger group, purpose of, 17
lateralization, 129
in large groups, 5
Lawler, M., xviii, xx
Leakey, R., 166
Leibniz, 63, 155, 158
Lenin, 42
Levi-Strauss, C., 51, 56, 82, 88, 92, 125, 130, 137, 139, 191
analytic structuralism of, 134-135
on antithesis between nature and culture, 81
on binary organization of thought, 72
on constellations of social relationships, 136
ecology of freedom, 171
esprit of, 127
on ethnology, 136
on first dialectic, 80
on intertextuality, 143
on marriage, 71, 81
on myth, 67, 71–72
on slavery, 138
on structuralism, 129, 133
on surface structuralization, 25
Levinson, D., 49, 50, 51
London Centre for Psychotherapy, x
London School of Economics, x

McDougall, W., 76
Mack, J., xix
Mahomet, 79
Main, ix
Malinowski, 117
Marlborough Family Service, x
marriage, 71, 81, 87–88
Marshall, T. H., 26
Marx, K., 42, 43, 63, 82, 114, 115, 118, 119, 130, 143, 144, 159, 174,
on primary infrastructure of materialism, 159
Maudsley Hospital, 12
Mauss, M., 23
meaning, principle of, 7
median group:
content of, 27–31
metastructure of, 31–34
optimum size of, 16
and post-oedipal community, 29
process in, 25–27, 36–38
structure of, 24–25
metastructure:
cultural context of, 32–34
of median group, 31–34
Mill, J. S., 169

Miller, E., xv
Miller, J. G., 107
Mills, C. W., 82
Moore, 152
More, Sir T., 85
Moreno, 95
Morowritz, 113
Mumford, L., 167

Neumann, E., 12
Newnham Community Mental Health Service, x
Northeastern Society for Group Psychotherapy, xviii
Northfield Military Hospital, ix, 11, 12, 168
Numbers, crucial, 165–166, 168–169

object:
 internal, 119, 128–129
 relations theory, 107–163
Oedipus complex, 31
Oedipus conflict, 105
oligarchy, 90

Paul, St, 30
Pausanias, 28
Pericles, 1, 5, 69
phobia, and large groups, 89
Piaget, J., 130, 134, 154
Pines, M., xi, 78
Piper, R., x, 189
Plato, 5, 26, 41, 42, 62, 74, 133, 143, 155
 on intertextuality, 143
population levels, optimum, 172
Portman Clinic, x
post-oedipal community, and median group, 29
post-oedipal considerations, of larger group, 11
post-structuralism, 65, 66
process, in median group, 25--27
projects, 119
Pugin, A., 174

Rice, A. K., 101
Rickman, J., ix, 168
Ricoeur, P., 5, 48, 72–73
 on symbols, 72
Roberts, J. P., 109
Rousseau, 138
Russell, B., 65, 74, 75, 115, 152, 153, 155, 159
 logical types of, 115
Rycroft, C., 45, 46, 77

Sahlins, M., 92, 117
Sale, K., 166, 167
Sartre, J.-P., 143
scale, human, 6
Schindler, W., 29
seating:
 effect of on group process, 6, 69, 174–175
 optimum, 16
semiology, 130
Shakespeare, W., ii, 75, 79
Shelley, P. B., 1
Simonides, 2
Singer, P., 156
size:
 effect of
  on group, 34–35
  on large group, 30–31
 increase in, characteristics engendered by, 177–178

Skinner, B. F., 84, 85
Socrates, 41, 65, 73, 79, 156
Spinosa, 155
Springmann, R., 97, 98
Steiner, P. P., xiii–xxiii
St George's Hospital, ix
St Joseph's Hospice, x
Stride, M., 33
structuralism, 25, 82–83, 107–163
  analytic, 134–135
  and post-structuralism, 65
structure:
  effect of on dialogue, 6
  of median group, 24–25
superego, and object choices, 122–123
symbol formation, 54
symbolic understanding, 55–56
symbolism, 149–150
  and cognition, 58
symbols, and thought, 5, 72–73, 91
systems thinking, 107–163

Tavistock Institute of Human Relations, xv
Taylor, R., 168
Thienemann, T., 5, 55, 56, 57, 162
thinking:
  dimensions of, 26–27
  types of, 46
Thompson, S., x–xi
Thucydides, 1
Toffler, A., 173, 174
transposition:
  and group analysis, 103–104
  in small group, 105
Trist, E., 169, 170
Tufte, E., 173
Turquet, P., 25
Turnbull, C., 139
Turner, V., 91, 92
Tweedie, J., 166

Utopia, B. F. Skinner on, 85

Van Gogh, V., 92
Volkan, V., xix

war, 69
Weber, M., 90, 137
Wellington, Cambridge, ix
Whitaker, D. S., 79
Wilden, A., 48
Wilmer, T., 97
Winnicott, 54, 77, 145
  transitional object of, 109
Wittgenstein, L., 43, 44, 108, 152–155, 156
Wollheim, R., 54
Worsley, P., 82, 115

For Product Safety Concerns and Information please contact our EU representative GPSR@taylorandfrancis.com
Taylor & Francis Verlag GmbH, Kaufingerstraße 24, 80331 München, Germany

www.ingramcontent.com/pod-product-compliance
Lightning Source LLC
Chambersburg PA
CBHW060742150926
51501CB00003B/68
9780367325282